Marquis of Dufferin and Ava

Speeches Delivered in India

1884-1888

Marquis of Dufferin and Ava

Speeches Delivered in India
1884-1888

ISBN/EAN: 9783337071905

Printed in Europe, USA, Canada, Australia, Japan

Cover: Foto ©ninafisch / pixelio.de

More available books at **www.hansebooks.com**

DELIVERED IN INDIA,

1884-8,

BY THE

MARQUIS OF DUFFERIN AND AVA.

LONDON:
JOHN MURRAY, ALBEMARLE STREET.
CALCUTTA: THACKER, SPINK & Co.   BOMBAY: THACKER & Co., LIMITED.
1890.

LONDON:
PRINTED BY WILLIAM CLOWES AND SONS, LIMITED,
STAMFORD STREET AND CHARING CROSS.

PREFACE.

It is the custom in India for the Viceroy's speeches to be printed in the Private Secretary's office, each speech being preceded by an introductory heading, descriptive of the circumstances under which it was delivered. Although Lord Dufferin, as he himself has told us, did not think it very desirable that the Viceroy should appear frequently on the platform, he was compelled during his term of office to deliver 177 speeches. The present volume consists of such of these as, from one cause or another, may be considered as possessing peculiar interest, and they are now published in the belief that some of them may prove useful to the large number of persons who have of late begun to turn their attention to the affairs of our Indian Empire.

Four non-Indian speeches have also been inserted. Two of these were delivered by Lord Dufferin before he went to India, namely, one at the Empire Club, and one at a dinner given to him in Belfast. The other two were made after his return to this country: one at the Mansion House on the 29th of May, 1889, and the other at a banquet given to him by the London Chamber of Commerce on the 30th of October, 1889.

DONALD MACKENZIE WALLACE.

London,
   15th February, 1890.

TABLE OF CONTENTS.

	PAGE
I. SPEECH AT THE EMPIRE CLUB. July 11, 1883 ..	1
II. BANQUET IN ULSTER HALL, BELFAST. Oct. 15. 1884	6
III. SPEECH AT THE NORTHBROOK CLUB. Nov. 1. 1884	16
IV. REPLY TO THE ADDRESS FROM THE MUNICIPAL CORPORATION OF BOMBAY. Dec. 8. 1884	20
V. REPLY TO THE ADDRESS FROM THE BOMBAY CHAMBER OF COMMERCE. Dec. 8. 1884	22
VI. REPLY TO THE ADDRESS FROM THE ANJUMANI ISLAM. Dec. 8. 1884	23
VII. REPLY TO THE ADDRESS FROM THE CORPORATION OF CALCUTTA. Dec. 13. 1884	25
VIII. REMARKS IN THE LEGISLATIVE COUNCIL. Dec. 19. 1884	27
IX. SPEECH AT THE CALCUTTA TRADES' ASSOCIATION DINNER. Jan. 30. 1885	27
X. THE BENGAL TENANCY BILL. Feb. 27. 1885 ..	31
XI. TENANT RIGHT IN BENGAL. March 5. 1885 ..	34
XII. THE BENGAL TENANCY BILL. March 9. 1885 ..	36
XIII. REPLY TO THE LANDHOLDERS OF BEHAR. March 10. 1885	37
XIV. THE BENGAL TENANCY BILL. March 11. 1885	39
XV. THE BENGAL TENANCY BILL. March 13, 1885 ..	44
XVI. ART IN INDIA. Sept. 18. 1885	46

TABLE OF CONTENTS.

	PAGE
XVII. Sir Donald Stewart. Oct. 13. 1885	48
XVIII. The New General Hospital, Delhi. Nov. 2. 1885	51
XIX. Opening the Mayo College at Ajmir. Nov. 7. 1885	52
XX. Speech at the Fortress of Gwalior. Dec. 2. 1885	57, 60
XXI. Reply to the Municipality of Lucknow. Dec. 4. 1885	61
XXII. License Tax Amendment Bill. Jan. 4. 1886	64
XXIII. License Tax Amendment Bill. Jan. 11. 1886	81
XXIV. Welcome to Foreign Officers at Delhi. Jan. 19. 1886	82, 86
XXV. The Countess of Dufferin's Fund. Jan. 27. 1886	86, 91
XXVI. Reply to the Address from the Inhabitants of Rangoon. Feb. 7. 1886	91
XXVII. Reply to the Address from the European Community at Mandalay. Feb. 8. 1886 ..	93
XXVIII. Reply to the Address from the Burmese Community, Mandalay. Feb. 8. 1886	95
XXIX. Reply to the Address of the Mahomedan Community of Mandalay. Feb. 18. 1886 ..	96
XXX. Military Operations in Upper Burmah. Feb. 17. 1886	97
XXXI. Address to the Members of the Hlutdaw ..	101
XXXII. Reply to an Address from the Chamber of Commerce, Rangoon. Feb. 23. 1886	102
XXXIII. Decoration of Burmese Gentlemen. Feb. 24. 1886	104
XXXIV. Reply to Address from Merchants on the Timber Trade	104

TABLE OF CONTENTS.

		PAGE
XXXV.	Reply to an Address from the Rangoon Bar	105
XXXVI.	Reply to an Address from the Burmese Community of Rangoon	106
XXXVII.	Reply to the Address from the Gee Heng Chinese Community	107
XXXVIII.	Reply to an Address from the Shan Community of Rangoon	108
XXXIX.	The Buddhistic Church in Burma	109
XL.	Reply to an Address from the Hokkien Chinese of Rangoon	110
XLI.	Reply to an Address from the Tamil and Telegu Christians of Rangoon	110
XLII.	The Countess of Dufferin's Fund. Feb. 24. 1886	111
XLIII.	Reply to Addresses at Madras. March 1. 1886	112
XLIV.	Infant Marriages among Hindus. March 2. 1886	117
XLV.	The Oudh Rent Bill. June 9. 1886	118
XLVI.	The Death of Sir Herbert Macpherson. Oct. 21. 1886	120
XLVII.	The Aitchison College. Nov. 3. 1886	121
XLVIII.	Address to the Convocation of the Punjab University. Nov. 4. 1886	124
XLIX.	Sir West Ridgeway. Nov. 4. 1886	128
L.	The Gaekwar of Baroda. Nov. 9. 1886	129
LI.	Reply to an Address from the Corporation of Bombay. Nov. 13. 1886	132
LII.	Reply to an Address from the Poona Muicipality. Nov. 19. 1886	133
LIII.	Banquet at Hyderabad. Nov. 24. 1886	138
LIV.	Banquet at Mysore. Nov. 30. 1886	139

		PAGE
LV.	Reply to an Address from the Mysore Representative Assembly ..	141
LVI.	The French in India. Dec. 10. 1886	143
LVII.	Educational Progress in India. Dec. 30. 1886	148
LVIII.	Address to the Convocation of the Calcutta University. Jan. 8. 1887	152
LIX.	The Countess of Dufferin's Fund. Jan. 26. 1887	154
LX.	The Queen's Jubilee. Feb. 16. 1887	156
LXI.	Burma Military Police. July 27. 1887	161
LXII.	French Scientific Travellers at Simla. Aug. 18. 1887	163
LXIII.	Investiture of the Countess of Dufferin with the Persian Order of the Sun. A Persian Speech. Aug. 30. 1887	164
LXIV.	The Punjab Tenancy Bill. Sept. 22. 1887	167
LXV.	Reply to Addresses from the Kurrachee Chamber of Commerce, the Inhabitants of Sind, the Mahomedan Central Association, and the Sind Sabha. Nov. 12. 1887	168
LXVI.	Durbar at Peshawar. Nov. 25. 1887	174
LXVII.	Reply to an Address from the Peshawar Municipality. Nov. 25. 1887	176
LXVIII.	The Dufferin Bridge, Benares. Dec. 16. 1887	177
LXIX.	Customs Duty on Petroleum. Jan. 27. 1888	181, 182
LXX.	Customs Duty on Petroleum. Feb. 3. 1888	182
LXXI.	Countess of Dufferin's Fund. Feb. 8. 1888	186
LXXII.	Announcement of Lord Dufferin's Resignation. Feb. 10. 1888	188
LXXIII.	Address to the Members of the Legislative Council, in Calcutta. March 23. 1888	190

TABLE OF CONTENTS.

	PAGE
LXXIV. Reply to Farewell Addresses, Calcutta. March 23. 1888	192
LXXV. Reply to Farewell Address from the Ooterpara Municipality. March 24. 1888	201
LXXVI. Reply to Farewell Address from the Central Mahomedan Association. March 24. 1888	203
LXXVII. Reply to Farewell Address from the Calcutta Mahomedan Literary Society. March 26. 1888	205
LXXVIII. Reply to Farewell Address from the Talukdars of Oudh. April 7. 1888	207
LXXIX. Reply to Farewell Address from Mahomedan Associations at Lucknow. April 10. 1888	212
LXXX. Speech at Farewell Ball at Simla. Sept. 24. 1888	215
LXXXI. Reply to an Address from the Municipal Committee of Lahore. Nov. 14. 1888	217
LXXXII. Reply to an Address from the Anjuman-i-Itihad, Lahore. Nov. 15. 1888	219
LXXXIII. Lady Dufferin's Reply to the Representatives of the Women of the Punjab. Nov. 6. 1888	220
LXXXIV. Speech at Durbar held at Patiala. Nov. 17. 1888	223
LXXXV. Speech in Proposing the Health of the Maharaja of Patiala. Nov. 17. 1888	226
LXXXVI. The Aligarh College. Nov. 20. 1888	227
LXXXVII. St. Andrew's Dinner, Calcutta. Nov. 30. 1888	229
LXXXVIII. Lady Dufferin's Reply to an Address from the Native Ladies of Bengal. Dec. 4. 1888	248
LXXXIX. Lady Dufferin's Reply to the Farewell Address of the Public Health Society. Dec. 7. 1888	250

		PAGE
XC.	REPLY TO THE FAREWELL ADDRESS FROM THE CALCUTTA MUNICIPALITY. Dec. 8. 1888	252
XCI.	REPLY TO AN ADDRESS FROM THE MUNICIPAL CORPORATION OF BOMBAY. Dec. 12. 1888	255
XCII.	REPLY TO THE FAREWELL ADDRESS FROM THE BOMBAY CHAMBER OF COMMERCE. Dec. 13. 1888	256
XCIII.	THOUGHTS ON ARRIVING IN AND LEAVING INDIA. Dec. 13. 1888	258
XCIV.	SPEECH AT THE MANSION HOUSE ON RECEIVING THE FREEDOM OF THE CITY OF LONDON. May 29. 1889	263
XCV.	BANQUET IN THE ULSTER HALL, BELFAST. Sept. 19. 1889	274
XCVI.	ENGLAND'S TRADE WITH INDIA. Oct. 30. 1889	282

SPEECHES.

On the 11th of July, 1883, Lord Dufferin was entertained at dinner by the members of the Empire Club, London, and in reply to the toast of his health spoke as follows :—

MY LORDS AND GENTLEMEN,—In rising to return thanks to those I see around me for the kind manner in which they have drunk my health, I cannot help asking myself, with some anxiety, what title I possess to the goodwill of my entertainers. The chairman has, indeed, referred to my public services in very flattering terms, but the reason for the cordiality you have evinced is further to seek, I fear, than anything contained in his indulgent observations. (Cries of "No.") My hosts upon this occasion are the members of the Empire Club, and perhaps I am justified in concluding that they have conferred upon me so signal an honour not so much on account of my individual merits, as because during the last twelve years I have been unremittingly occupied in maintaining and promoting in different parts of the world the "imperial" as distinguished from the domestic interests of our common country. (Cheers.) In Canada, in Russia, at Constantinople, and in Egypt, home politics, and the bitter strifes engendered by party warfare, have naturally faded from my view, and my one thought by day and by night has been either to safeguard the honour, the influence, and the commerce of Great Britain in its relations with foreign Governments, or to draw still more closely together the ties which unite her to the most powerful as well as the most loyal of all her colonies. (Loud cheers.) Under these circumstances, it must be forgiven me if, without indulging in any vulgar or selfish spirit of Jingoism—and, after all, an Ambassador or Colonial Governor is almost a Jingo by profession—I have come to look at England—

> "This sceptred isle, this earth of majesty,
> This other Eden—demi-Paradise,
> This precious stone set in the silver sea—
> This happy breed of men"—

not as she exhibits herself in the recriminations of Parliamentary warfare, or the denunciatory eloquence of the platform, but in an aspect softened by distance and regret, as the happy home of a great and noble-hearted people, whom it is an honour to serve, and for whose sake it would be a privilege to make any possible sacrifice—to look at her, in fact, with the same loving, loyal, all-embracing pride and affection as she is regarded by those widespread communities to whom she has given birth, who are filling the most distant regions of the earth with her laws, her liberties, her language, and her civilization, many of whose most distinguished representatives are here to-night, and to whom it is the special object of this club to extend the right hand of brotherhood and good fellowship. (Cheers.) If, therefore, I fail, gentlemen, in adequately expressing to you my deep sense of obligation for having invited me to this splendid banquet, it will not be from any want of sympathy with the guiding idea which has drawn you together. I am well aware, indeed, that some of the most influential thinkers of the day are disposed to stand aghast at the accumulating responsibilities, the increasing calls upon our resources, the widening vulnerability entailed by England's imperial position, and the outlook may well suggest the necessity of caution, and, above all, of preparation. But, after all, it is with nations as with individuals. The burden of a man's duties, cares, and preoccupations gathers weight in proportion to the expansion of his faculties, the richness of his nature, the increase of his wealth or influence. The very children who people our homes are so many hostages that we have given to fortune. Nay (but I say it beneath my breath), the wives of our bosoms seldom fail to provide us, each on her own account, with a whole chapter of startling accidents. (A laugh.) Yet what man of spirit ever turns his back upon opportunity, or disdains the tender ties of a love-lit fireside, through fear of the obligations which might be entailed by a fuller and more complete existence? (Cheers.) But, even did she so desire, it is now too late for this country to disinherit herself of the destiny with which I firmly believe she has been endowed by Providence. The same hidden hand which planted the tree of constitutional liberty within her border, which called upon her to become the mother of Parliaments, has sent her people forth to possess and fructify the waste places of the earth's surface. How the desert is being planted and turned into a paradise in every quarter of the globe those who hear me can best tell. Yet what has been done is nothing in comparison with what may well be accomplished within the lives of our own grandchildren. According to the computation of one of the most sober of our statisticians, before another century is brought to a close the English-speaking populations will have expanded to a thousand millions. Of these, forty millions will probably be found in Canada alone, seventy millions in the British Islands, and a corresponding proportion along the coasts of Africa, in India, and in our Australian possessions. If united, co-ordinated, and inspired by a common impulse, what a powerful influence, as compared with that likely to be possessed by any other nationality, whether for good or for evil, whether considered from a moral or from a material point of view, this multiplication of the English race implies! (Cheers.) For that they will remain Englishmen—if not in name, at all events in their common feeling and in their affections—who can doubt? (Cheers.) Chance and change, the increasing momentum acquired by the progress of civilization, forbid us to forecast or anticipate the future too minutely. Moreover, the gigantic forces operating over these large spaces preclude almost the hope of human prescience or human wisdom directing the course of events. But one thing at all events is obvious—namely, that for many a generation those communities must necessarily be deeply impressed by English sentiment, English habits and customs, English literature, and English institutions. (Cheers.) That this should long continue to be the case is the object dearest to the heart of those I am addressing. (Cheers.) It is their desire to see our statesmen so conduct their relations with our colonies and dependencies as to retain unimpaired those affectionate feelings with which they are instinctively disposed to regard the mother-country. Whatever else may happen, it is certain that the people of England will never allow their Government to repeat the errors which led to the separation of the United States. (Cheers.) However well contented we may be with the relations now existing between ourselves and the great Transatlantic Republic, there can be little doubt that, but for the violence of the disruption, those relations would at the present moment have been more mutually advantageous. The catastrophe occurred through the Minister of the day failing to appreciate the force and direction of colonial sentiment. There can be no greater mistake than for statesmen to overlook the important part which sentiment plays in the conduct of human affairs. (Hear, hear.) More of the wars which have desolated the earth have been occasioned by outraged sentiment than by the pursuit of material advantage. Nay, even commerce itself, the most unromantic and sagacious of interests, follows for lengthened periods in the wake of custom, consanguinity, sentiment, and tradition. This is one of those truths of which the English people are but imperfectly aware. Indeed, until lately, they scarcely realized the yearning desire felt by the British colonial populations for the due recognition of their kinship. Happily, increased facilities of intercourse, the ever-widening stream of emigration, and the exigencies of trade, have changed all this. The fact has now been brought home to the imagination of Englishmen that beyond the narrow seas which encircle their island, there lie vast regions peopled by powerful communities, owing allegiance, and proud to owe it, to Queen Victoria, animated by the same ideas as themselves, in their material resources richer, and destined, perhaps, some day to become more powerful than themselves, and yet who will never have a higher ambition, if only they are properly dealt with, than to continue co-heirs of England's illustrious past, associates in her empire, and sharers in her future fortunes, whether they be for good or evil, until the end of time. (Cheers.) Gentlemen, I believe it is the desire of the members of this club to propagate such ideas as these, however imperfectly I may express them, and I feel that, in returning thanks to you for the great honour you have done me, I cannot show my gratitude in a more acceptable manner than by telling you how cordially and enthusiastically I subscribe to them.

The conclusion of his Lordship's speech was received with great enthusiasm, the company rising to their feet and continuing to cheer for some minutes.

SPEECH IN BELFAST.

On October the 15th, 1884, the inhabitants of Belfast and of the neighbouring counties entertained Lord Dufferin at a banquet in the Ulster Hall, on the occasion of his appointment to the Viceroyalty of India. In reply to the toast of his health, which was proposed by the mayor, Sir David Taylor, his Lordship spoke as follows :—

MR. MAYOR, MY LORDS, AND GENTLEMEN,—I am sure that there is not one in this room who will not understand how impossible it is for me to give anything approaching an adequate expression of that deep emotion which is stirring the very inmost recesses of my heart as I rise to respond to the toast which you have just received in so enthusiastic a manner. Standing as I do in this well-known hall, surrounded by the friends and neighbours of my early manhood, with the cheers and plaudits of all Ulster ringing in my ears, and overwhelmed, as I have been, by the kind words of welcome and encouragement pronounced on your behalf by the president of this banquet, I am almost driven to take refuge in silence from the bewildering thoughts that crowd on my mind. How at such a moment can I help remembering the many occasions upon which during the last thirty years I have appeared before you, only to receive fresh proofs of your goodwill and indulgent sympathy? Least of all, how can I forget that memorable night when, on the eve of my departure for Canada, this splendid chamber was filled with friends who had assembled to bid me God-speed and to assure me that, in the opinion of those who had known me best and longest, the honour then conferred upon me by Her Majesty was not considered misplaced or undeserved ? (Cheers.) The fact that I am again standing before you in analogous circumstances authorises me to entertain the pleasing conviction that none of you regret the pledge you then gave for my good behaviour, or consider that I have done disgrace to your *imprimatur*. (Cheers.) The occasion ushered in the brightest and happiest period of my life—a period passed in one of the fairest regions within the confines of the empire, amongst a people animated by the most generous instincts, endowed with all the noblest gifts and qualities which distinguish the British race, and to whom I owe a debt of gratitude and affection whose welcome burden I shall carry to the grave. Since that auspicious celebration twelve years have passed, during which in different capacities I have done my best to render faithful and loyal service to my Queen and country—(cheers)—and now again that I am about to proceed to a distant land, to undertake a task more arduous, more responsible, and, I may add, more honourable, than any which has ever been imposed upon me, can it be wondered at if, like the hero of old who was invincible so long as he was in contact with his mother earth, I come back here amongst you to gather fresh strength and vigour and renew my youth by once more looking around on your familiar faces, by listening to your genial words of welcome and encouragement, by taking a farewell grasp of your thousand friendly hands. (Cheers.) It is true that the powers of Antæus faded into impotence as soon as his enemy lifted him from the ground, but I feel that, no matter how high the sphere to which I may be elevated, the fortifying influences with which I am surrounded to-night will follow me wherever I go, and in the darkest moments of lassitude and depression the recollection of this glorious scene will restore my faltering spirits and make me more than equal to deal with any emergency which may occur. (Cheers.) And yet the fable to which I have referred carries with it a wholesome warning and some melancholy reflections. It may simply mean that the promotion of a man to a situation beyond the scope of his abilities is certain to be followed by his speedy overthrow. But though, I trust, future events may prove that this is not its true interpretation so far as I am concerned—(hear, hear)—I cannot help being aware that the unanimity with which you, gentlemen, who sometimes are temporarily divided by differences of opinion in the fields both of political and of religious thought—(hear, hear)—have been pleased to hail my nomination as Viceroy of India, together with the cordial manner in which my appointment has been endorsed, and which it would be an affectation as well as an act of ingratitude on my part not to recognise and take pride in, is a condition of public sentiment which can never again recur to me. (Cheers.) Never again, I fear, no matter what my efforts or exertions, can I hope so completely to unite in their present harmonious concord the suffrages of my countrymen. The government of India is not only a laborious task, but it is one presenting problems of the very greatest doubt and intricacy. From day to day the most complex questions are submitted to the attention of the Executive, which from their very nature are incapable of an altogether satisfactory solution; and in regard to which the choice does not lie between the absolute good and the absolute bad, but is dependent upon such a delicate comparison of advantage and disadvantage upon either side as to render it very difficult for even those who have every opportunity of acquainting themselves with the elements of the case to come to a sound conclusion. Out of these circumstances must arise a vast amount of intelligent and conscientious criticism; and, while on the one hand it can scarcely be expected that he who is ultimately responsible for what happens will be invariably in the right, it is certain that he will frequently appear to many intelligent observers to be altogether in the wrong. Hence it must inevitably follow that very conflicting estimates will be formed of the success with which the Governor-General of the day is conducting the arduous administration over which he presides. Nor is he in any way entitled either to deprecate the most searching examinations into his conduct, or to be irritated at the blunt and angry criticisms to which he may be exposed. All regard for his personal susceptibilities will naturally be postponed and disappear in the presence of the great questions at stake, affecting at the same time the happiness of millions of our fellow-subjects in India itself, and nearly touching the honour, the conscience, and the safety of that

Imperial Power to whom Providence has entrusted the superintendence of their destinies. (Cheers.) All that a person in such a situation can demand is that one thing, and one thing alone, should be remembered in mitigation of any impending condemnation which public opinion may be disposed to pass upon his conduct, and that is, that he is the man upon the spot; that he is the man who must know a great deal more intimately than anybody else what may be the requirements of the situation—(hear, hear)—that there may be many a consideration present to his mind possessing the most cogent force which is naturally hidden from the gaze of those who are watching the drama from a distance—(hear, hear)—that the temporary puffs and flaws of fleeting public opinion are not always a true indication of the direction in which the wind is blowing; and that it is but just and fair to credit your servant, to whom you have once given your confidence, at least with the presumption of being in the right until the contrary is shown to reasonable demonstration. (Cheers.) Above all, let me remind you, my lords and gentlemen, that when dealing with such vast subjects as those which occupy the statesmen of Calcutta; when handling the tremendous forces which are evolved out of the complicated and multitudinous political systems which exist within the borders of the Indian peninsula; when endeavouring to mould by slow and cautious efforts the most ancient, the most continuous, and the most artificially organised civilisation to be found on the face of the earth, into forms that shall eventually harmonize more and more with those conceptions which the progress of science and the result of experience have shown to be conducive to human happiness, the result of the ruler's exertions and the flower of his achievements are seldom perceptible at the moment, but far more frequently bring forth their fruit long after those that tilled the field and sowed the seed have rested from their unrecognised and sometimes depreciated labours. (Hear, hear, and cheers.) The days when great reputations are to be made in India are, happily perhaps, as completely past as those in which great fortunes were accumulated. Famous Indian Pro-Consuls are no longer required by their superiors or compelled by circumstances to startle their countrymen by the annexation of provinces, the overthrow of dynasties, the revolutionising of established systems, and all those dramatic performances which invariably characterise the founding and consolidation of new-born empires. Their successors must be content with the less ambitious and more homely, but equally important and beneficent, work of justifying the splendid achievements of those who have gone before them, by the careful and painstaking elaboration of such economical, educational, judicial, and social arrangements as shall bring happiness, peace, contentment, and security alike to the cabin doors of the humble ryot, to the mansions of the loyal zemindar and enterprising European settler, and to the palace gates of Her Majesty's honoured allies and princely feudatories. (Cheers.) Nor let it be imagined that this humble programme is not enough to exhaust the energies and strain to the utmost the abilities and statesmanship of India's most experienced servants, and England's wisest counsellors. (Hear, hear.) Things go very fast with us nowadays, and the changes in their conditions and relations are as multiplex and instantaneous as those in a kaleidoscope. Yesterday India was an isolated region, remote from the disturbing influences of foreign contact. To-day we have an European neighbour on our north-western frontier, and ere long we may have another on our eastern boundary. Happily I have the good fortune to be united to the foreign Minister of Russia by the ties of personal intimacy and regard. I am convinced that a more moderate-minded, wise, and unaggressive statesman does not breathe in Europe. I believe his great desire is that Russia should live in amity with England—(hear, hear)—and that no causes of disagreement and suspicion should be generated in Central Asia between the two countries. (Hear, hear.) He has more than once assured me that he regarded the expansion of Russia in a south-easterly direction with regret, and his most earnest wish is for such a condition of affairs to come into existence as should impose upon that expansion its natural and permanent arrest. I rejoice to think that it should have fallen to my lot to co-operate with a personal friend in arriving at this desirable and necessary result. (Hear, hear.) Nor within the confines of India itself have matters remained a whit more stationary. The spread of education and the extension of railways, the congestion of populations, slow moving as are the habits of Indian thought and sentiment, have created new requirements and demand fresh readjustments, the successful accomplishment of which will call for the most extensive knowledge and the acutest insight. It would be altogether inappropriate at to-night's celebration to trouble you with the crude speculations of one who is still an outsider and a neophyte in regard to Indian politics; but in one respect, at all events, I am to be congratulated, and it is this: that when I come to address myself to the study of these subjects I shall be assisted by as able a body of public servants, both English and native, as has ever been at the disposal of any ruler. (Cheers.) I believe, my lords and gentlemen, that the civil service of India is unrivalled for integrity, intelligence, loyalty, and a sense of public duty; and probably nothing has contributed more effectually to impress it with these characteristics than the recruits it has received from Ireland, and especially from Ulster. (Loud cheers.) I might perhaps be straining our native privileges too far if I connected Wellington with the civil service, though India's greatest soldier was a civil servant, and some of her ablest civil administrators have been soldiers. But, keeping within the letter of the allusion, where has there existed a more capable and benevolent representative of the Crown than Marquis Wellesley? (Cheers.) What Governor-General has ever so captivated the affections of the Indian people as the late lamented Lord Mayo? (Cheers.) What statesman in either hemisphere can point to such an heroic record as that of the immortal Lawrence? (Cheers.) Where can you find a name surrounded by a brighter halo of blameless fame and honour than that of Sir Robert Montgomery? (Cheers.) Nor in this connection can I altogether pass over the allusion made by a previous speaker to one of the most heroic and noblest individuals with whom it has ever been my good fortune to come into contact. During the period I spent at Constantinople I had become acquainted with Colonel Stewart's exceptional qualities. He had served under my orders in Asia Minor, and again in Egypt. He was sent out by her Majesty's Government in a diplomatic capacity, with orders to repair to Khartoum to report on the condition of affairs which he found there. It was a matter of astonishment to me to hear of his reported death; and I am happy to think that I have recorded in an official despatch the capacity, the industry, and the ability with which, under most unpropitious circumstances, that noble officer discharged the task entrusted to him. He sent home a series of despatches which are unrivalled for their lucidity, for the mass of complicated information which they conveyed, and, above all, the noble spirit of humanity which they breathed. Gentlemen, it is a melancholy pleasure to me—if, indeed, it is true that we must give up the hope of ever seeing him again—to have this opportunity of paying this public tribute to the memory of Colonel Stewart. But, to return to India, behind and beyond the fortunate few whom accident and happy chance, seconding their inherent merits and native genius, have made known to the world, there are hundreds and hundreds of noble and high-minded officials, unknown and unrewarded, who in the solitude of their several districts, burdened with enormous responsibilities, compelled to sacrifice almost everything that renders human life delightful, are faithfully expending their existence for their Queen, for their country, and for those committed to their charge, with nothing but their conscience to sustain them, reinforced by the conviction which is inherent in every Briton's breast, that the sense of having done one's duty is better than name or fame, Imperial honours, or popular approbation. (Loud cheers.) It is to join these men that I go, and though I dare say there may be many amongst them superior to myself in ability, as they all must be in experience, one thing I can promise you, that neither amongst those who have lived and laboured and who have disappeared from the scene, nor amongst those who are still working for the good of England and of India, will any have set forth more determined to walk fearlessly and faithfully in the unpretending paths of duty. (Hear, hear, and cheers.) So convinced am I, indeed, of the truth of what I say, that I imagine the greatest success and triumph I can obtain is that, from the time that I depart from these shores and wave a grateful response to the farewell you are saying to me to-night, even the echo of my name may never be wafted to your ears until at the end of my official term I stand again amongst you, having won from the historian of the day no higher encomium or recognition than that my administration was uneventful, but that I had kept the empire entrusted to my guardianship tranquil and secure. (Loud cheers.) And now, gentlemen, I have done. In the few words I have addressed to you I have made but a poor return for the honour you have conferred upon me, for the kindness you have shown me, and for the confidence you have placed in me. What the future may bring forth none can foretell, but of this at least you may be sure, that no act or thought of mine shall be unworthy of my country and its Sovereign, who have entrusted this charge into my hands, of the Indian Empire I am required to administer, or of that greater Empire of which India is but a part—of that Empire whose laws and liberties, whose honour and repute, whose past and whose future are the birthright and the legitimate care and pride of every Englishman in every quarter of the globe! (Loud and prolonged applause.)

On the same occasion Lord Dufferin, in responding to the toast of Lady Dufferin's health, said:—

MR. MAYOR, MY LORDS AND GENTLEMEN,—I hope you will remember that during the last four years of my life the chief obligation imposed upon me was that of silence—(laughter)—and that consequently the effort of addressing a public assembly after so long an interval of desuetude is extremely difficult; but all the married men amongst you will understand that, when any one hears his wife praised in such chivalrous and eloquent terms as those to which we have just listened, his heart begins to burn within him and he cannot hold his tongue. (Laughter and applause.) I myself, my lords and gentlemen, have always considered that amongst Lady Dufferin's great and eminent qualities the most pre-eminent, and the one of which I was proudest, was the very one alluded to by my honourable friend—namely, that she was an Irishwoman—(applause)—and, having already ventured to treat you to a classical allusion, I will venture to refer you to another, in order that you may thoroughly understand how completely I endorse the sentiments which have been so cordially received by all present. In ancient times there was a certain well-known—I dare not call him distinguished—Grecian chief who wandered over many seas and visited many cities and conversed with many men, but wherever he went he was followed by the mysterious influence of the goddess, who suggested to him at all times and seasons what he was to do and say, who smoothed his path before him, and rendered his progress miraculously successful. (Applause.) My lords and gentlemen, it is no exaggeration to say that during the course of my public career no ancient goddess of Grecian mythology could have rendered me more effective aid, could have extended to me more completely the ægis of her sweet wisdom and comforting counsel than that of the lady to whose health you have just paid this tribute of respect. (Applause.) It has been a deep regret to her not to be able to be present on this occasion, but I assure you I shall not fail to make her understand how kindly you have expressed yourselves towards her, and I assure you in her name that she is most deeply grateful to you for the friendship and consideration with which you have honoured her. (Cheers.) And now, my lords and gentlemen, it is my pleasing duty to discharge a most important, and to me most imperative task. Amongst the many regrets which, in the midst of all this pleasure, I cannot help experiencing, is the regret of finding myself in the midst of so many personal friends and neighbours and acquaintances without having the power of shaking them by the hand or exchanging with them—with each individual—a friendly word of greeting; but I feel that I cannot better consolidate and concentrate the gratitude which I feel towards you one and all than by endeavouring to convey it to this great and generous assembly by calling upon you to drink the health of your honourable representative on this occasion—the Mayor of Belfast—(applause)—who has presided over this banquet with so much propriety and dignity, who by the cheers with which his various speeches were greeted has evidently expressed so completely to your satisfaction those sentiments which you desire to make known. (Hear, hear.) I am well aware of the estimation in which the Mayor is held by his fellow-citizens, but in one respect I will not follow his example. I will really abstain from doing what might embarrass him by enlarging at too great length upon his many amiable qualities. I beg leave to propose to you " The Health of the Mayor," and with the toast I venture to couple " Prosperity to the great town of Belfast." (Applause.)

SPEECH AT THE NORTHBROOK CLUB.

On the 1st of November, 1884, the members of the Northbrook Club entertained Lord Dufferin at dinner in the Westminster Town Hall, previous to his departure from England to assume the duties of the Indian Viceroyalty. In reply to the toast of his health Lord Dufferin spoke as follows :—

In rising to return thanks for the kind reception you have just given to the mention of my name, I cannot help expressing at the same time my deep sense of the favour shown me by the large attendance of members who have assembled in this magnificent apartment to bid me "God-speed." One sometimes hears of a person not being able to contain himself for joy, and of a man's heart being too full for words, but it is an unprecedented honour when a club, in its generous enthusiasm for its guest, is content to emigrate from its accustomed haunts in order to find elbow room for its feelings in the ample precincts of an alien hall like this.

And now, gentlemen, I scarcely know in what way to continue. When I look around me upon this august assemblage, composed as it is in a great measure of illustrious and distinguished persons who have passed their lives in India, who are intimately acquainted with every nook and corner of that great peninsula and the intricate mysteries of its administration, I feel that it would be the height of presumption on the part of one so ignorant and inexperienced as myself in Indian matters to hazard any observations in reference to our great dependency. A newly-appointed viceroy, when called upon to make a speech under such circumstances, must seem to the onlookers very like a man who is playing at blind-man's buff. While the room and the company present are flooded with light, he is floundering about with outstretched arms in utter darkness, with great danger of breaking his shins over the furniture, or, what would be more dreadful still, of knocking over any amount of delicate bits of china, to the great indignation of the mistress of the house—who on this occasion is not inaptly represented by my noble friend the Secretary of State—as she watches in an agony of indignant trepidation his indiscreet and ungainly rhetorical gambols. Happily, however, there is nothing your kind consideration has not taken into account, and I understand that all of us who may have the privilege of addressing you will do so in the happy consciousness that they are revelling in the luxury and licence of unreported speeches. Be that, however, as it may, there are one or two things I can say with a perfectly clear conscience. In the first place, it greatly enhances my pleasure to know that the favour shown to me emanates from a society which in a great measure owes both its name and its existence to one of my earliest and most constant personal friends, a statesman who has rendered the greatest services to his country, whose name is equally beloved and honoured in India and at home, and whose bright example it will be my highest ambition to follow and emulate. Neither can I refrain from expressing my satisfaction at finding myself in contact—I may say for the first time, and under such agreeable auspices—with so many of our Indian fellow-subjects. Ignorant as I am of many matters connected with India, I am not ignorant of the claims the native gentlemen I see around me possess to my respect and consideration. Their acquirements, their princely charities, their loyalty, and their personal qualities are well known to me, and I regard it as a most happy omen that they should have thus met together in such large numbers to give me a foretaste of the cordial welcome which never fails to await the representatives of their Queen at the hands of their countrymen at home.

I am also entitled to express my deep gratitude for the kind words of encouragement and approval in which Sir Barrow Ellis (the chairman) has been good enough to refer to my nomination. Though I do not dare to accept all the pleasant things he has said in my regard, I may certainly hope, without incurring the charge of presumption, that my previous official experiences may prove of advantage to me in my new position. I believe that it will be by no means a bad thing for the Viceroy of India to have established friendly relations both with the Court of Russia and with that of Constantinople. During the whole time of my stay in Turkey, I experienced nothing but the greatest kindness and many personal favours at the hands of his Imperial Majesty the Sultan, who is distinguished amongst the monarchs of the day for the unrivalled courtesy of his manners and the greatest consideration for those who come into personal relations with him. Nor can the acquaintances and friendships I formed with the Turkish statesmen at Constantinople, and the knowledge I acquired of the habits and modes of thought of the inhabitants of the Turkish Empire, fail to be of the greatest service to me in a country where Mahomedans compose a very large and influential section of the population. Of my regard for the distinguished minister who conducts the foreign affairs of Russia, I have already had occasion to speak, and as far as the ties of personal friendship can influence such matters, I am sure that nothing will be wanting on Mr. de Giers' part or on my own to promote the most friendly understanding between the two countries. At the same time I trust that the people of England will not forget, as certainly I will not forget, that national security must not be allowed to depend upon the moderation of a minister of a foreign State whose hand may be forced at any moment by rivals or subordinates, or upon the friendly intentions of a neighbouring monarch, who is as often compelled to follow as to lead—but that the only trustworthy guarantee for the integrity of national boundaries is the vigilance and valour of those who dwell within them.

And now, gentlemen, in conclusion I will merely say that in proceeding to the fulfilment of the task which has been set me, my highest ambition will always be to illustrate in practice, and carry out in spirit, those praiseworthy purposes for which this club was founded. In doing this, I believe I shall be making the best return in my power for the hospitality you have extended to me to-night. These purposes as I understand them are to promote by every means in our power the best possible relations between the native populations of India and their British fellow-subjects; to unite them in the bonds of a common loyalty; and, under the ægis of an impartial executive, to extend to all and each of them the blessings of justice and good government. Those honoured and distinguished persons who are sitting around me are the men who, in their day and generation, have inextricably interwoven these principles with the most sacred traditions of Indian administration, and I may observe in passing that these principles have never been more vigorously enforced than by the present courageous, unselfish, and high-minded Viceroy. The wisdom, integrity, and devotion to their Queen and country which these high-minded and conscientious men have displayed, have established immutably upon this righteous basis what I believe to be the most beneficent empire the world has ever seen. Your society has been impregnated by the same lofty and generous spirit, consequently I regard it as a fortunate circumstance (to borrow a simile from oriental philosophy) that I have had an opportunity of thus passing within the sphere of your influence and of becoming incorporated with your essence, before I go forth as an emanation temporarily severed and separated from your august communion, to pass through the stages of a troubled existence in a distant world of anxiety and labour. Should fortune favour, however, and no misdeeds or miscarriages of my own render me unfit for such enjoyment, I have at least the prospect of at length returning to find in your approval and welcome that Nirvana and perfect rest which the justified great ones I see around me have attained to in your placid halls.

ADDRESS FROM THE MUNICIPAL CORPORATION OF BOMBAY.

The Earl and Countess of Dufferin, accompanied by Lady Helen Blackwood, Miss Thynne, Mr. Mackenzie Wallace, Major Cooper, and other members of His Excellency's staff, arrived in Bombay Harbour by the P. and O. steamship *Tasmania* on the morning of the 8th December, 1884. Their Excellencies landed at half-past four in the afternoon, and an address of welcome was presented to Lord Dufferin by the Municipal Corporation of Bombay at the Apollo Bunder. In the course of their address, the Corporation referred to Lord Dufferin's distinguished career in other parts of the world, and, remarking on the fact that the success of His Excellency's administration of Canada was largely due to his personal intimacy with the various communities and outlying regions of that country, they hoped that he would be able to visit the various provinces of India and become personally acquainted with the people and their leaders. They referred to some of the more important administrative measures with which Lord Dufferin would have to deal, such as railway and irrigation works, the advancement of free Municipal Government, and other measures of internal reform, and in conclusion drew His Excellency's "serious attention to the danger which one-half of the sea-borne commerce of India incurs from the utterly defenceless condition of Bombay Harbour." Lord Dufferin replied as follows:—

Mr. CHAIRMAN AND GENTLEMEN,—No servant of the Crown could desire his arrival in India to be more auspiciously inaugurated than by the cordial words of welcome and encouragement you have addressed to me on behalf of the inhabitants of this prosperous and famous city; and the impressive picture you have drawn of the opportunities, duties, and responsibilities attaching to the great office I am about to assume, is well calculated to afford me matter for serious and wholesome reflection. It has been your pleasure to extend similar courtesies to several of my predecessors when they stood—as I do now—on the threshold of their career in this country, unwitting of the good or evil fortune which might be in store for them. These illustrious persons have greatly differed from each other in their antecedents, their dispositions, their attainments, and their intellectual idiosyncrasies. But there is one quality which all of them have possessed in common—a deep-rooted and unswerving determination to sacrifice ease, health, leisure, nay, as some of them have done, even life itself, at the welcome and spirit-stirring call of duty. (Hear, hear; and cheers.) It is this characteristic which has impressed the Government of India, from its foundation to the present day, with a loftiness of aim and intention, and an energy in execution, which I believe to be unparalleled in the history of the world. (cheers.) Though not presuming to compare myself with the statesmen who have gone before me, in this last respect at least I trust to prove their equal, by preserving unimpaired the noble traditions of devotion and self-effacement which have been established by their heroic examples, and by none more signally than by your present illustrious and eminent Viceroy. (Loud cheers.) Whatever criticisms may be justly passed on my future administration, it shall be in the power of no man to allege that either from fear or favour, or any personal consideration, I have turned aside from whatever course was most conducive to the happiness of the millions entrusted to my care (cheers), or to the dignity, honour, and safety of that mighty Empire with which this great dependency is indissolubly incorporated. (Renewed cheers.) Only partially acquainted as I am at present with the indigenous customs and ancient civilization of its multitudinous races, I hope to find at your provincial centres advisers and counsellors, both British and native, whose experience will enable me to discharge with success the task I have undertaken; and to no set of men could I address myself with greater advantage for such information as I may require, than to the representatives of the great community of Bombay, whose industry, enterprise, and sagacity have created a city vying in its prosperity and wealth with any capital that has ever been called into existence by Caliph or Mogul. Should fitting opportunities present themselves to my Government of still further promoting your welfare, stimulating your trade, increasing your security, or enlarging the scope of your municipal activity, you may rest assured that it will be my most anxious desire to take advantage of them. Under any circumstances I shall always retain a grateful recollection

of the considerate manner in which you have made me feel that
in landing upon the shores of India I have come to a home
already rendered bright and attractive by the presence of hosts
of fellow-workers, well-wishers, and friends. (Loud and prolonged cheers.)

ADDRESS FROM THE BOMBAY CHAMBER OF COMMERCE.

The Bombay Chamber of Commerce next presented an address to Lord
Dufferin, in which His Excellency's attention was specially directed to the
importance of developing railway communication not only in the Bombay
Presidency, in which the Chamber indicated certain lines requiring more
immediate attention, but throughout India generally. Reference was also
made to the defects of the Indian Insolvent Act, and the Chamber pointed
out the desirability of extending the provisions of the new English Bank-
ruptcy Act of 1883 to India. The appointment of a Commission to inquire
into the defences of Bombay Harbour was suggested; and the Chamber
remarked that, in common with the Chamber of Commerce at Manchester,
they would welcome any efforts having for their object the development of
the overland trade with Western China and the early termination of the
present unsatisfactory state of affairs in Upper Burmah. His Excellency
replied as follows:—

Mr. CHAIRMAN AND GENTLEMEN,—I have to thank you
cordially for the words of welcome and confidence which I have
just heard, and for the suggestions which you have made concerning the measures for increasing and intensifying that
commercial and industrial enterprise with which your
magnificent city is so intimately associated. It is hardly
necessary for me to say that I thoroughly sympathise with you
in your desire for still further developing the natural resources
of the country, and that it will be my constant endeavour to aid
and encourage, within the limits of the means at our disposal,
all legitimate and practical schemes which have that object as
their aim. Before leaving England I had the advantage of
having your views regarding railway extension presented to me
by very competent authorities, and I was fully impressed with
the necessity of constantly keeping the means of communication
on a level with industrial and commercial requirements. That

the principle is a sound one there can be no doubt; but I cannot of course express any opinion as to how it is to be applied until I have had time to consider the question carefully in all its bearings. All that I can say, therefore, for the present is, that I shall consider your suggestions with the care and attention which are due to a body so deeply interested in the question and so competent to form a sound judgment upon it. In conclusion, gentlemen, I have to thank you personally, and through you the great mercantile class which you so worthily represent, for the very kind reception which I have met with in Bombay.

ADDRESS FROM THE ANJUMANI ISLAM.

The President and Members of the Anjumani Islam of Bombay, on behalf of themselves and of the Mahomedan community of Western India, then presented an address of welcome to His Excellency. After expressing a hope that the contact into which Lord Dufferin's duties had brought him with Mussulman communities in other parts of the world had created a sympathy for them in his Lordship's mind, the address proceeded to draw Lord Dufferin's attention to the backward condition of the Mussulmans in India as compared with that of other communities; while these had risen socially, intellectually, and morally, the Mussulmans had not even remained stationary, but had declined and decayed, and unless the causes were at once traced and remedies applied, the address went on to remark, " the poverty and decay of the fifty millions of the Mussulman subjects of Her Majesty cannot but prove a source of danger to the State." Pressure of work, the address stated, had prevented Lord Ripon from dealing with the question, but the deputation looked to Lord Dufferin for support, and expressed every confidence in his ability to deal adequately with the evil. His Excellency replied as follows:—

GENTLEMEN,—Few things could have given me greater pleasure on my arrival in India than to find myself welcomed by the representatives of Her Majesty's Mahomedan subjects. A considerable portion of my public life has been passed in endeavouring to be of service to Mussulman communities in different parts of the world. I am well acquainted with their history, their literature, and their modes of thought and feelings. The personal kindness I have received from His Majesty the Sultan of Turkey—who excels all the monarchs of the day in the urbanity and charm of his manners and in the gracious consideration he shows to those who have the happiness of being admitted to his presence—would of itself have made a lasting impression on my mind; and in taking leave of His Majesty I was glad to assure him of my determination to watch over the interests of his co-religionists with a fatherly solicitude. It pains me much to learn that the Mussulman community of India should entertain the misgivings you have expressed in regard to their actual condition. It is both the pride and the desire of the Imperial Government to provide impartially for every class and section of Her Majesty's subjects in India, fair and equal opportunities of improving their material condition, and of multiplying their means of moral advancement. If one member of the body politic lags behind the rest, it is a misfortune for all. I am too new to the country to be able to form an opinion as to the causes of the exceptional circumstances you signalize; but I have been glad to learn that of late you have been making great exertions to improve your educational system. When I remember that it is to Mussulman science, to Mussulman art, and to Mussulman literature that Europe has been in a great measure indebted for its extrication from the darkness of the middle ages, I find it impossible to believe that the Mahomedan communities of India should have any difficulty in keeping abreast of the rest of their fellow-subjects in the general progress of the nation. Should they be labouring under any exceptional disabilities which might militate against so desirable a result, I will endeavour to see them removed, and I have no doubt that your present illustrious Viceroy, who has had your welfare so much at heart, will place me in possession of his views on the subject to which you refer. Under any circumstances you must allow me to assure you that I have been very much touched by the terms of personal goodwill in which your address of welcome to me has been couched.

ADDRESS FROM THE CORPORATION OF CALCUTTA.

On Saturday afternoon, the 13th December, the Earl and Countess of Dufferin, accompanied by Lady Helen Blackwood, Miss Thynne, Mr. Mackenzie Wallace (Private Secretary), Major Cooper and Lord Herbrand Russell (Aides-de-Camp), and other members of His Excellency's staff, arrived in Calcutta from Bombay. Their Excellencies were met at the Howrah Railway station by the Secretaries to Government in the several departments, Brigadier-General Wilkinson and his staff, Lord William Beresford (Military Secretary to the Viceroy), and various other civil and military officers. Their Excellencies drove at once to Government House, receiving *en route* a very enthusiastic reception from the crowds who thronged the streets. On arriving at the foot of the grand staircase at Government House Lord and Lady Dufferin were received by the Lieutenant-Governor of Bengal (Mr. Rivers Thompson), and at the head of the staircase by Lord and Lady Ripon, the members of the Executive Council, the Judges of the High Court, and a large number of English and native gentlemen. Lord Dufferin was shortly afterwards conducted to the Council Chamber, where the ceremony of installing His Excellency as Viceroy and Governor-General of India was gone through with the usual formalities. Lord Dufferin then proceeded to the Throne Room, where a Deputation from the Corporation of Calcutta was in waiting to present him an address of welcome. The principal points touched upon in the address will be apparent from His Excellency's reply, which was as follows:—

Mr. CHAIRMAN AND GENTLEMEN,—No man acquainted with the history of our Indian Empire and with the annals of Calcutta could fail to be moved when addressed for the first time by the honoured representatives of that illustrious city. The friendly words of welcome and encouragement with which you have been pleased to greet my arrival amongst you add a peculiar grace to the impressive ceremony in which I have just taken part. India appears to differ so much even from the Oriental countries with which I am acquainted, that I scarcely dare attach the value to my past experiences which you are good enough to attribute to them; but at all events I trust that my familiarity with different races, forms of government, customs, and habits of thought alien to our own, have endowed me with a faculty for appreciative sympathy with what does not exactly square with Western ideas, which may prove of service to me in my new position.

In alluding to the subject of Local Self-government and to

the exceptional impulse it has received under the benign auspices of Lord Ripon, you have touched upon a matter which has already attracted my attention. If there is one principle more inherent than another in the system of our Indian administration, it is that of continuity. Nothing has struck me more than the loyal and persistent manner in which successive Viceroys, no matter what part they may have played in the strife of party politics at home, have used their utmost endeavours to bring to a successful issue whatever projects their predecessors may have conceived for the benefit of the people. It is by adherence to this principle that we have built up in this country the majestic fabric of our Government; and it is needless for me to assure you that I shall not fail to follow a line of conduct consecrated by the example of Cornwallis, Bentinck, Canning, Mayo, and those who followed them. The Marquis of Ripon and his predecessors have prepared the soil, delved, and planted. It will be my more humble duty to watch, water, prune, and train; but it may not be out of place for me to remind you that the further development of the principle of Local Self-government rests very much in your own hands. It is by an intelligent discharge of your duties, by a conscientious care of the public purse, by purity of administration, by the vigorous and economical promotion of whatever operations come within your sphere, that you will vindicate your title to enjoy the privileges conferred upon you.

In conclusion, allow me to express the satisfaction with which I have listened to your loyal reference to Her Majesty the Queen and Empress. The good of her Indian subjects is never absent from Her Majesty's mind; and it will be a gratification to her to know that you appreciate her claims to your love and devotion.

REMARKS IN THE LEGISLATIVE COUNCIL.

In opening the Proceedings at the Legislative Council, held at Government House, Calcutta, on the 19th December, 1884, the first Council at which Lord Dufferin presided, His Excellency made the following remarks:—

YOUR HONOUR AND GENTLEMEN,—I cannot take my seat for the first time at this Council Board without desiring to express to you the extreme satisfaction which I feel in being associated with so many distinguished persons in the government of this great dependency. For a very long time I must be little more than a learner in regard to the details of many of those important questions which will come up before us. But it makes me happy to think that I shall have for my colleagues and advisers men so thoroughly acquainted as yourselves with everything that is connected with the administration of India, and in whom both Her Majesty's Government and the general public possess such confidence. I only hope that I, on my side, will be able to do what is incumbent upon me for expediting the public business to your satisfaction.

The ordinary business of the Council was then proceeded with.

CALCUTTA TRADES' ASSOCIATION DINNER.

The Annual Dinner of the Calcutta Trades' Association took place in the Town Hall on Friday, the 30th January, 1885, His Excellency the Viceroy being present. Amongst the guests were also Sir Rivers Thompson (Lieutenant-Governor of Bengal), General T. F. Wilson, and Messrs. Hope and Ilbert (Members of the Viceroy's Council), Messrs. Cunningham, Pigot, Norris, and Prinsep (Judges of the Calcutta High Court), besides a large number of civil and military officials and gentlemen, including the representatives of the various Consulates in Calcutta, and of the Press, European and native.

After the toast of the Queen-Empress and the Royal Family had been honoured, the Master of the Association (Mr. A. H. Wallis) proposed the health of the Viceroy, his speech being frequently interrupted by applause. Mr. Wallis remarked that the Association were deeply sensible of the honour which the Viceroy had done them in accepting their invitation, "thus giving the city an opportunity of personally renewing that warm and heartfelt welcome with which all classes of the community received His Excellency on his arrival in Calcutta." He expressed the gratification they all felt at Lord Dufferin's appointment, than whom, he said, no servant of the British Crown was more eminently fitted to fulfil the duties of a ruler; he referred to Lord Dufferin's distinguished services in other positions, and observed that it was a happy augury for India when England could send out such sons to do her service, and he expressed his conviction that "the wise and just and honest and political administration of India would have a staunch interpreter" in the Viceroy.

His Excellency, who, on rising to respond to the toast, was greeted with loud and continued cheering, said :—

Mr. CHAIRMAN, YOUR HONOUR, AND GENTLEMEN,—In rising to return thanks for the cordial reception you have given to the mention of my name, I hasten to express my satisfaction at finding myself surrounded by the representatives of the trading community of Calcutta. (Cheers.) At the same time I confess that it was with some hesitation that I accepted your invitation. I knew that I should be expected to address those whose hospitality I was permitted to share, and I had some doubts whether it was altogether desirable that the head of the Executive Government of India should indulge, otherwise than upon exceptional and rare occasions, in oratorical displays. It is his duty to listen to others rather than to speak himself; to examine and decide rather than to explain or advocate; and, if I am right in considering that such ought to be the general rule of his conduct, it is still more imperative that he should follow it when he is but newly arrived in a land which presents to his consideration so many problems of the greatest magnitude and importance, and where a casual word pronounced in ignorance, or under misapprehension, may occasion numberless embarrassments. Still, as I am here, it would be ungracious upon my part were I not to take so fitting an opportunity of expressing my deep appreciation of the friendly feeling which has been manifested towards me from the time I landed in Bombay to the present moment, by all ranks and conditions of men, by the various communities which compose our body politic, and by my British and Native fellow-subjects. All have made me feel that they are ready to give me their confidence; that they are willing to believe in my sincere desire to do my duty faithfully by each of them; that they appreciate the difficulties of the task which lies before me, and that I can count on their conjoint sympathy and united assistance in my endeavours to promote the well-being of the common weal. (Cheers.) Now some of those present are probably anxious that I should define the character of the policy I am disposed to follow. I do not know that there is any reason why I should not gratify their curiosity. In doing so, I shall disclose no secret, nor initiate them in a new revelation, for my policy will be guided by those ancient principles upon which the British Empire in India was originally founded, which have ever since been interwoven with its structure and vindicated in turn by each of my illustrious predecessors: namely, a justice which neither prejudice nor self-interest can pervert; an impartiality between all religions and races, which refuses to be irritated by criticism, or cajoled by flattery; and a beneficence of intention which seeks to spread abroad amongst the many millions of Her Majesty's subjects in this country, contentment, prosperity, wealth, education, professional advancement, a free scope to municipal institutions, and every other privilege which is compatible with authoritative Government and Imperial supremacy. (Cheers.) And in saying this, remember I am not speaking in my own name, nor merely as the head of the Indian administration. I am speaking in the name of the Queen-Empress herself, and not only of the Queen, but of the Parliament and people of England, who are fully determined that English rule in India shall be so blamelessly and vigorously conducted as to become the crowning glory of our country's history; and that any grievance and wrong of which Her Majesty's subjects can complain, whether Princes or People, whether native or British-born, shall be examined into, and so far as the imperfection of all human administration will allow, abated or redressed. (Cheers.) That I may be able, under God's providence, during my brief residence among you, to perform the part allotted to me in a satisfactory manner, is my dearest ambition. There is no sacrifice, whether of time, labour, health or strength, I am not prepared to make in pursuit of it; and though it is only by painful and slow degrees that so vast and inchoate a community as ours can expect to move towards the consummation of an ideal, I trust that when the time arrives for me to quit these shores, I may have perceptibly contributed towards the advancement of the country and the realization of the just and legitimate aspirations of its inhabitants, and to the fair fame and stability of the British Empire. That you, gentlemen, as organisers of labour, as promoters of the industrial arts, as creators and distributors of wealth, are powerful factors in our national development, none can doubt; and it is on that account I again repeat I have so much pleasure in finding myself associated with you in to-night's celebration. (Loud cheers.)

<small>The toasts of "The Lieutenant-Governor of Bengal," "The Legislative Councils," "The Army, Navy, and Auxiliary Forces," and other toasts followed, and at the close of the proceedings the Viceroy proposed the health of the Chairman (Mr. Wallis) in the following terms:—</small>

Before we separate I have received the permission of the chairman to propose a toast. I dare say that many are under the impression that the toast that I am about to propose is that of the ladies. As a married man I could not do justice to that toast under half an hour. (Laughter.) Therefore it will be a relief to you to know that it is not the toast of the ladies but the health of your chairman. (Cheers.) It will not be necessary for me to detain you by any observations in support of that toast, because I have only to ask you to cast your memory back along the whole course of to-night's pleasant proceedings and to consider that it is under the auspices of your chairman, and thanks to the Trades' Association of Calcutta, that we have enjoyed one of the most genial entertainments, and I may add, as far as I am concerned, one of the most profitable we have ever attended. (Loud cheers.)

<small>The chairman, Mr. Wallis, briefly responded to the toast; and the proceedings came to a close at about half-past twelve o'clock.</small>

THE BENGAL TENANCY BILL.

The first meeting of the Legislative Council, to discuss the Bengal Tenancy Bill, took place on 27th February, 1885, there being a full attendance of members. Sir Steuart Bayley (the Member in charge of the Bill) moved "that the Reports of the Select Committee on the Bill to amend and consolidate certain enactments relating to the law of landlord and tenant within the territories under the administration of the Lieutenant-Governor of Bengal be taken into consideration." Sir Steuart Bayley delivered an exhaustive speech on the motion. He reviewed the work of the Select Committee and showed the nature of the principal alterations made, the reasons for them, and how far the Bill as altered was likely to succeed in securing the results which the Council had in view. He claimed for the measure that it was an improvement on the old law, and without any injustice to the landlord fulfilled the object of Government, which was "to give reasonable security to the tenant in the occupation and enjoyment of his land," while the just interests of the landlords were not lost sight of in any way. Having answered the charge that the Bill was being passed with undue haste, he concluded by asking the Council to reject the amendment that the Bill should be republished, and to decide on proceeding at once with the consideration of the Select Committee's report and of the amendments of which notice had been given. Mr. Quinton followed Sir Steuart Bayley and spoke in support of the Bill as amended. The Mahárájá of Darbhunga offered unqualified opposition to the measure, and urged its withdrawal, as the Bill was distasteful to zámindár and raiyat alike. Mr. G. H. P. Evans delivered an able speech reviewing the whole position. He regarded the kernel of the Bill as sound and the general object and scope of it as salutary, but argued that many portions of it, as now amended, were ill-advised and mischievous. The Council adjourned at five o'clock, and re-assembled on the following Monday (2nd March), when the debate was resumed. Mr. Goodrich supported the Bill, and held that the necessity of immediately regulating the law between landlord and tenant was proved. He believed the Bill would limit the landlord's right no further than the public interest demanded. Bábú Peári Mohan Mukerji urged strongly the postponement of the passing of the Bill, in order to afford members of Council, the outside public, and parties interested in the measure, an opportunity of studying it. Mr. Vishvanatha Narayan Mandlik, Messrs. Reynolds, Hunter, Gibbon, Ilbert, and Sir Rivers Thompson spoke in support of the Bill and against its postponement. His Excellency the Viceroy in closing the debate said :—

I do not think it necessary that I should trouble the Council with any observations of my own at this stage of our proceedings. I shall have ample opportunity, when we come to discuss the several points in this Bill with respect to which amendments are to be moved, of expressing my opinion in regard to them. I will therefore content myself by saying that, although it is likely that during the course of our deliberations this Bill will be considerably improved in many of its particulars, I have no hesitation whatever in giving to its general features my most cordial and sincere support. I have convinced myself that it is, as my honourable colleague has just said, a very honest and conscientious piece of work. I am quite certain that those who have engaged in advancing it to its present stage have been actuated by the sole desire of doing equal justice to all those interests which are dealt with under the Bill. It cannot be seriously urged that this Council has not a right to legislate in the direction proposed. It so happens that I became Under-Secretary of State for India while the legislation, which resulted in Act X. of 1859, was still under discussion, and I then came to the conclusion, which further examination has only confirmed, that it would be idle to contend that legislation of this description is any invasion whatever of the rights accorded to the zamíndárs under the Permanent Settlement. If I thought that any clause of the Bill interfered with rights which have been granted to any class of Her Majesty's subjects in India by the Imperial Government, I certainly would not be found among its supporters; but, on the contrary, I believe that this Bill is in perfect harmony with those principles which inspired the authors of the Permanent Settlement; and I am quite certain that hereafter, when the present controversies have subsided, even those who consider their interests most injuriously affected by what it is proposed to do will acknowledge that this legislation has benefited the agricultural interests of the country. With regard to the special point which is before us, namely, whether or no the present Bill should be hung up for another year, I can only say that, in the presence of the all but unanimous opinion which has been delivered by my colleagues in favour of proceeding at once to the immediate consideration of the Bill as amended by the Select Committee, it would be impossible for me, even if I myself did not share that opinion, to undertake the responsibility of delaying a measure, the postponement of which, I am told by so many persons competent to speak with authority on the subject, would be so disastrous. In conclusion, I may observe that I for one have listened with the greatest interest and pleasure to the discussion which has taken place. Although I have certainly done my best to acquaint myself with all the facts and arguments bearing on this question as far as they are contained in the voluminous literature connected with the subject, this is the first occasion on which I have had the advantage of hearing it discussed by persons so capable of handling it. I have been specially struck with the moderation, the temper, good sense, and the eloquence with which my several colleagues have placed us in possession of their respective views, and I may be permitted to add that the native members of this Council were certainly not those who have shown the least ability in dealing with the question.

Sir Steuart Bayley's motion that the Report of the Select Committee be taken into consideration, was then put and carried.

The motion of Bábú Peári Mohan Mukerji that the Bill as amended be republished and the consideration of the measure be deferred for at least three months from the date of its republication, was then put and declared lost, the Honourable Mover and the Mahárájá of Darbhunga only voting in favour of it.

Bábú Peári Mohan Mukerji then moved that the consideration of the Bill be postponed for two or three weeks, to enable members who were not on the Select Committee to study the amended measure, and the English-knowing landlords and tenants to give their opinions on the subject.

Sir Steuart Bayley pointed out that such postponement meant delay for another year, and asked the Council to reject the proposition. The amendment was put and lost, and the Council adjourned.

At the sitting of the Council on Thursday, the 5th of March, Mr. Amír Alí brought forward the following amendment :—

After this section (section 24) insert the following section :—

"An occupancy-raiyat shall be entitled in Bengal Proper to transfer his holding in the same manner and to the same extent as other immovable property:

"(a) Provided, however, that in the case of a sale the landlord shall be entitled to a fee of five per cent. on the purchase-money.

"(b) Provided also that a gift of an occupancy-right in land shall not be valid against the landlord unless it is made by a registered instrument.

"(c) The registering officer shall not register any such instrument except on payment of the prescribed fee for service on the landlord of notice of the registration.

"(d) When any such notice has been registered, the registering officer shall forthwith serve notice of the registration on the landlord."

Before moving the amendment, Mr. Amír Alí obtained the permission of the Council to make the following alteration in clause (a).

"Provided, however, that where the right of transfer by custom does not exist in the case of sale, the landlord shall be entitled to a fee of ten per cent. in the purchase-money."

Mr. Amír Alí having spoken in support of his amendment, he was followed by Sir S. Bayley, who pointed out that the Executive Council of the Government of India had decided that the transferability of these tenures should not be made a principle in the Bill, and he therefore asked the Council to reject the amendment. Bábú Peári Mohun Mukerji, Mr. Mandlik, Messrs. Reynolds, Hunter, Gibbon, and the Lieutenant-Governor opposed the amendment, and thought the mover, in view of the opinion expressed against it, should withdraw it. His Excellency the President said :—

As a reference has been made to my connection with this part of the subject, I should like to have an opportunity of expressing my own opinion upon it. In the first place we have to consider the matter from the point of view of right and equity. Sir John Shore, a contemporary authority upon the subject, has stated in the most positive manner that the occupancy-right does not include the right of sale or transfer, and the Courts of Bengal, as I understand, have hitherto maintained this view. It is therefore a question as to how far we should be justified in giving the occupancy-tenant a right carrying a money value to which he has not hitherto been entitled by law. That he should have it by custom is a totally different question. It stands to reason when a landlord has allowed such a custom to grow up, when the landlord has permitted sales of occupancy interests to take place, it is but fair and just that the actual tenant, who has paid consideration for the occupancy-right, should be allowed to dispose of it upon the same conditions as those upon which he bought it. Without, however, wishing to pronounce dogmatically upon this part of the question, I have to observe that when the matter was brought to my notice, the Government of Bengal had already decided that the legalising of the custom was at all events not desirable in Behar. It was also decided that its application to Bengal must be hedged and restricted by various safeguards, one of which consisted of the right of the landlord to bar the transfer where the transferee was objectionable to him. Thus it became apparent that even its application to Bengal might be also questioned. I can quite understand that the honourable member who has moved this amendment should take a different view of the question, because I believe that he is more immediately connected with a part of the country where the raiyats are in a very satisfactory and strong position; and undoubtedly where that is the case transferability is not only a convenience, but works without injury to the raiyat and with advantage to the public. But, on the other hand, we must remember that if the amendment were to be adopted, we should at once confer upon vast numbers of indigent men the right and opportunity of mortgaging the land on the unembarrassed condition of which the salvation of themselves and their families depends. However, I need not enlarge upon this view of the question, because the remarks which have already fallen from the Lieutenant-Governor I think amply justify the view which has been taken of the subject by the Government of India. I think it right, however, to say, on behalf of myself and my colleagues, that if, at this stage of the proceedings, arguments had been adduced in favour of such an amendment as that which has been proposed by Mr. Amír Alí, we should have been quite prepared to give to them that attention which they deserve. But so far from that being the case, even those other members of the Council who are disposed to look with an indulgent eye upon the principle in the abstract, announce to us that they do not feel themselves in a position to support it. Under these circumstances, we—I for one, and I imagine all my colleagues—feel that there is no reason whatever why we should depart from the conclusion at which we originally arrived.

The honourable Mr. Amír Alí said that under the circumstances he would ask the permission of the Council to withdraw his amendment.

The amendment was accordingly withdrawn.

THE BENGAL TENANCY BILL.

In the course of a discussion which took place on the 9th March, Babu Peárí Mohun Mukerji moved that sections 101 to 115 of the Bill be omitted. He said that both landlords and tenants were opposed to this portion of the Bill more than to any other. Speaking not in the interests of either class, he conscientiously thought the provisions of this chapter would give rise to a great deal of litigation and create bitter feelings and irritation amongst both those classes. These provisions were altogether unnecessary, and all that this chapter contemplated might be much more simply and effectually done by the provisions of section 158, to which reference had already been made.

Messrs. Reynolds, Gibbon, the Lieutenant-Governor, and Sir Steuart Bayley spoke against the amendment.

His Excellency the President observed that he had been very much struck by the almost complete unanimity of opinion which prevailed in the Council as to the utility of this chapter. At the same time he was perfectly able to comprehend the natural anxiety which its unreserved application over very extensive areas would occasion both to the raiyats and the zamíndárs. Regarding the question in the abstract, it was obvious that one of the first steps towards the cessation of litigation and ill-feeling between two antagonistic interests, was that they should each know exactly what belonged to them; therefore no one, His Excellency imagined, not even the honourable member himself, could in theory be opposed to the introduction of this chapter. At the same time His Excellency could assure the honourable member that not only in deference to the suggestions made to them by the Secretary of State, but also from their own appreciation of the exigencies of the case, the Government of India would be indisposed to consent to the application of the sections referred to otherwise than in the sense and spirit recommended by Lord Kimberley. By applying the machinery of the chapter to a special and limited area in a tentative manner they would be able to observe how the clauses were likely to work, and there was every hope that by that cautious method of procedure they would be able to obviate those objections to which the honourable member had referred.

The motion was put and lost.

DEPUTATION FROM THE LANDHOLDERS OF BEHAR.

On Tuesday, the 10th of March, 1885, a deputation from the landholders of Behar, headed by the Mahárájá of Darbhunga, waited on the Viceroy at Government House, and presented a memorial to His Excellency on the subject of the Bengal Tenancy Bill. The memorial, which was read by the Mahárájá of Darbhunga, set forth that zamíndárs and raiyats alike regarded the Bill with most unfeigned alarm, as a novel departure from the existing law and the precursor of future taxation. The memorial went on to say that the zamíndárs and raiyats "look upon the Patwarí Bill now before the Bengal Council as an indication of the measures of taxation by which the present Bill will be supplemented. They feel that the Patwarí Bill will soon be followed by another Bill to impose additional taxation to meet the expenses of a survey and preparation of a record-of-rights, and burdened as they already are with a road-cess and public works cess, they look with despair on the prospect before them. They desire a final measure, and not a measure which will have to be supplemented by legislation in another Council." The memorial further pointed out the disastrous effects which would follow the preparation of a record-of-rights, as endless litigation would follow, and, in conclusion, respectfully asked whether the Government of India would distinctly declare whether the zámindárs had any, or what, special rights under the Permanent Settlement, and in what respect they differed from the zamíndárs of a district which had not been permanently settled.

His Excellency the Viceroy replied as follows:—

MAHÁRÁJÁ AND GENTLEMEN,—It has been some satisfaction to me, in listening to an address which criticises the Bengal Tenancy Bill, to find that the complaint with which it begins and ends is not directed against the actual Bill under discussion by the Government of India, but to what is at present merely inchoate or contingent legislation to be initiated hereafter under the auspices of the Local Government. Almost all the points you have brought to my notice have been so ably discussed by your representatives in the Legislative Council—and I cannot sufficiently acknowledge the ability, the patience, and the temper evinced by those gentlemen during the discharge of their arduous duties—that it would be altogether inopportune for me to re-open them. There is one matter, however, you have mentioned to which it is desirable I should refer. You have stated on behalf of the zamíndárs of Behar that you regard with special apprehension that chapter which relates to the survey and to the record-of-rights. Now I must ask you to remember that the provisions of that chapter cannot, in their most important particulars, be applied by the Local Government except with the consent of the Government of India, and the Secretary of State has especially recommended that when they are applied it should be done in a cautious and tentative manner, and that the experiment should be confined to a small and special district. Under these circumstances I cannot but hope that you will go away with the conviction that nothing rash or detrimental either to the interests of the zamíndárs or of the raiyats will be likely to take place under the operation of that particular chapter.

As to that which is, I may say, the main question of the Bill, *i.e.*, whether too much or too little has been done for the raiyat, I must remind you that there are several members of my Council—gentlemen of high standing and of large experience, gentlemen to whose opinions I am bound to pay the very greatest attention—who maintained that so far from the present legislation having erred against the zamíndárs, it still fails, on the contrary, to give adequate protection to the raiyats. After having given to this vital question my most anxious attention, I have not, nor have the majority of my colleagues, been able to acquiesce in that view; but, on the other hand, such a contention naturally strengthens us in the belief that we have not gone too far in the other direction. I believe that upon the whole this legislation does fair and equal justice between the two interests concerned, though, perhaps, it may be found—indeed it could hardly be otherwise—that in the application of so intricate a measure to such large areas and varied agricultural conditions, exceptional cases may arise here and there where its operation will fall short of effecting the results desired by its framers, but such consequences are incident to all legislation of the kind. Apart, however, from inevitable imperfections of this description, I have every reason to hope that the condition of affairs created by the Bengal Tenancy Act will turn out to be a very considerable improvement upon the existing state of things, a state of things which successive Governments,

Commissions, and other authorities have agreed in pronouncing intolerable.

<small>Sir Steuart Bayley added a few words in addition to what had fallen from His Excellency the Viceroy, and confined himself more particularly to the subject of the objection made in the memorial to the proposed survey and record of rights in Bengal. Sir Steuart Bayley pointed out that this survey and record of rights, when made, would operate beneficially, both in the interests of the raiyat and of the zamíndár, and that he could not see what objection there could be to it.</small>

<small>At the sitting of the Legislative Council on Wednesday, the 11th March, after the last of the amendments before the Council had been disposed of, Sir Steuart Bayley moved that the Bill be passed. The members who spoke on the motion were the Mahárájá of Darbhunga, Mr. Evans, Bábú Peári Mohun Mukerji, Mr. Mandlik, Messrs. Reynolds, Hunter, Amír Alí, Gibbon, and the Lieutenant-Governor. Sir Steuart Bayley having replied at some length to the various objections raised against the Bill, His Excellency the Viceroy addressed the Council as follows :—</small>

It is perhaps as well that I should say a few words before putting the motion. Sir Steuart Bayley, in his admirable speech, has explained so fully the views of the Government of India, and has anticipated so many of the points upon which I had felt inclined to touch, that there is but little for me to add. At the same time it is but fair to my colleagues that I should take this opportunity of saying how glad I have been to associate myself with them in the passing of this measure. It is true I have only come in time to take part in its recent stages, but I should be very unwilling on that account to withdraw in any degree from the full responsibility which rightly attaches to the head of the Government of India for any Act passed by this Legislative Council. Moreover, it must be remembered that before reaching Calcutta I was perfectly familiar with almost all the issues raised in this Bill. Similar discussions took place in reference to Act X. of 1859 when I was Under-Secretary of State for India, and other circumstances have for some years past called my special attention to questions connected with land legislation. It was urged at that time that Act X. of 1859 was an infringement of the Permanent Settlement; but I was convinced then, as I am convinced now, and as the British and Indian Governments of that day and of this were and are convinced, that the "permanency" of Lord Cornwallis' Settlement applied to the pledge given by His Excellency never to demand from the zamíndárs an increase of the assessment which at that date was imposed upon them, but that, so far from any quality of permanency having been then officially impressed upon the relations subsisting between the zamíndárs and their raiyats, the Indian Administration of the day and the East India Company reserved to themselves in the most explicit and express manner the right of interfering in the interests and for the protection of the raiyats whenever circumstances might require them to do so. But I have no hesitation in adding, that even if no such reservation had been made by Lord Cornwallis and his colleagues, there would have remained an inherent and indefeasible right in the Government of India to enter upon legislation such as that we have undertaken as a matter of public policy, and in the interests of the community at large. I do not presume, however, to say that, in spite of my conscientious endeavours to master all the intricacies of the Bill, I have felt myself in a position to pass an authoritative opinion upon all the subordinate points which are involved in it. A great number of those points are of a technical character, and can only be properly decided by those who have a practical acquaintance with the agricultural conditions of the country. Again, there are some parts of the Bill to which I have assented with a fuller and more satisfactory conviction than to others, while there are some with regard to which I have subordinated my indefinite impressions to the opinions and authority of those who were more competent than myself to come to a decision upon them. It was impossible that this should have been otherwise, but taking the measure as a whole, I have no hesitation in saying, both with respect to its principle, its general features, and its chief details, that the Bill as it stands has my hearty and sincere support. I believe with Mr. Reynolds that it is a translation and reproduction in the language of the day of the spirit and essence of Lord Cornwallis' Settlement; that it is in harmony with his intentions; that it carries out his ideas; that it is calculated to ensure the results he aimed at; and that it is conceived in the same beneficent and generous spirit which actuated the original framers of the Regulations of 1793. Lord Cornwallis desired to relieve the zamíndárs from the worry and ruin occasioned by the capricious and frequent enhancements exacted from them by former Governments; and it is evident from his language that he expected they would show the same consideration to their raiyats. I am happy to think that all of us assembled here to-day, no matter what our individual opinions upon various points of this measure may be, are actuated by the same honest and conscientious desire to do justice to each of the interests concerned, and to regulate their relations in such a manner as to secure the rights of the one and to respect those of the other. Nor is there one of us who would not have been ready to have submitted to any amount of additional labour or inconvenience had there been any hope that by further discussion we could have arrived at a more satisfactory conclusion than that which we have reached.

These few observations are all that it is necessary for me to make on the Bill generally; but there is one accusation which has been brought against the Government of India and against its responsible head, so extraordinary and unfounded that it is right I should vindicate both myself and my colleagues in the matter. In consequence of a telegram which has been sent to England for the purpose of being used in Parliament, a statement is about to be made that the Viceroy of India has rushed this Bill with indecent haste through the Legislative Council, in order that he might hurry off to Simla. That statement ought never to have been made. So far from any haste or desire for haste having attended the passing of this measure, I would venture to remind the Council that, independent of the long consideration it has received since it was introduced in 1882—I may say ever since the letter of the Government of India was written in March, 1881—the most ample opportunity has been given to those interested on either side of stating their objections, and of bringing to the notice of the Legislature any alterations they might have to suggest. After lengthy debates in Council upon its first introduction, it was referred to a Select Committee. There were sixty-four meetings of that Select Committee, each meeting lasting nearly four hours—periods which, if added together, would amount to nineteen or twenty days of twelve hours each. At these discussions the representatives of the zamíndárs had the most ample opportunities given them of pressing their views upon their colleagues, and so far from their representations having failed to produce any effect, so far from the observations of an honourable Member being true that amendments proceeding from the zamíndárs' representatives always failed to meet with due consideration at the hands of the Committee, even since I myself have been in the country, that is to say, within the last two or three months, amendments of the most important kind, amendments which the zamíndárs represented as being vital to their interests, have been incorporated with the Bill. Amongst these amendments I may mention the elimination of the word "estate," which gave to the clause in which it was found an operation so wide as to be very disadvantageous to the interests of the zamíndárs. The right of transfer, which was found in the original Bill, was also removed at the instance of the zamíndár party. It was agreed for the same reason that no limit should be placed upon the initial rent to be demanded from the non-occupancy-raiyat, that is to say, that there should be no interference with freedom of contract in respect of rent between the zamíndár and his ordinary tenant, for it will be observed that the Bill has been careful to discriminate between the ancient customary and acknowledged rights of occupancy and its attendant incidents, universally acknowledged to be inherent in the resident raiyat, and the unprivileged status of the non-occupancy raiyat. Again, it was proposed in the original draft of the Bill to introduce a universal limit to rent, represented by one-fifth of the value of the gross produce. That limitation has been abolished. In the original Bill fractional limitations were imposed upon enhancements in Court. These fractional limitations have disappeared. There was also a clause which nullified all contracts which had been entered into between the zamíndárs and their raiyats during the last twenty years. That clause was recognised as unjust, and has been excised. There was another chapter giving to the non-occupancy tenant compensation for disturbance on eviction. It was pleaded by the representatives of the zamíndárs that the introduction of a novel principle of the kind would work a great deal of injustice, and it was therefore dropped. In the chapter relating to agreements for enhancements out of Court, the representations of the zamíndárs have been taken into account, as far as circumstances permitted, and a subsidiary clause has been introduced with the object of redressing the hardships entailed by the hard-and-fast application of the twelve per cent. rule. Liberal reclamation clauses were also introduced in the interests of the zamíndárs, and no later than this morning a most important amendment, moved by the honourable Mr. Hunter, was unanimously accepted by the Council in their anxiety to encourage the zamíndárs to improve their properties and to relieve them of all unnecessary restrictions in dealing with any tracts of land they might themselves bring under cultivation. I do not say that, in agreeing to these modifications, we were actuated by any other motive than a desire to do equal justice between the two parties. We did not adopt these alterations in order to conciliate the zamíndárs or by way of offering a compromise. That would not have been consistent with our duty to the raiyats, nor is it within the province of the Government of India to enter into compromises. The Government of India distributes justice, and that is what we have endeavoured to do in the Bill. We agreed to these concessions, because we thought the demand for them was just, but I have mentioned the circumstance, in order to rebut the assertion that the amendments introduced in the interests of the zamíndárs and by their representatives have been uniformly rejected or disparaged. I fear that the enumeration I have made of these modifications which have told so largely in favour of the zamíndárs, will have renewed the pang felt by those of my honourable colleagues who were opposed to their being made, and who, so far from admitting that the zamíndárs have been hardly dealt with, contend, on the contrary, that this Bill still falls short in giving adequate protection to the raiyat. At all events, if there is one thing more obvious than another, it is this, that the Government of India has had to exercise a very severe watch over its conscience in order to discriminate with justice and impartiality between the elaborate arguments advanced on either hand by the eloquent representatives of the zamíndár and raiyat seated at this Council Board. We have been told that we have undertaken a great responsibility in promoting a measure of this description. I should be the last person to deny the truth of the assertion. The measure is a momentous one, affecting vast interests, and calculated to produce far-reaching consequences; but I maintain that a far graver responsibility would have weighed upon those who, if their opposition had succeeded, would have stood between the occupancy-raiyat and those rights which every one acknowledges to be his, and which every one is equally aware but for this legislation he would have been in the greatest danger of losing.

The motion was then put and carried, and the Bill was passed. The only members who voted against the Bill were the Mahárájá of Darbhunga and Bábú Peári Mohan Mukerjí.

The Legislative Council re-assembled on Friday, the 13th of March, for the despatch of ordinary business, when the Viceroy took the opportunity of making a further statement with regard to the Bengal Tenancy Bill. His Excellency spoke as follows:—

I have to apologise to my colleagues for having called them back in Council, but the recent adjournment was an accident. I was detained in my room unexpectedly, and requested Mr. Gibbs to take the chair, but the business before the Council was transacted so rapidly, that when I came to take my place the Council had adjourned. I regretted the circumstance, more especially as I was anxious to have had an opportunity to thank honourable members for the cordial and effective assistance they have been good enough to give me during the conduct of the legislative business of the session, but I was also anxious to make a few observations.

At the last meeting of Council, it was my unpleasant duty to allude to a most unfounded statement forwarded from this country, to the effect that the Bengal Tenancy Act had been rushed through the Legislative Council with indecent haste in order that the members of the Indian Executive and the Viceroy might hurry off to Simla. This misstatement has been repeated in Parliament, and it has now been supplemented by another assertion equally devoid of truth, namely, that the Bill had been forced through the Council over the heads of its opponents by the dead weight of an official majority. It is sufficient to observe, in reply, that so far from the official majority having attempted to coerce the independent section of the Council, only two dissentient voices have been raised against the Bill. Consequently it has been passed at the instance, and with the all but unanimous consent, of our entire body, of that body which the wisdom of Parliament has associated with the Viceroy for the purpose of making laws for India.

On a previous occasion I have mentioned the extraordinary length of time devoted to the most minute examination of this Bill, and to the unprecedented number of sittings—64 I think —of the large Committee of eleven members, of whom only two, I may mention, were members of the Government of India. We ourselves have consumed seven days of six or seven hours each in its further consideration, and when eventually we came to a final vote, there was not a single member who dreamt of suggesting that it had not in every particular been subjected to a most minute and exhaustive discussion. Had it been otherwise, I need not say that there is no one amongst us who would not have been ready and glad to have sat on for another six months, if by so doing there had been any prospect of arriving at a different conclusion from that which had been reached, or the slightest chance of the opinion of members being modified by further debate.

I have gone at length into this subject for a specific purpose, namely, in order to show what embarrassments must be occasioned to the Indian Executive, and what mischief must arise from members of the British Legislature bringing forward motions in Parliament founded upon no better authority than the inaccurate statements forwarded for party purposes by the agents of particular interests in this country. The Bill upon which this discussion has arisen may be a good Bill or a bad Bill; that has nothing to do with the subject: but at all events this is manifest, and cannot be gainsaid, that every clause, and, I may add, every word in every clause, has received a most minute, patient, and conscientious examination at the hands of this legislative body, and that the idea of its having been passed with haste, or forced through the Council by the dead weight of the official members of the Government of India, is in contradiction with the facts of the case. Having thus vindicated the honourable and the upright intentions of this Council; having placed upon record, and in a permanent manner, the real facts of the case, I do not propose hereafter to take further notice of any similar misrepresentations, either in respect of this or any other cognate matter.

The Council was then adjourned *sine die*.

FINE ARTS EXHIBITION AT SIMLA.

The Fine Arts Exhibition at Simla was opened by the Viceroy on Friday afternoon, the 18th September, in the presence of a large assembly. The proceedings were commenced by a speech by Mr. W. W. Hunter, who, on behalf of the society, welcomed His Excellency. The following is an extract from the speech made by Lord Dufferin in declaring the Exhibition open:—

But passing from the immediate scene before me, and taking a somewhat wider view of the subject to which our attention has been directed by to-day's celebration, I cannot help expressing my surprise that there should not exist in India a more favourable field for the exertions of the professional artist than there appears to be. In many of its social aspects the India of to-day resembles the Italy of the 15th century. There, as here, there existed a great number of sumptuous

Courts, ruled over by Princes of wealth, education, and refinement. There, as here, there were rich and splendid nobles, landed proprietors, merchants, and traders. There, as here, there were numerous nascent municipalities, entrusted with the charge of great works of civic utility. There, as here, there rose on every side the most exquisite examples of the artistic genius of an older civilization : while there, as here, the characteristics of the climate and other corresponding circumstances endowed the magnates of the land with opportunities of leisure and inducements to the cultivation of Art unknown to less favoured regions and to busier and more prosaic ages. Why, then, should not here, as there, the leading classes of the country create for Art among themselves such a home and second birthplace as was given to it in Italy by the Leos, the Medicis, the Colonnas, the Dorias, and the Strozzis of the days of the Renaissance? In doing so, they would engage in an enterprise as patriotic as it would be agreeable ; for if there is one need more evident than another in the present stage of our social evolution, it is that of discovering for the generations who are being so rapidly educated at our schools, colleges, and universities, fresh channels in which they can exercise the new intellectual powers with which they have been endowed, and multiplied opportunities of following such honourable and remunerative professions as shall provide their industry and ability with appropriate rewards and merited distinction. At present the native youth of India seem but to have three outlets for the exercise of their faculties—official employment, the Bar, and the Press. But it is very evident that at the rate at which our educated thousands are being manufactured, each of these three walks of life will soon become overcrowded. If, however, a real and genuine love of Art were widely diffused amongst our wealthier Indian fellow-subjects, a highly honourable, lucrative, and useful career would be opened to hundreds and hundreds of our aspiring young men, whether as painters, engravers, sculptors, architects, designers, illuminators, enamellers, or otherwise; while, what is even more important, a corresponding stimulus would be communicated to those manufacturing industries which are peculiarly suited to the genius of the people. However, this is too large a subject to be touched upon on so chance an occasion as the present, and I almost feel that I owe you an apology for having done so. It only remains for me to congratulate you heartily upon the number and diversity of the works of Art which have been gathered together this year at Simla as well as upon the wide geographical area which is represented.

SIR DONALD STEWART.

On the evening of Tuesday, 13th October, 1885, the Viceroy and Lady Dufferin entertained Sir Donald and Lady Stewart at dinner at the Viceregal Lodge, Simla, previous to their departure from India. There was a large number of guests present; and after dinner His Excellency proposed the Commander-in-Chief's health in the following terms:—

LADIES AND GENTLEMEN,—I am about to do a thing which may not perhaps be altogether pleasing to the person in this room whose feelings and wishes I should of all things have been most anxious to consult; for, in the whole range of my acquaintance, I know no one who would be probably less gratified in having his services referred to in his own presence than Sir Donald Stewart; and yet it is the health of that distinguished officer I am about to propose to you. (Cheers.) Unfortunately the Viceroy of India is seldom able to consult the inclination of his friends; and I should have justly exposed myself to criticism, and have caused great disappointment to every soldier—nay, to every servant of the British Crown in this country—had I allowed our illustrious Commander-in-Chief to quit the shores of India without attempting, in however imperfect a manner, to make him feel with what infinite regret we shall watch his departure, and with how tender and affectionate a regard we shall ever cherish the memory of his presence amongst us. It is just forty-five years since Sir Donald Stewart joined the army of India; and in the military annals of this country it would be difficult to point to a career more deeply impressed with all those characteristics which ensure the success and adorn the renown of a great commander. Abnegation of self, simplicity of purpose, devotion to duty, freedom from all taint of jealousy or personal ambition, professional industry, combined with those natural gifts and talents which are native to the genius of every born soldier, have—unassisted by any adventitious advantages of favour or patronage—raised Sir Donald Stewart to his present enviable and eminent position; have earned him the unbounded confidence and gratitude of his Sovereign; and have rendered his name at this moment more honoured and respected than that of any other man in India. (Cheers.) It is not necessary that I should enumerate to those around me my guest's especial services. In recording the annals of the last half century, the hand of History herself will emblazon in imperishable characters his successive achievements, and mark the stages of his ever-widening reputation; for scarcely any considerable operation of war has taken place within living memory in which he did not play a distinguished part,—whether while engaged, in early days, with the wild hill tribes upon our frontier; or, at the outbreak of the mutiny, when his calmness, enterprise, and courage will never be forgotten by those who were eye-witnesses of his conduct; or during the siege and storming of Delhi; or at the capture of Lucknow; or subsequently while heading the Indian contingent under Lord Napier of Magdala in Abyssinia; or later still when, after winning a decisive battle, he took possession of the enemy's capital, and by the wisdom of his policy, his moderation and humanity, and above all, by the energetic and effective manner in which he sped his distinguished lieutenant, Sir Frederick Roberts, on his successful march to Candahar, he crowned his career in the field in a manner so noble and generous as to send a thrill of loving admiration through the hearts of all his countrymen. (Great cheering.)

But my task would be unfulfilled if, in thus imperfectly glancing at Sir Donald Stewart's achievements as a soldier, I did not also allude to the equally valuable services he has rendered at the Council Board (hear, hear): and here, Ladies and Gentlemen, I am able to speak from my own experience, and with all the force of grateful and earnest conviction which a ruler must ever feel when, in troublous times and in the presence of great anxieties and responsibilities, he finds at his side a colleague in whose sagacity, calmness, experience, and loyalty he can place implicit confidence. And in saying this much, I feel that I am speaking, not only in my own name, but on behalf of every other member of the Indian Government. One and all of us are deeply sensible that we are sustaining an irreparable loss in the departure from amongst us of so kind, so courteous, and so straightforward a coadjutor, who possesses the art of urging his opinions with as much engaging suavity as lucidity and force. (Cheers.) On behalf, then, of all your colleagues; in the name of the Army you command—and I will add of both the Civil and Military Services of India—as the representative of your Sovereign and of her Government; as the spokesman of the Natives of India, from amongst whom the major part of the gallant battalions you led to victory were recruited, I now bid you farewell. And from the bottom of my heart I trust that you will long live to enjoy your well-merited honours, and to assist with your fresh experience and ripe wisdom the counsels of the Indian Administration in England. (Long and repeated applause.)

I need not say that, in losing you now, it is a great consolation to me, and to all of us who are responsible for the proper conduct of Indian affairs, that your connection with the Government of India is still to remain unbroken. Arriving in England at a time when external circumstances have necessitated the reconsideration of many difficult military and political problems, your presence among the official advisers of the Secretary of State cannot fail to prove of the greatest service and utility; and glad am I to think that, while the memory of your noble example and great deeds will be stimulating every one of us out here—from the junior ensign in the army to the highest officials in the land—to emulate your patriotic devotion to the service of your Queen and country, you yourself will be pursuing at home, I trust with unabated strength, vigour and success, that splendid and blameless career which, to the deep and unspeakable regret of your comrades, friends, admirers, and fellow-subjects, is so soon to reach its destined close in India. (Loud and continued cheering.)

LAYING THE FOUNDATION STONE OF THE NEW GENERAL HOSPITAL, DELHI.

On the morning of the 2nd November, 1885, the Viceroy, who was accompanied by Lady Dufferin, laid the foundation stone of the new General Hospital at Delhi. Mr. Smyth, the Deputy Commissioner, read an address, in which the prominent position the city of Delhi had always occupied in the world of medical science was touched upon and the history of the hospital briefly related. In asking His Excellency to perform the opening ceremony, Mr. Smyth explained that it was the unanimous desire of the Native gentlemen, who were the largest subscribers to the fund for the new building, that the hospital should, with His Excellency's consent, be called "The Dufferin Hospital" instead of "The Delhi Hospital," as was originally contemplated. This decision to rename the hospital was come to only on the previous evening and after the leading members of the Native community had met and been personally introduced to His Excellency at the *conversazione* which was held at the Town Hall.

The Viceroy in declaring the hospital to be open spoke as follows:—

GENTLEMEN,—I can assure you it gives me the very greatest pleasure to have had an opportunity of participating in the ceremonial of to-day. I am always glad to evince by every means in my power my deep sympathy with all enterprises which are conducive to improving the sanitary condition of the people of India, the prevention and cure of disease, and the mitigation of human suffering; and I am especially touched by your kind thought in suggesting that my name should be connected with so noble an institution as that whose foundations I am about to lay. I am glad to see that you have referred in becoming terms to the well-known excellence of the local Native physicians of this place in former days; nor should it ever be forgotten how great is the debt of gratitude which the Science of Europe, and especially the Science of Medicine, owes to the East. It was Arabic literature that preserved intact the fruit of the world's earlier experience and research during those dark ages which almost submerged and obliterated for a time the intellectual achievement of the classic nations. But the centre of gravity of all human excellence, whether in the fields of art or of science, is perpetually shifting. Yesterday it was here, to-day it is in Europe, to-morrow it may move still further west; but, wherever it may be, thanks to the rapidity of modern communication, its results are soon universally disseminated and become the property of all. The past history of India is a sufficient guarantee that the seed we are now sowing will fall in fertile soil, and will be certain, I trust, to bear the most beneficent fruits. That this Hospital may not only become a source of relief to thousands, but also a successful witness to the true principles of medical science, is my earnest hope; and most heartily do I congratulate its founders and promoters upon the successful issue of their labours and this day's auspicious inauguration.

OPENING THE MAYO COLLEGE AT AJMIR.

On the afternoon of the 7th November, 1885, the Viceroy opened the Mayo College at Ajmir and Lady Dufferin distributed the prizes to the assembled students. The immense hall of the College was crowded with Europeans and Natives, who gave Their Excellencies, on their arrival, a most enthusiastic reception. Amongst those present were Sir Charles Aitchison, Sir Oliver St. John, Sir Edward Bradford, and a number of political officers, the Maharajas of Ulwar and Kishenghar, and several other native chiefs. The Viceroy, who was accompanied by Lady Dufferin, Lady Helen Blackwood, and Miss Thynne, was received by Sir Edward Bradford and Major W. Loch, Principal of the College. On Their Excellencies taking their seats, Major Loch read an interesting account of the origin and growth of the College, the facts of which, briefly, were that, in 1870, at a durbar held within a few yards of the present building, Lord Mayo proposed to the Rajputana Chiefs then assembled a project he had much at heart, namely, the establishment of a college to be devoted exclusively to the education of the sons of the Chiefs, Princes, and leading members of the aristocracy of Rajputana. After Lord Mayo's death, Sir Charles Aitchison, then Foreign Secretary, proceeded to give effect to Lord Mayo's wishes, and nearly six-and-a-half lakhs of rupees were eventually subscribed towards the College by the Rajputana Chiefs. The scheme had been completed by the addition of boarding-houses for the students from the various states, as well as ornamental grounds. The foundation stone was laid in July 1877 by Sir Alfred Lyall, then agent to the Governor-General in Rajputana, and the building, which was designed by the late Major Mant, was virtually completed in June 1883. The style of the building is Hindu-Saracenic, which was selected by Lord Northbrook as the most suitable to adopt in a part of the country where the palaces and finest buildings bear witness to its popularity. The entire cost of the building was over three-and-a-half lakhs of rupees. The attendance had been steadily increasing up to the present, and there were now seventy-nine young Chiefs on the rolls of the institution. In concluding his statement, Major Loch asked the Viceroy to declare the College open, and called upon the Chiefs and Sirdars for whose benefit the building had been erected, to remember the precepts and example of the great statesman whose name the College bore.

The Viceroy then rose to reply to Major Loch's address and was very heartily cheered, while in the course of his speech he was frequently interrupted by bursts of enthusiastic applause.

His Excellency spoke as follows:—

LADIES, PRINCES, CHIEFS, AND GENTLEMEN,—It is almost superfluous for me to tell you that I experience exceptional satisfaction in taking part in this day's celebration. The late Lord Mayo was a personal friend of my own, and I am naturally glad to have the opportunity of showing my interest in the prosperity of an institution which bears his name, and to join with you in paying a well-merited tribute to his memory. But, however grateful such an act might be to my private feelings, it is in my public capacity and as the representative of Her Majesty and the British Government that I desire more especially to mark my admiration of the intention and ideas with which Lord Mayo was inspired when he founded this College, to emphasize my approval of the special objects for which it was designed, and to assure you of my earnest desire to extend the sphere of its usefulness. And in doing this I feel that it is not to the statesmanlike views of Lord Mayo alone that I am according the acknowledgments which are their due, but that I am also conveying, in as marked a way as circumstances permit, my appreciation of the public-spirited manner in which the Princes, and leading Chiefs and inhabitants of Rajputana have associated themselves with his noble work. Though the idea of such a foundation originated with Lord Mayo, it is to the generosity and wise liberality of the Rajput Rajas and aristocracy that the realisation of the project is due, and most heartily do I congratulate them on the effective manner in which they have been able to give effect to the intention of their late lamented Viceroy. (Cheers.)

And now, turning for a moment to those for whose benefit so many have laboured and so much has been done, I would wish to address to them a few words of earnest and friendly advice. In the first place, I would remind them that, whether as the scions of ancient houses, as the heads of historical families, as destined to fill public positions of importance in Rajputana, or as the future Chiefs of independent States, there has already fallen upon their young lives the shadow of heavier responsibilities and stricter duties, as well as the sunshine of loftier aspirations and wider possibilities, than any which encompass the existence of the bulk of their countrymen. The happiness of thousands, the tranquillity of vast territories, and the general prosperity of the Empire at large, may be advanced or retarded in a sensible manner in proportion to the degree to which they may take advantage of the opportunities of self-improvement afforded them within these walls. For this reason it is exceptionally incumbent upon you, my young friends, to cultivate certain special qualities, and to avoid certain special dangers. Inasmuch as Providence has placed you in a position of considerable social dignity, has relieved you from the pressure of sordid cares and the anxieties incident to straitened circumstances, it should become a matter of pride and conscience with you to clothe yourselves with those manly virtues and characteristics which in all ages have been recognised as the proper adornment of the well-born, such as self-restraint, fortitude, patience, the love of truth and of justice, modesty, purity, consideration for others, a ready sympathy for the weak, the suffering, and the oppressed, and, above all, with that noble courtesy which does not merely consist in grace of manner and a veneer of conventional politeness, but which is the outcome of an innate simplicity and generosity of spirit which instinctively shrinks with scorn and disgust from anything approaching to egotistical vanity and vulgar self-assertion. On the other hand, you should be equally watchful against those temptations to which wealth, with its opportunities of self-indulgence, in all ages and all countries, has been peculiarly exposed, such as sloth, idleness, sensuality, effeminacy of mind and body, and all those baser influences which render a man a burden to himself, a disgrace to his family, and a curse to his country. And in saying this I would warn you that we are living in a shifting world,—in a world in which those very privileges and advantages upon which you have been led—I do not at all say illegitimately—to pride yourselves, are being continually exposed to the criticisms of public opinion and the ordeal of intellectual competition. If, then, Rajputana is to maintain her historical position as one of the leading provinces of Hindustan, and the ancient home of all that was high-bred, chivalrous, and heroic, it is absolutely necessary that the sons and representatives of its famous houses should endeavour to retain as leaders of the people in the arts of peace, and as their exemplars in the van of civilisation, that pre-eminence and renown which their forefathers won, fighting sword in hand at the head of their clans on many a field of battle. (Cheers.) And, believe me, such peaceful triumphs, promoting, as they do, the well-being of multitudes of our fellow-creatures, are far more worthy of your ambition than any which were gained in those miserable days when scarcely a twelvemonth passed without the fair fields of India being watered with the blood of thousands of her children.

But, passing from these general topics, I would have wished to have made a few specific recommendations in regard to matters of detail. Having, however, already detained you longer than I intended, I will confine myself to a single point which has been already frequently referred to on similar occasions, namely, the great desirability of your becoming thorough masters of the English language. In doing so, I will not particularly insist upon the obvious advantage of your acquaintance with a tongue so rich and varied in its literature, and through which you can make yourselves acquainted at first hand with the ideas of some of the greatest men that have ever lived, as well as with the latest results of modern philosophic thought and scientific research. I would rather remind you of the practical benefits which the due prosecution of your studies in this direction will confer upon you. English is the official language of the Supreme Government under which you live, and of the books which deal with the public affairs, the domestic administration, and the general interests of your country, and it will be of continual use—indeed, I may say of absolute necessity—to you in the positions which you may be called upon to fill. The keen-witted inhabitants of many other parts of India have fully appreciated this fact, and all their energies have consequently been devoted to the acquisition of English. As a consequence, many of them both speak and write it with an eloquence and fluency beyond all praise. Now, I trust that those I am addressing have sufficient self-respect and take a sufficient pride in their province not to wish it to fall behind the other component parts of the Empire in this particular; and therefore, again I say, let it be one of the principal objects of your ambition while within these walls to acquire the English language. (Cheers.) Already in the Councils of Providence the edict has gone forth that English should be the language chiefly prevalent upon God's earth. Within another hundred years it has been calculated that the English-speaking races of the world will number upwards of a thousand millions. Under such circumstances, it would indeed be a disgrace if any of Her Majesty's subjects in India with any pretensions to belong to the educated classes should remain ignorant of it. (Cheers.)

And now, Ladies, Princes, Chiefs, and Gentlemen, it only remains for me to congratulate those present—and especially those who, like my honoured friend Sir Charles Aitchison, and your first Principal,* happily present upon this occasion, were the first promoters of this great and noble institution—on the practical success it has attained, and on the favourable future extending before it. Already it has turned out pupils possessed of those characteristics which we in England most highly value; nor need I go further in illustration of this fact

---

* Sir Oliver St. John.

than to point to the first and as yet the only Rajput Prince whose State I have yet visited, and with whom I have had the pleasure of a few days' personal intercourse, the Raja of Ulwar —(cheers)—an honoured pupil of the Mayo College, who has more than kept the promise of his youth by the intelligence of his government, and by the personal industry which he brings to the management of his affairs. He is administering his State in a way to conduce to the prosperity and contentment of his people, his own reputation, and the honour and welfare of the Supreme Government. (Cheers.) If only the Mayo College will continue to turn out such rulers, we may well envy the illustrious Viceroy to whose wisdom we are indebted for its establishment, and whose honoured memory it is destined, I trust, to preserve in the land for many and many a generation. (Loud and continued applause.)

RESTORATION OF THE FORTRESS OF GWALIOR.

On 1st December, 1885, the Viceroy and Lady Dufferin, accompanied by Sir Frederick Roberts (the recently-appointed Commander-in-Chief in India), with their personal staffs, left Agra by special train for Gwalior, which was reached in the afternoon. On the following morning the Viceroy, with Sir Frederick Roberts, visited the Fortress, and in the afternoon His Excellency held a special durbar for the purpose of formally announcing to Maharaja Scindia the restoration to him of the Fortress of Gwalior, with the neighbouring cantonment of Morar. The scene was one of unusual magnificence. Over one hundred and fifty of Scindia's Sirdars attended, and were seated according to their rank in the durbar, while in another portion of the hall were assembled Sir Frederick Roberts and his staff, the General commanding the division and his staff, and a brilliant company of civil and military officers. Lady Dufferin and a number of ladies were also present. The Viceroy entering the Durbar Hall in procession with his staff, was received by the Maharaja and Sir Lepel Griffin at the entrance, and conducted to a chair of state on the dais. The Maharaja was seated on His Excellency's right and Sir Lepel Griffin on his left. After a short interval the Viceroy rose and addressed Maharaja Scindia as follows:—

YOUR HIGHNESS,—I have invited you to meet me here today, in order that I might formally communicate to you the intelligence that Her Majesty the Queen-Empress of India has resolved to bestow upon you a signal mark of her confidence and favour.

Twenty-eight years ago India was shaken by a great convulsion; and, in common with many other Native Princes, Your Highness found yourself involved in the gravest difficulties and dangers.

These eventually culminated in the overthrow of your authority by a misguided soldiery, which had risen in revolt alike against Your Highness and against the British Government. The rebels were speedily defeated and dispersed by Her Majesty's troops; but in the interests of peace and order, it was thought desirable that the Fortress of Gwalior and the neighbouring Cantonment of Morar should be temporarily garrisoned and held by a British force. This arrangement has been maintained up to the present day. Time, however, with its healing hand, education with her divine light, and the irresistible and subtle influences of civilization, have in the meanwhile been making great changes around us. Order and tranquillity have succeeded to disturbance and unrest. Convinced both of the power and of the intention of the British Government to protect the weak, to control the unruly, and to reward the well-disposed, the inhabitants of the Native States of India, with few exceptions, have for many years past been following the path of progress in peace and contentment, while their rulers have long since recognised the benefits accruing to them from the predominance of a government which unfeignedly desires the perpetuation of their dynasties and the maintenance of their rights, demanding only in return that they should be loyal to their Empress, and should administer their important governments in such a way as to promote the happiness of their subjects, for whose welfare the paramount Power is ultimately responsible.

One of the results of this change has been that some of the precautions which were at one time necessary both for the protection of the Princes themselves and for the maintenance of the imperial authority, have become superfluous.

For these reasons, and because the Ruler of this State, as is well known to all present, holds an exalted place among the loyal and capable feudatories of the Crown, Her Majesty the Queen-Empress has determined to restore to Your Highness's possession and keeping the noble Fortress which towers above the capital of your State.

In accepting this important trust, Your Highness need have no apprehension that the support which you have hitherto received from the British Government will be in any way diminished. In consequence of the extension of railways and the changes which have taken place in the military requirements of the situation, we can act as effectively from a distance as from the positions we now occupy; and Your Highness may rest assured that if ever the necessity should arise, the British Government will fulfil with promptitude and energy the obligations imposed upon it by existing engagements.

Her Majesty the Queen-Empress well knows that in restoring to Your Highness the Fortress of Gwalior, she is gratifying one of the most ardent wishes of your heart, and I may add that it is a personal pleasure to myself to be the instrument of conveying to Your Highness this fresh proof of Her Majesty's favour. At the same time the Queen-Empress hopes that this act will be regarded throughout India, not merely as a personal favour bestowed upon the individual Chief to whom it has been accorded, but as an indication that Her Majesty and the English nation have not failed to appreciate the universal loyalty to the imperial rule, and to the throne and person of Her Majesty, which has recently been displayed in so striking a manner by the Princes, the Native States, and the people of India.

Mr. Durand, the Foreign Secretary, then read a translation of His Excellency's speech in the vernacular; and after a brief pause the Maharaja replied in a short speech, which was rendered into English by Sir Lepel Griffin as follows:—

"In the first place I desire to express to Your Excellency my thanks for the honour you have done me in visiting my capital, and in the second place, my gratitude for your having fulfilled the deepest wish of my heart in restoring to me the Fortress of my ancestors. So long as I live I shall never forget the kindness and honour that have been bestowed upon me by former Viceroys, your predecessors, and especially by Your Excellency. I trust that you will always consider me among your sincere friends and well-wishers, and that I may be counted among those who are most warmly attached to the service of Her Most Gracious Majesty the Queen-Empress."

The proceedings then came to a close, and the Viceroy, taking leave of Maharaja Scindia, left the hall in procession as he had entered it.

In the evening the Maharaja entertained the Viceroy and a large number of guests at a banquet in the palace. Towards the close of dinner the Maharaja entered and was seated close to the Viceroy. Sir Lepel Griffin, on behalf of the Maharaja, having proposed the health of the Queen-Empress, and of Lord and Lady Dufferin, the Viceroy spoke as follows :—

LADIES AND GENTLEMEN,—In rising to acknowledge on behalf of the Queen-Empress the courteous terms in which the Maharaja has been good enough to propose her health, I am anxious to take the opportunity of offering him my sincerest congratulations on this morning's proceedings. When I received him in durbar, I was speaking as Viceroy and in the name of the Government of India. My language was of necessity formal and restrained. Now, however, that I am addressing him as a personal friend and as a guest under his roof, I may indulge in a more familiar strain. I may tell him what intense personal satisfaction I have derived at being the fortunate instrument through which the natural and legitimate desires of his heart have been gratified. In restoring to his keeping the noble Fortress of his ancestors, which, with its historical monuments, its picturesque characteristics, and its commanding position, the greatest monarch might be proud to possess, I well know that it is to one of the most loyal feudatories of Her Majesty, to one of the best friends of the Government of India, to a fine soldier, and to a brave and honourable prince, that this great trust has been confided. (Cheers.) And, furthermore, let me assure him that the gift thus conferred upon him by his Sovereign is conveyed freely, ungrudgingly, and untainted by any misgivings or regrets. Long, I trust, may His Highness live to look forth from its coronet of towers over the noble expanse of territory at the feet of his Fortress of Gwalior, and for many and many a generation hereafter may his descendants refer with gratitude and reverence to the name of their distinguished ancestor through whose merits and good fortune so bright a jewel of the State was restored to the family. And in saying this, I feel that indirectly I am addressing the Princes of India at large, and that the especial honour which peculiar circumstances have enabled the Queen-Empress to confer upon one of their most illustrious representatives, is in a certain sense shared by them all, as no more striking proof could be given to the world of the deep trust reposed in their loyalty as a class by their Sovereign and the British nation. At all events, it is in this light that Her Majesty and her Government hope that the matter may be regarded. (Cheers.)

And now, Ladies and Gentlemen, before I sit down, I will ask you to drink the Maharaja's health. The major part of this company is composed of the officers and of the inhabitants of the neighbouring cantonment of Morar. I know that I am expressing the feelings of those gentlemen and of all connected with them, when I say that it is with extreme regret they have learned that the arrangements following upon the cession of the Fort of Gwalior will remove them from the vicinity of the munificent Prince and considerate host and neighbour, within whose territories they have enjoyed such a pleasant sojourn, and of whose personal kindnesses they have had so many proofs. (Loud cheers.)

ADDRESS FROM THE MUNICIPALITY OF LUCKNOW.

The Viceroy arrived at Lucknow at 9 A.M. on the 4th December, 1885. At the railway station His Excellency was met by a deputation from the Municipality, who presented him with an address of welcome. The address remarked on the general satisfaction which was felt at Lord Dufferin's appointment as Governor-General, as well as the confidence in his ability to deal with pending questions—a confidence which had since been amply justified by the firm and able manner in which His Excellency had dealt with the complications on the North-Western Frontier. It referred to Lady Dufferin's sympathetic efforts to further the cause of medical education among the women of India, which had "called forth the admiration and affection of all classes," and it concluded with some observations on the progress of municipal administration in Lucknow and with the warmest expressions of confidence in Lord Dufferin as Viceroy. His Excellency replied as follows:—

GENTLEMEN,—It is with the utmost sincerity that I offer you my best thanks for the kind and friendly address with which you have welcomed me to the city of Lucknow—a city round whose walls there cling many sad and solemn, as well as many triumphant, memories, and within whose precincts there passed to his rest one of the most heroic, chivalrous, and unselfish soldiers and servants of the State that ever sacrificed health and life in India for his Queen and country. His name, and the names and fame of hundreds of others who were his brave companions in that time of trouble, will not only long live in the pages of history, but have received additional and undying lustre at the hands of the greatest poet of our age, whose son, I am happy to think, has to-day accompanied me to the spot which has inspired one of his father's noblest poems. Though we also in our generation have our troubles, anxieties, and preoccupations, those miserable times have passed away, and the India of to-day, her face averted from the past, and not discontented with the present, is pressing forward with high hope and widening aspirations to what I trust will prove an ever-brightening future.

I have remarked with pleasure the modest terms in which you speak of your own efforts as a civic body to contribute to the general progress and prosperity of the community with which you are connected; and that very spirit of modesty which characterises your address is in itself the best guarantee we can wish to have of the success with which your efforts will be undoubtedly crowned. My illustrious predecessor said on one occasion, if I remember right, that, rather than discourage or damp the spirit of local self-government by any over-severity of remonstrance, it would be better for us to put up for a time with the initial mistakes and shortcomings of our newly-fledged municipalities, even though their first inexperienced and tentative efforts should fall short of the efficiency which might otherwise be required. Though you yourselves stand in need of no such indulgence, I may be permitted to say that, however closely and strictly the Government of India may be disposed to watch, and, if need be, to criticise, the proceedings of older and more responsible urban administrations, in the soundness and wisdom of this considerate opinion of my predecessor I fully concur.

And now I must thank you for the friendly allusions you have made to the endeavours of the Government to maintain peace along our North-West Frontier, and to the successful issue of our campaign in Burma. Fortunately, we have attained the object for which the Burmese Expedition was undertaken, without serious loss of life either to ourselves or to those who were unhappily opposed to us; and I have been informed by our authorities on the spot that nothing could be more satisfactory than the goodwill and friendly spirit displayed by the population of Upper Burma and of Mandalay towards us. The future arrangements to be introduced into that region will now have to be considered carefully, deliberately, and after a full examination of the various elements of a most momentous question. It is undoubtedly necessary to the peace and security of Lower Burma, as well as of our Eastern Indian Frontier, that our political ascendancy should prevail throughout the upper valley of the Irrawaddy. Whether this may be best secured by the union of both sections of the Burmese people under British rule, or by the re-constitution, under certain conditions, of the Kingdom of Upper Burma, is a very grave and serious matter, not to be settled hastily or without the most anxious examination as to what will be conducive to the interests of India, to the welfare of the Burmese people themselves, and to the requirements of the Empire at large. Of this at all events you may be sure, that the Government of India will not approach the question in any light or thoughtless spirit, nor will it in any way seek to commit the Government of Her Majesty prematurely to a line of action which may not approve itself to the English people. We commenced the war against our will, and our chief cause of satisfaction in the conquest of the kingdom has been that the event has neither brought disaster upon the country we have taken, nor engendered feelings of animosity towards us amongst its inhabitants.

In conclusion, Gentlemen, allow me to thank you for your kind allusion to Lady Dufferin's efforts to improve the medical education of the women of India. I have already had so many opportunities of expressing my own and her deep sense of the sympathy with which her proposals have been met, that I need not again refer to the subject. My not doing so, however, must not be misinterpreted as any want of gratitude upon our part for the kind expressions you have made use of in regard to them. (Applause.)

LICENSE TAX AMENDMENT BILL.

In the Legislative Council which assembled at Calcutta on the 4th January, 1886, the Hon. Sir Auckland Colvin moved for leave to introduce a Bill for imposing a tax on income derived from sources other than agriculture. He concluded an exhaustive speech on the motion as follows: "In the necessities of the time—in the interest of all classes of the community—in the present incidence of our Indian taxation—in the legitimate and necessary result of the financial policy pursued by our predecessors, in the admissions of those who oppose an income tax, will be found the justification of the measure which I now have the honour to ask Your Lordship to allow me to introduce. I have shown what our financial position is; I have added that, while we are not forgetful of economies, we cannot hope, in the ensuing year, for any great relief in this direction; I have stated why, in our opinion, resort to indirect taxation is undesirable; I have pointed out that direct taxation is the necessary outcome of the financial policy of the last eight years; I have drawn attention to the provisions of the Bill to prove that it is framed with a view to profiting by the great experience which in a quarter of a century we have acquired; I have glanced at the objections which may be urged in view of the silver exchange, and while deploring its effect on the position and the circumstances of so many here in India, I have given my reasons for thinking that, objection for objection, there is more to be said in favour of the struggling silent masses than of the few to whom I have just referred; and I now look to the candour and intelligence of my hearers to decide whether in these circumstances some revised form of direct taxation is not inevitable, and whether direct taxation in the form embodied in the Bill which I wish to lay before the Council is not unquestionably a course which is more free from objection than any which can be urged upon our attention as an alternative."

His Excellency the President spoke as follows:—

As Sir Auckland Colvin has made so complete and lucid a statement of our present financial position and the reasons which have compelled the Government of India to introduce the present Bill, it would have been scarcely necessary for me at this stage of the proceedings to trouble you with any observations of my own, did not I think it my duty to seize the earliest opportunity of taking upon myself, as the head of this Government, the full responsibility of a measure which, however imperative, must by its very nature prove extremely unpopular. The Financial Member in taking the initiative has merely discharged the technical duties attaching to his office, and he is no more responsible for the policy upon which we have determined than any other member of the administration, inasmuch as the causes which have created the difficulties with which we are about to grapple have in no way resulted from circumstances over which the Financial Department have had the slightest control. Before, however, I touch upon that part of the subject which concerns the future, it is but right that the Indian tax-payers, and the Indian public generally, should receive a full explanation in regard to the past, and to the causes which have occasioned the actual deficit which will confront us at the conclusion of the present financial year. That deficit, as you have been already told, will probably amount, in round numbers, to £2,800,000. The principal portion of this sum, which may be put roughly at a couple of millions, is due to those preparations which we were compelled to make on our side of the water in view of a possible contest between Great Britain and Russia. The nature of the crisis to which I allude was thoroughly understood from one end of India to the other. Its gravity was fully appreciated, and there probably has never been a more gratifying feature in the history of this country than the way in which all classes of Her Majesty's subjects came forward, not merely with a unanimous expression of loyalty and devotion to the throne and to the person of the Queen-Empress, but, in numerous instances, with offers both of personal and material assistance. In these circumstances, it scarcely is necessary for me to show that the expenditure which we at that time incurred was necessary and inevitable. It will be sufficient for me to point out that so imminent was war considered by Mr. Gladstone and his colleagues that the reserves were called out and a powerful fleet was equipped by the British Government, at an expense of six and a half millions. I imagine that no one will care to suggest that, while these sacrifices were being made by the English tax-payers with the view of maintaining the sanctity of the north-western frontier of India, India herself should have remained a listless spectator of the scene and have done nothing for her own defence. But though we felt it incumbent upon us to prepare for what then appeared the probable contingency of war, we restricted our precautionary measures to those which the barest necessities of the case required. We contented ourselves with providing such an amount of transport and stores as would enable us to place a *corps d'armée* of observation on our own frontier. We did not mobilise a regiment, or move a man, or spend a penny otherwise than on these initial and elementary measures, and had any Government done less, it would have deserved impeachment.

The other items of the deficit have been occasioned by the construction of a temporary line through the Bolan Pass from Rindli to Quetta, and by our military operations in Upper Burma, the cost of the latter of which has been estimated for the current year at £270,000. With regard to the first of these projects, the Bolan line, I need not say much. It is well known how fatal to the lives of our soldiers and how intolerably expensive has been in times past the despatch of troops on foot along this fatal road. A considerable period must of necessity elapse before the Hurnai route can be completed, and were a war to occur there is no doubt that the existence of direct and through railway communication to Quetta would save thousands of lives, as well as the original cost of the railway many times over.

As to the Burmese war, though it is not perhaps a very fitting opportunity for explaining the policy of the Government, there are one or two observations it might be opportune for me to make in regard to it. That our proceedings in the matter have been almost unanimously approved of in England has long since been sufficiently apparent. In this country, however, a different view has been taken of the affair by a considerable proportion of the native press. That this should be the case has not at all surprised me, and I readily admit that the instinctive aversion so many of our native friends have shown to the Mandalay expedition has been both natural and reasonable. As a general principle, it is not desirable that either the limits or the political and financial responsibilities of the Indian Empire should be extended, and every Indian tax-payer is perfectly justified in apprehending that every war, no matter upon how moderate a scale it may be conducted or how successful its issue, must add to the public burdens. Nor, indeed, can we expect that those larger and predominant considerations which dictated the line of action we have followed should be present to the minds of the great mass of the Indian people. To them Burma is a remote and foreign country. The history of our relations with the Government of King Theebaw during the past years is alike indifferent and unknown to them, and we must not be surprised if the inhabitants of Lahore, or of Trinchinopoly, Benares or Multan, should fail to remember that, for thirty years, Lower Burma has formed an integral part of the Indian Empire; that it has contributed its full share, and, as the Burmese allege, more than its full share, of taxation to the Imperial Exchequer; and that anything which affects its security or welfare must of necessity prove of as deep concern to the Government of India as if it lay in the heart of Her Majesty's Indian possessions. A variety of concurrent circumstances made it only too evident that the future of Lower Burma would be seriously compromised unless we came to some satisfactory understanding with the Government of Mandalay in respect to the various outstanding complaints which for years past we have been vainly preferring to the Burmese King. An honest and sincere endeavour was made to reach an amicable settlement, but our well-meant intentions were frustrated by the folly of the ruler, and we were forced very reluctantly to undertake the conquest of the country. Thanks to the skill, the prudence, and the humanity with which the expedition has been conducted by General Prendergast, and to the zeal and energy displayed by Her Majesty's forces of both services, English and native, the capital of Upper Burma has been occupied, it may be said, almost without bloodshed, and certainly without engendering any bitterness of feeling between ourselves and the Burmese people. That these proceedings will entail a certain amount of cost cannot be denied; but, without endorsing the complaint of the representatives of Burmese interests, who maintain that the Indian Exchequer has unduly profited for many years past by the exorbitant amount of Burmese revenue which it absorbs, it will probably be found, when the debtor and creditor account between India and Burma is finally examined, even after the expenses of the present war have been duly debited, that an ultimate balance sheet will be shown which may by no means prove unsatisfactory to the Indian tax-payer. As to the degree to which the revenues of Upper Burma may suffice to provide for the wants of its own administration in future, nothing at present can be said. It was necessary, of course, once the conquest of the country had been effected, to determine and to declare for diplomatic purposes its international status. This has been done by the Proclamation of the 1st of January, under which the authority of the Viceroy is substituted for that of the late King. Such an arrangement, however, though required by the actual circumstances of the case, will eventually be replaced by a more fully regulated system, the nature of which will, in all probability, not be determined until I have myself visited Mandalay, and been in a position to submit a report to the Queen's Government at home.

Having now dealt with the causes of our actual deficit, and one or two subjects cognate to them, I will ask permission to make a few further observations in regard to the Bill we purpose to introduce. The object of that Bill is to impose a tax upon those classes who at this moment contribute nothing, or only contribute in a very imperceptible degree, to the Indian revenues. On the necessity for strengthening our present financial position I will not enlarge. Sir Auckland Colvin has clearly shown that the financial position of the country is gravely imperilled by a harassing uncertainty in regard to the future of silver. The fall of a penny in the price of silver at once adds, in round numbers, a million to our expenditure. In this manner, since I entered upon the duties of my office, an additional charge of a million sterling has been laid upon our shoulders; and, though I trust that the depression of the metal may have reached its lowest limit, the possibility of a further fall, and the consequent presence of an element of uncertainty in all our accounts, renders it absolutely incumbent upon the Government to take such precautionary measures as the circumstances of the case permit. After consultation with a number of persons, both English and native, who are entitled to speak with great authority upon such questions, we have framed the provisions of the present Bill, and from first to last the utmost care has been taken to render their application both equitable and as consonant to the habits and feelings of those affected by it as possible. I am aware that in all Eastern countries there is a great objection to anything approaching to direct taxation, and I might have hesitated to give my assent to such a measure as the present if it had been an unprecedented essay in that direction; but so far from this being the case, direct taxation has for some years past formed a portion of the fiscal system of India. The license tax is a tax essentially direct both in its principle, its incidence, and its application, and so far as I have been able to learn by enquiry, or to gather from the public prints, the opposition which this impost originally encountered has in a great measure subsided. Its assessments have been gradually brought into harmony with the real status of those who have been subjected to it. Its inquisitorial character has been eradicated, and it is now submitted to with as much cheerfulness and good humour as is compatible with the infirmity of human nature. The necessity then of some addition to our public revenues being admitted, the Government naturally considered that the extension of a tax similar in principle to the license tax to those classes of the community who are not subject to its operation, was both a just and a desirable expedient. The only alternative open to us was to re-enhance the salt tax; but, though this would have been an indirect tax, and consequently not so unpopular as the one we are about to impose, its operation would have chiefly affected the poorer masses of the community. Now, I am very far from wishing to say that in the presence of any overwhelming necessity, such as that of a great war or a great famine, it might not be necessary to raise the duties upon salt. It would be by such a measure alone that a great emergency of the kind could be met, and all minor considerations would have to be postponed to the imperative necessities of the hour ; nay, even something short of either of these calamities might justify us in resorting to it. But when the situation merely requires a comparatively slight addition to our current revenue, it is obvious that any honourable man who had to chose between taxing the most indigent classes who already contribute a considerable share of the public burdens, and taxing those classes who, though in easier circumstances, scarcely contribute anything, it is to the latter alternative that he would resort. This at all events is the conclusion that the Government of India has come to in the matter. We look abroad, and we see that the peasant pays his salt tax, which, though it has been reduced, still supplies us with a yearly net revenue of £6,000,000 ; that the landowner pays his land tax and his cesses ; that the tradesman or the merchant pays his license tax ; but that the lawyer or doctor, the members of the other learned professions, the officers of Government, and other persons occupying an analogous status, and the gentleman at large, pay little or nothing. I look around this very table, and what do I see ? That there is not one of us into whose pocket Sir Auckland Colvin is able to get so much as his little finger. For instance, take my friend Mr. Mandlik, a most eminent and distinguished member of the legal profession. He will admit, I am sure, that his qualifications to rank as a tax-payer are of the most microscopic proportions. The same may be said of my friend Mr. Peari Mohan Mukerji, except in so far as he may be a landowner ; but whatever revenue he derives from land are exempted from the operation of this Bill. I might make the same appeal to most of our other colleagues, and, what is equally sad, I am forced to make an identical confession in regard to myself and to the members of the

Government. There is not one of us who pays any really serious sum from his income into the Imperial Exchequer.

Now, surely this cannot be right, and to such an anomaly it is no answer to say that direct taxation is repugnant to oriental customs. Justice is the inhabitant neither of the East nor of the West. She admits no geographical limits to her supremacy; her throne is on high, and sooner or later, in spite of prejudice or custom, she never fails to vindicate her title to the respect and veneration of mankind. It is then in the name of justice that we propose the imposition of this tax, and we feel assured that every fair and right-thinking man in the country, no matter how his private interest may be affected by our action, will recognise that no other course was open to us. Indeed, already I see that no less intelligent a body than the congress of Indian delegates lately held at Bombay have forestalled our conclusions, and have passed a resolution, recommending, in default of other expedients, the extension of the license tax to those members of the community who hitherto have enjoyed an undeserved immunity from the visits of the tax collector.

But though I do not anticipate that any serious objections will be raised to the principle of the Bill, it is possible that adverse criticisms may be passed upon some of its details. I need scarcely say that the most searching criticism, especially if accompanied by practical suggestions, will be very welcome and will receive from the Government most careful and impartial consideration. I do not anticipate, however, that any great changes will be necessary, because great care has been taken to divest it of all those unsatisfactory characteristics which have hitherto rendered the imposition of direct taxation so unwelcome. Warned by the experiences of those who have gone before us, we have carefully eliminated from our Bill everything that rendered former measures of the kind odious and obnoxious. In fact, our project is merely an expansion of the license tax. The license tax is a one-storeyed house, and on the top of it we are putting a second storey, but the order of architecture in both will be the same; and as the foundations of the one have stood the test of time and of popular criticism, so I trust will the walls of the other possess the same solid characteristics.

But there is now another aspect of the question to which I am bound to refer. Following in the steps of Sir Auckland Colvin, I have shown, I trust in a perfectly conclusive manner, that the instability of silver, and the loss by exchange we have sustained during the current year, have compelled us to strengthen our financial position in the manner I have described; but, besides this, other unexpected calls upon our revenue have arisen, which have also had their influence in determining us to introduce the present Bill. A few short years ago, India was an isolated region, cut off from the rest of the world, on two sides by the sea, and on the third by a range of mountains whose further slopes were inhabited by populations destitute of modern arms, unskilled in the arts of war, and from whom no serious acts of aggression were to be apprehended. But within a period of startling brevity this situation has been completely revolutionised. A great European Power has advanced its confines by sudden leaps and bounds into what by comparison may be called close proximity to our own frontier. It is true several hundred miles still separate the territories of India from those of Russia, but the intervening space is ruled by a Prince in close alliance with ourselves, whose interests are cognate to our own, and the invasion of whose territories we are solemnly pledged to resent so long as he conducts his external relations in accordance with our advice and wishes. I do not propose to waste the time of the Council by entering upon any justification of the arrangements out of which the foregoing obligation has arisen. They were made by my illustrious predecessor, to whose good management and wise conduct of the affairs of the North-West we are indebted for a united Afghanistan and a friendly Afghan ruler. But whatever their character, they have to all intents and purposes brought, though in an indirect manner, the area avowedly dominated by our political influence and ascendancy into direct contact with one of the greatest military monarchies of the day. Under these circumstances it would be the height of folly upon our part if we did not recognise the change which has taken place in the external position and relations of the Indian Empire. My own opinion is that the councils of Russia are controlled by a just and peace-loving Emperor, and inspired by a moderate and unaggressive statesman; but those who have watched the recent current of events in Europe and the origin and causes of some of the most bloody wars of the last thirty years, must be aware that the hands of monarchs, however powerful, and of ministers however conscientious, are violently forced and their most earnest desires countervailed by a hundred disturbing influences. The accident of a moment, a wave of popular prejudice or passion, the influence of a subordinate but powerful party in the State, a chance collision between distant pickets, each one of these, or all combined, have been and will be again sufficient to bring the nations of the earth into disastrous collision. But for the accidental circumstance of the Amir being in my camp at Rawal Pindi, and the fortunate fact of his being a Prince of great capacity, experience, and calm judgment, the incident of Penjdeh alone, in the strained condition of the relations which then existed between Russia and ourselves, might of itself have proved the occasion of a long and miserable war. But, not only so, there are other contingencies and untoward possibilities which must occur to the mind of every one, though it may not be desirable or prudent to specify them in detail, which, were they to happen, would still further accentuate the change in our circumstances which the entry of Russia into the valley of the Hari-Rud, and her advance to the borders of Maruchak, Maimena, and Balkh, have occasioned. If then the situation is such as I have described,—and I have endeavoured to shape my language in accordance with absolute fact and the suggestions of plain common sense,—it is evident that we should be neglecting a grave and obvious duty did we not follow the example of all civilised communities under such circumstances, and place our frontiers in such a position of defence and impregnability as will render us comparatively indifferent to the changes and chances of the outside world, and restore to us that feeling of security and independence of others which is absolutely essential to the stability of our credit and the healthy condition of our finances. These necessities have been equally admitted by the late and the present Governments of Great Britain. During a remarkable debate which took place last year, the representatives both of the Conservative and of the Liberal parties united in recognising the necessity of completing with as little delay as possible such a system of defensive railways, fortifications, and other works along our north-western frontiers as would effectually bar our doors against all chances of annoyance from beyond them, no matter from what source they might proceed —whether occasioned by a foreign foe or by any change of policy on the part—I will not say of the present ruler of Afghanistan, for of his steadfastness and fidelity we have received satisfactory proofs—but on the part of any of his successors. With such a consensus of opinion in the Parliament of Great Britain, the Government of India had no difficulty in discerning what line of action to adopt. Some very complete and well-considered projects for the construction of military railways wherever strategic considerations might require them to be laid had already been drawn up by the late Viceroy and accepted by the Secretary of State, and during the past summer the military authorities here, in conjunction with those at home, have been elaborating a plan for the erection of such places of strength, fortresses and fortified positions, as may be best adapted for the purpose we have in view. In doing this we shall be merely following the example of every other nation in the world, who, no matter how friendly may be its relations with its various neighbours, rightly feels that its security and peace should not be allowed to depend upon their good-will, however genuine, or their professions of amity, however sincere, but upon its own valour and prudence, aided by such means as military science can suggest for the protection of its borders.

It has also been determined for the same reasons to increase to a moderate degree the numbers both of the British and of the native forces in India. This is a measure which the late Commander-in-Chief, one of the most economical, sagacious, and prudent officers that ever occupied that high position, most earnestly counselled, and the necessity for it has been impressed upon us in an equally emphatic manner by his present distinguished successor, as well as by other persons entitled to speak with scarcely less authority. But, though anxious and ready to give every proper consideration to the recommendations of those who are the legitimate advisers of the Government of India in these matters, we felt that due regard had also to be paid to the financial exigencies of the situation. Consequently, the addition we propose to make to our present forces falls considerably short of the figure desired by Sir Donald Stewart and other high military authorities both here and at home. In coming to this conclusion the Government has felt that it was incurring a very grave responsibility, but still, on balancing the conflicting considerations forced upon our attention, we are convinced that the more moderate limit we have adopted is the one best suited to the circumstances of the case.

Unfortunately, precautions of this kind cost money and the necessities of the case require them to be pushed with energy and rapidity; and although the expenditure needed for the greater proportion of these works will be, as heretofore, provided by loan (and by sums refunded to us from time to time by the private companies to which Government railways may be transferred) we shall have of course to pay the interest on whatever sums we borrow. Then again there are three Famine Railways which have been already commenced, and which the Government are determined to complete with all despatch,— namely, two in Madras and one in Northern Bengal. And here perhaps I may take an opportunity of correcting an error which has been frequently made, and which seems to return to new life each time that it is corrected—namely, that an inroad has been made upon the Famine Grant. When I arrived in the country, I found that the system which had been followed by my predecessor had been to apply half a million a year from the Famine Grant to Famine Railways; £250,000 to irrigation works; and the remainder of the grant to the diminution of debt. The justification for its application to this latter purpose has been so fully set forth and explained in a speech of Sir Evelyn Baring's that I need not say any more upon that head. Such was the system I found in vogue when I arrived in India, and during the current year that is the exact system which has been followed. These facts are perfectly well known to all who are acquainted with the subject, and now that I have myself re-stated them in Council, I trust that the foolish ghost of this perennial fiction has been once and for ever laid. In fact, I may say that, so far from diverting the Famine Grant to extraneous purposes, there is nothing which myself and my colleagues have so strongly urged upon the Secretary of State as the desirability of continuing the policy sanctioned by our predecessors, at all events until we shall have reached a stage when our Famine Protective Railways shall have sufficiently multiplied to compress within tolerable bounds the chance of such casualties from famine as have desolated the land in past times. But, though such is our intention and desire, we have thought it perfectly consonant with the principles I have enunciated to ask the Secretary of State that, instead of making all these Famine Protective Railways ourselves, we should be permitted to apply a small proportion of the Famine Grant to the payment of interest to certain companies whom we propose to entrust with the construction of special lines which possess a protective character, and which, by their completion, will diminish the evil consequences of bad seasons in various threatened districts.

Such, gentlemen, are the circumstances under which the Government of India have asked this Council to give leave for the introduction of the present Bill. Stated briefly, our chief justification for the measure is to be found first of all in the extraordinary fall of silver which has recently taken place, and in the uncertainty which prevails as to the future fluctuations which may affect its value. In the presence of such a state of things, the strengthening of our financial position became an absolute duty, and the performance of this duty has been rendered still more incumbent upon us by the necessity, which has been equally recognised by every shade of public opinion in England, of strengthening our frontier defences, and prosecuting with energy the completion of our frontier railways. In determining the amount of money to be raised, we were very careful to limit it to the minimum sum which we thought it safe to ask for, and you may be satisfied that in carrying out the programme which has been determined upon, the Government will be careful to square its efforts with the means at its disposal. All the works which are contemplated cannot, of course, be carried out at once, and by the exercise of prudence and discretion, and by a wise adaptation of the means at our disposal to the ends in view, it may fairly be hoped—unless some unforeseen catastrophe should overset our calculations—that with this slight addition to the taxation of the country, which as I said before will merely touch those who hitherto have contributed but slightly to the public burdens, we shall be able to carry out our programme. Nor need we by any means despair of a very considerable proportion of the expenditure to which I have referred proving remunerative. Railways of course which are simply constructed for strategical reasons cannot be expected, as they are not intended, to prove profitable commercial speculations; but it so happens that the two principal railways which are to subserve our military needs will run in such a direction as in all probability to become of the greatest service to commerce. As everyone knows, the caravan route which connects Hindustan with Persia and Central Asia runs through Quetta, and the goods which are now conveyed on camels' backs to the proximity of the Indus may be expected to feed the chief of these lines with a continually growing traffic. Again, the Sind-Saugar Railway, which will enable us to move our troops along the whole face of our frontier, may from the peculiar circumstances of its location eventually become a considerable commercial artery. These results, however, are only subsidiary to the main purpose of the two lines in question, and I merely mention them as affording some consolation to those of us who like myself have an instinctive dislike to purely military expenditure.

It only remains for me, gentlemen, to thank you for the patience with which you have listened to me, and to apologise for the length of my observations; yet there is one thing which I desire to say before I conclude. Although I have not the slightest doubt or difficulty in recommending you to agree to the introduction and to the eventual passing of this Bill, I cannot help desiring to express my extreme and heartfelt regret that the occasion should have arisen for legislation of this description. The imposition of taxes is always an ungrateful task to any Government, even when its measures have received, through their representatives, the sanction of a majority of the people. The performance of such a duty to persons situated as are my colleagues and myself is still more irksome. When I reached the shores of India, I had marked out for myself a very different programme. For five years the country had been administered by a wise, cautious, and distinguished statesman, who had devoted his attention to the internal welfare of Her Majesty's Indian subjects. Peace reigned from one end of the land to the other; and though our Financial Member could not boast of more than an actual equilibrium between our resources and our expenditure, there was no reason to anticipate, until some months after my arrival, that anything was likely to disturb the even tenor of our way. My predecessor having had such exceptionally favourable opportunities for introducing reforms, and of bringing the institutions of the country into harmony with its growing wants and aspirations, my ambition was confined to the humble intention of watching the effects of his policy, and tending and watering what he had planted. We all know how rapidly these prospects have been overclouded by a succession of adverse circumstances over which this Government has had no control; and now, at the expiration of the first year of my term of office, I and those associated with me in the government of the country find ourselves driven to a course of action which cannot fail to cause inconvenience to certain classes of our fellow-countrymen, whose worldly trials and troubles are already sufficient, I dare say, to try their patience and fortitude to the utmost. Let me assure them that, at all events, neither my colleagues nor I have failed to comprehend the many sacrifices which the imposition of this taxation, moderate as is the scale we have adopted, and comparatively few as are the individuals it will affect, cannot fail to entail upon many of them; and most deeply do we lament the necessity of subjecting them to the ordeal. These observations more especially apply to those Anglo-Indian servants of the State who are compelled by their domestic necessities to transmit to England the greater part of their hard-won earnings for the support of their children. That very depreciation of silver from which the revenues of the State have so greatly suffered has also made itself felt in their case with the most bitter severity. On the other hand, however, it must be remembered that only five years ago three millions of taxes were remitted by the Government of the day. The amount of taxation which we are about to impose will not probably bring in more than six or seven hundred thousand pounds, so that, when all is said and done, the inhabitants of India will be still left the enjoyment of more than two millions of the taxation which was remitted in 1882 by Sir Evelyn Baring. Indeed, if an actual calculation were made, I think it might probably be shown—at all events in the case of the wealthier classes we are now bringing into our net—that the gain they have derived from the remission of the import duties compensates them in a considerable degree for the additional impost to which they are being subjected. Be this, however, as it may, whatever the sacrifice, whether it affects the Anglo-Indian or the native servants of the British Crown —of this I am sure, that if they are once convinced that the measures proposed by this Bill are necessary to maintain unendangered the honour of the Queen-Empress and the safety and security of the Indian Empire, and of the millions of hearths and homes it contains, as well as the stability of our public credit, they will cheerfully submit to them. The offers of assistance forwarded to me during the course of last summer in so generous a manner by the princes, zamíndárs, and leading men of the country more than justify such an expectation. But the days are past for supplementing the resources of the State by private benevolences. The only fair and effectual way of accepting the assistance we have been proffered is by recommending to the generous acceptation of the people a fair, just, and equal measure of taxation. This in our hearts and consciences we believe we have done. But there is one other measure by which we intend still further to fortify our financial position, and to protect it from whatever changes or chances the future may bring forth. Although from time to time during past years frequent endeavours have been made to examine the great machine which constitutes the Indian Government, with the view of rendering its operation more effective and economical, much, I cannot but believe, still remains to be done in that direction. As you are aware, the Government of India itself controls but a part of the expenditure of the country, so large a proportion of the Imperial resources having been confided to the control of the provincial and subordinate administrations. Very soon, however, the provincial contracts instituted between ourselves and the local governments will expire; and it will be necessary, especially in view of the circumstances to which I have referred, most carefully to review them. At a time when fluctuations in the currency are threatening the stability of our whole financial system, and when the possibility of external commotion is darkening the political horizon, it is very evident that the duty of economy and retrenchment ought to be prosecuted with the utmost energy and decision. Already we have initiated this policy with effect; and by an appeal to the provincial governments, which I must say was answered with the greatest loyalty, we have to a very considerable extent been compensated for our additional military expenditure. But this was a temporary measure to meet an equally temporary need. It is now desirable to ascertain whether it would not be possible to add considerably to the margin of our resources by a careful revision of our Imperial and Provincial expenditure, as well as by the addition to our income with which the present Bill will provide us. With this view the Government of India have determined to issue a Financial Commission, so strongly constituted and furnished with such instructions as to ensure that the task entrusted to them will be conscientiously performed, and to prove conclusively that the Viceroy and his colleagues are thoroughly in earnest in their determination to adapt the administration in all its branches to the financial exigencies of the Empire.

The motion was put and agreed to. Sir Auckland Colvin then introduced the Bill, explaining its more important provisions, and the Council was adjourned.

LICENSE TAX AMENDMENT BILL.

On the 11th January the License Tax Amendment Bill was again considered in the Legislative Council. Sir Auckland Colvin moved that the Bill be referred to a select committee consisting of the Honourable Messrs. Ilbert, Hope, Quinton, Hunter, and Steel, the Honourable Rao Saheb Vishvanath Narayan Mandlik, the Honourable Peari Mohan Mukerji, and the mover, with instructions to submit their report on the 22nd instant.

The speakers on the motion were Messrs. Hunter, Steel, Quinton, Evans, Goodrich, Babu P. M. Mukerji, Rao Saheb V. N. Mandlik, the Lieutenant-Governor of Bengal, Sir A. Colvin, and Mr. Hope.

His Excellency the President closed the discussion as follows:—

Before putting the question, I may be permitted to express the very great satisfaction I have derived from the generous unanimity with which the various members of this Council have expressed their approval of the measure which is before them. Quite independent of those who are connected with the Government, we have amongst us the representatives of the three most important interests in India affected by the present Bill. We have a most distinguished member of the mercantile interests, to whose incisive and weighty speech I am sure we have all listened with the greatest pleasure and profit. We have an equally distinguished representative of the interests of the learned professions. And we have also amongst us two gentlemen who are exceptionally authorised to speak on behalf of the interests of the native community. When, therefore, we find that the representatives of these three interests have been good enough to acquiesce in a measure which any Government would have introduced with a considerable amount of anxiety, we may well congratulate ourselves upon the result. But there is another view in which

I personally may be permitted to regard this question, which gives me even more satisfaction than that which I derive from the consciousness that a Government measure has been unanimously approved by this Council. As the representative of the Queen-Empress, and as in some sort the spokesman of the British people, I feel that the unity of effort which we have agreed to make in common for the protection of the Indian Empire is a better proof and test than any which could be produced of the solidarity of interests which unites Her Majesty's Native and British subjects in one common bond of loyalty towards the Queen and the Empire. And let me assure those gentlemen who represent so ably native interests in this Council that the fact that through them the native community has stepped forth so cheerfully and patriotically to support the policy of the Government on this occasion, will not fail to be appreciated at its true value by their fellow-subjects at home.

The motion was then put to the Council and carried, and the Council was adjourned till the 22nd instant, when Sir Auckland Colvin presented the report of the select committee.

The report of the select committee was discussed at a meeting of the Council which took place on the 29th January, the members who took part in the discussion being Sir A. Colvin, Mr. Steel, Babu P. M. Mukerji, Rao Saheb V. N. Maudlik, Mr. Hope, and Mr. Evans. At the close of the discussion, Sir Auckland Colvin moved that " the Bill as amended be passed," and the motion was put and agreed to.

THE FOREIGN OFFICERS AT DELHI.

On Saturday morning, the 16th January, 1886, the Viceroy left Calcutta by special train for Delhi to witness the march past of the troops, numbering about 40,000, who had been engaged in the winter manœuvres, and arrived at Delhi on the evening of the 17th. On the morning of the 19th, before the march past took place, he breakfasted at Colonel Upperton's camp in order to meet the Foreign Military Officers who had been deputed by their respective Governments to attend the manœuvres. A number of guests, including many ladies, were also present. After breakfast His Excellency rose and spoke as follows :—

LADIES AND GENTLEMEN,—As this, I fear, is the only opportunity I shall have of doing so, I hope I may venture, in the name of the Government of India, to express how highly we consider ourselves honoured by the presence of those European officers who have come from so great a distance to witness the military manœuvres in which so considerable a portion of Her Majesty's forces in India, both British and Native, have lately been engaged. On behalf of my colleagues, and as the representative of the Queen-Empress in this country, I now bid them most heartily welcome. All are distinguished representatives of the respective armies to which they severally belong, and I have no doubt we shall derive very great profit from such observations and criticisms as may have occurred to them. But not only do I desire to welcome them as head of the Indian Government; I also wish to express my great personal satisfaction at receiving them in our midst. It so happens that there is not one amongst them to whom, had he come as an ordinary traveller, I should not have felt bound to show special courtesy and attention. For instance, there is Prince Esterhazy, from whose grandfather at an early period of life I experienced great personal kindness, and who has received his mission here at the hands of Count Kalnoky, the Austro-Hungarian Minister for Foreign Affairs, who was an intimate friend and colleague of my own at St. Petersburg. In company with Count Kalnoky, I was permitted to be a spectator of Russia's annual great manœuvres, when I had ample opportunities of appreciating the splendid and gallant appearance, and of noting the efficiency of the men and officers of the Imperial Russian army, as well as of receiving most considerate kindness at the hands of His Majesty the Emperor. Not only so, but one of the Russian officers present wears the uniform of the regiment who were good enough, when we left St. Petersburg, to depute some of their number to say farewell to Lady Dufferin at the station, when they almost smothered her with bouquets. Again, I see opposite to me two officers representing the most venerable and one of the mightiest of European monarchs. Through accidental circumstances, during a period of thirty years, I have experienced from time to time, at the hands of the Emperor of Germany, repeated marks of his never-failing urbanity and goodness of heart, and I hope that when the representatives of the German army return to their native land they will lay my respectful homage at the feet of their sovereign, and assure His Majesty of the unspeakable pleasure it has given me to show them whatever attention lay in my power. On my left I am honoured by the presence of the representatives of the French army. One of them is well known to be more respected and universally liked in London than any one who has occupied a similar position. His colleague is an old acquaintance, and both represent a country with most of whose distinguished statesmen and generals I have had the good fortune to be upon terms of intimacy. We have also many friends in common. To extend to these two officers my most respectful greetings is naturally, therefore, a labour of love. With the officers who come from Italy I can boast no personal acquaintance, and yet. probably I am united in sympathy with them by far stronger ties than they themselves suspect. Though an Englishman, or rather an Irishman, by nationality, by birth I am an Italian, and I never hear their beautiful language spoken without its recalling many agreeable memories. They can, therefore, well understand how pleasant it has been to me to welcome them to India. Again, on the other side, are two other officers whose presence here is as grateful to my feelings as that of any of their colleagues, inasmuch as they represent the army of the United States—a country which I had often occasion to visit when Governor-General of Canada, and whose border I never passed without experiencing at the hands of its inhabitants such an amount of kindness and hospitality as it would be impossible for me to forget. If, therefore, I have ever found myself in the midst of any company whose presence I should welcome, it is that of those distinguished officers now present at the table. At the same time there is one consideration which, perhaps, mars the harmony of my greetings. As followers of the profession of arms, it is the duty of our military visitors to bring to the utmost efficiency those means of mutual destruction to which nations are forced to appeal in the last resort. Now it has been my duty, as a diplomatist for several years, to apply whatever faculties I am possessed of to rendering those armies, whose organization they are so eager to bring to perfection, as inoperative as possible. Wars are the reproach and disgrace of diplomatists, whose ambition should be the reverse of that of our military friends—namely, to render war a lost and forgotten art. Unfortunately hitherto the soldiers have too often got the better of us. But whatever my professional instincts might have been as an Ambassador, I am free to confess that, as Governor-General of this country, my desire for the maintenance of peace has been still further intensified; and most heartily do I pray that the wisdom of all our Governments, and the calmness and moderation of public opinion in the various countries of the world may confine the efforts of all nations to such mimic warfare as that which you, gentlemen, have lately witnessed on the plains of India, and that in Asia, as in Europe, the beneficent triumphs of civilisation may never be marred or interrupted by the terrible necessities of war. In conclusion, I have only to express my regret that my proximate voyage to Burma will prevent me from entertaining our foreign visitors in Calcutta in the manner I should desire. If they will permit it, however, I will commission my daughter to welcome them to Government House in Lady Dufferin's name and my own, and to give a ball in their honour, in order that they may have an opportunity of convincing themselves how favourable is our climate to feminine beauty; that our ladies' eyes are more fatal than our artillery; their wit more pointed than our bayonets, and that they are ready to give them as kind, though, perhaps, a more dangerous welcome to the capital of India as that which we have endeavoured to extend to them in our camp at Delhi. And now, ladies and gentlemen, I beg to propose the health of the Emperors, Kings, and Chiefs of States of those countries whose officers have done us the honour of visiting India.

THE "MARCH PAST" AT DELHI.

After breakfast with the Foreign Officers, the Viceroy accompanied by his staff proceeded to view the march past of the troops. The weather proved very unfavourable, and heavy and incessant rain fell during the day. At the conclusion of the march past, the Viceroy addressed the Commander-in-Chief as follows :—

GENERAL ROBERTS,—I beg to offer you my heartiest congratulations on the noble and imposing spectacle which has been presented to us this morning, and which has proved a fitting termination to the series of useful and interesting manœuvres which Her Majesty's army has been recently executing. I must request you to convey to the generals of division and to the officers and men of all arms under your command my great satisfaction at their fine appearance and bearing, as well as at the very creditable manner in which they marched past this morning under somewhat trying circumstances. I believe that the army in the field to-day is the largest which has ever been brought together in India, and I congratulate you most heartily on finding yourself at the head of such gallant troops. It will be my duty to acquaint the Queen-Empress with the circumstances attending this day's performance, and I am sure that Her Majesty cannot fail to derive the very greatest pleasure from the excellent account I shall be able to give her of her army in India and of the individual regiments, whether British or native, whom I have had the privilege of inspecting.

The Viceroy returned to Calcutta on Thursday evening, the 21st January.

THE COUNTESS OF DUFFERIN'S FUND.

A general meeting of the National Association for supplying female medical aid to the women of India was held at the Town Hall, Calcutta, on the afternoon of 27th January, 1886. The Viceroy presided, Lady Dufferin being seated on His Excellency's right, and the Lieutenant-Governor of Bengal on his left. The meeting was largely attended by the European and native community of Calcutta. In opening the proceedings Lord Dufferin spoke as follows:—

LADIES AND GENTLEMEN,—I do not remember ever having taken part in any public proceedings with greater pleasure than I now experience in presiding over this meeting—one of the most important perhaps that has ever been held in India, and upon the successful issue of which a vast amount of human happiness is dependent. In the first place, it is always a delight to me, as it is to all her subjects, to obey the behests of our Sovereign; and in endeavouring to launch a scheme for the improvement of the medical treatment of the women of India, we are fulfilling the special injunction of Her Majesty the Queen. In the next, I am standing before you as the advocate of an undertaking which has been initiated and shaped by one for whose goodness, wisdom, and simplicity of purpose I have the most respectful admiration. But, however strongly the considerations I have mentioned may lead me to plead with all the earnestness I can the cause of the association we are about to found, a still more powerful inducement than either has been constantly present to my mind, and that is the firm conviction I entertain that, if only we are able to carry out in its full integrity, and to the required extent, the programme we have settled, there will ensue in the course of time a greater alleviation of suffering among the million homes of India than has been afforded them during the whole of the present century either by the spread of civilisation or by the efforts of the Government. After all, ladies and gentlemen, if we analyse the conditions of human life and catalogue the material sources of its sorrows, where shall we find a more fruitful cause of anguish than in bodily pain and sickness and in the multiform miseries of ill-health. Not only do they paralyse our physical energies and activities, and render us incapable of those pursuits and industries upon which the well-being of those nearest and dearest to us is so dependent, but they prostrate our mental faculties, and what is even worse, they too frequently enfeeble and undermine the healthy tone and temper of our moral dispositions. Happily Providence in this case as in every other has provided us with the means, if not of extirpating, at all events of diminishing to an extraordinary degree, much of the suffering to which I have referred. Within the last few years the true principles of sanitation have been recognised, the cause and sources of many preventible diseases which raged like a plague amongst the human race have been discovered, and their propagation has been almost completely arrested. Means have been found of assuaging the intolerable agony with which surgical operations were formerly accompanied, and the average duration of human life in those countries where the medical art is afforded a fair field has been sensibly prolonged. It is perfectly true that India, in common with other Asiatic countries, has greatly benefited by the triumphs of the medical science of the West, which is thus paying back the benefits which at the early dawn of modern history she received from the physicians of the East. But, however admirable and efficacious may be the native school of medicine in this country, it is a patent fact that the benefits it is able to confer remain almost completely beyond the reach of one half of the Indian community. Custom, decorum, the traditions—I will not say of immemorial ages, because I believe the expression would be historically incorrect, but of many generations—coupled with an instinctive delicacy of sentiment, which indeed is by no means absent in other countries—have more or less closed the doors of the zenana to the visits of properly qualified members of the medical profession. As a consequence, the duty of combating those terrible bodily afflictions to which women even more than men are liable has necessarily fallen into the hands of a class of female practitioners who, however great their deftness and zeal, are utterly incapable of fulfilling the heavy responsibilities imposed upon them, and whose modes of dealing with their patients at certain critical conjunctures are, I understand, of a deplorably clumsy and inefficient character. The object then of our present effort is to found an association which in its ultimate development shall supply the women of the land, from one end of it to the other, with proper medical advice and attendance, under conditions consonant to their own most cherished ideas, feelings, and wishes; and in considering this object we must remember that in some respects the importance of maintaining a high average standard of health amongst the women of the country is even greater than that of doing so among the men. The sickness of a man indeed may mean loss of employment and many other distressing consequences; but the ill-health of the women of a household is tantamount to perpetual domestic wretchedness and discomfort as well as a degradation in the strength and virility of subsequent generations. Whether, therefore, from the point of view of pure humanity, or from that of utility, we are bound to strain every nerve to remedy this great defect in our present social system. Now, if there is one direction in which science has made progress, it has been in the means which have been discovered of alleviating the special sufferings and trials to which women are particularly liable; and knowing what we do about the system in accordance with which they are at present treated in India, we may well comprehend how grave and urgent is the obligation of placing within the reach of our native female fellow-subjects those merciful alleviations which have been so providentially revealed to modern surgery. If the efforts of this association were confined to this one object, it would amply justify its existence. But our ambition extends much further than this. It is with the whole range of maladies to which flesh is heir that we are about to contend, not only in the great centres of wealth and population, like Madras and Bombay, where the battle indeed has been waged for some years past under very encouraging auspices, but throughout the whole region of the mofussil. Our ambition is eventually to furnish every district, no matter how remote, if not with a supply of highly-trained female doctors, at all events with nurses, midwives, and female medical assistants, who shall have such an acquaintance with their business as to be a great improvement upon those who are now employed. Of course where the circumstances of the locality permit of a more highly-organised and effective system, there our efforts will be more ambitious. It would be altogether out of place for me, however, to attempt to explain the practical details of our scheme. I have already detained you too long; but I trust there is no one whom these words may reach who will not be willing to come to our assistance, to join with us in this noble work, and in their respective spheres to do their best to lighten the burden of physical misery by which at this moment and for ages past the women of India have been oppressed. Sickness and pain is the common lot of humanity. Rich and poor, the people of all lands and the professors of all religions, are engulfed in this universal liability. Well may we hope then that on this occasion the various communities of India will unite in one determined national effort to countervail its effects. The response which has been already made from all sides to our original appeal proves that this will be the case. From a hundred different quarters, both from small and from great, from the princes of the land and from individuals in more humble stations, sympathetic replies, as well as considerable material assistance, have been received. The sum already subscribed to the central fund amounts to a lakh and a half, and the branches are also doing well. But I need not remind you that this amount is altogether inadequate to what will be required for any extensive operations. What is wanted is a permanent annual income, whether derived from the interest on our capital, or from yearly subscriptions. Those who will hereafter address you will explain more fully the nature of our requirements. For the moment I will simply content myself with expressing the hope that, when our report has been distributed and has been fully considered by the leaders of public opinion and by those upon whose assistance we must so largely depend for success, what has already been done will receive a still more energetic impulse, as well as material assistance upon a far larger scale and in a more permanent form.

The meeting was then, in turn, addressed by Mr. Ilbert, the Bishop of Calcutta, Mr. Justice Chunder Madhub Ghose, Surgeon-Major Cleghorn, Sir Steuart Bayley, Messrs. Keswick, Goodrich, and Broughton, Sir Jotendra Mohun Tagore, and Syed Amir Hossein. A vote of thanks having been proposed to the Viceroy for presiding, His Excellency rose and said:—

LADIES AND GENTLEMEN,—Up to this point I have not thought it necessary to interrupt the proceedings of the meeting by asking you to accept one by one the various resolutions which have been submitted to you by the speakers who have had the honour of addressing us. I thought it more convenient, as all those resolutions are but part of a whole, to put them to this assembly *en bloc*. Before, however, I do so, I may perhaps be permitted briefly to express to all those present my sincere thanks for the kind manner in which they have been good enough to receive the observations relative to myself which have been submitted to them by the three last speakers. This is the first occasion upon which I have found myself surrounded by such large numbers of my native fellow-subjects, and I cannot help expressing to them my deep and heart-felt satisfaction at the thought that we should be thus united in a common endeavour on behalf of an object which I can assure them is as dear to the hearts of their European fellow-subjects as it can be to their own. I do indeed believe, and fervently trust, that the auspications of the Bishop of Calcutta will be fulfilled, and that a community of interest and endeavour will still more indissolubly unite in the bonds of a common loyalty and a common friendship, all those who, whether natives or Europeans, are proud to be subjects of the Queen-Empress, and citizens of the great Imperial dominions.

His Excellency then put to the meeting the series of resolutions which had been proposed by the various speakers. These were unanimously adopted, and the proceedings terminated.

ADDRESS FROM THE INHABITANTS OF RANGOON.

On Wednesday morning, the 3rd February, 1886, the Viceroy left Calcutta for Upper Burma. His Excellency, accompanied by the Countess of Dufferin, Mr. Mackenzie Wallace (Private Secretary), Lord William Beresford (Military Secretary), Major Cooper and Lord Clandeboye, Aides-de-camp, Dr. Findlay, and Mr. J. McFerran, left Government House at half-past seven o'clock and drove to the Sealdah station, whence they proceeded by special train to Diamond Harbour. Here the Government S.S. *Clive* was in waiting to convey Their Excellencies to Rangoon. On board the *Clive*, to accompany the Viceroy to Upper Burma, were His Excellency Sir Frederick Roberts (Commander-in-Chief in India) with his Military Secretary, Colonel Pole Carew, and Mr. H. M. Durand, Foreign Secretary to the Government of India. The *Clive* left Diamond Harbour on the forenoon of the same day, and on the afternoon of the 7th February arrived in Rangoon Harbour. The Viceregal party was met at the mouth of the river by the Chief Commissioner, Mr. Bernard, and Mr. Mackenzie, Home Secretary to the Government of India. Great preparations had been made in Rangoon to welcome the Viceroy and Lady Dufferin. At the landing-stage a large building was erected, reproducing the front of Killyleagh Castle, the ancestral home of both Lord and Lady Dufferin's family. The Viceroy was received on landing by a large assemblage, comprising the chief officials, the leading merchants, the representatives of all the various nationalities in Rangoon, and by a guard of honour composed of the local volunteers. As the vessel approached the stage, a salute of thirty-one guns was fired by the Rangoon Volunteer Artillery, while at the same time the men-of-war in the harbour, the *Bacchante*, the *Woodlark*, the *Turquoise*, and the *Sphinx*, manned their yards and saluted.

The Viceroy then proceeded by a covered passage to a large temporary building, profusely decorated and gilded, and copied from a Burmese pagoda. It was filled with many hundreds of persons of different nationalities— Europeans, Burmese, Karens, Chinese, and natives of India. An address, numerously signed, was presented by an influential deputation, comprising a large number of the leading inhabitants of Rangoon. Mr. Thompson, chairman of the Viceroy's reception committee, read the address, which, after welcoming His Excellency on behalf of the inhabitants of Rangoon, went on to say that the Viceroy had come to Burma at a most important crisis in its history. The Province of Upper Burma, which, by the valour of British arms, had just been added to the Empire, was still suffering from disorder which was the outcome of years of misgovernment. The committee looked to the wisdom and experience of His Excellency with the confident hope that order would speedily be restored, and that the people would be rendered happy and prosperous under the British administration, which, they felt convinced, was the only possible guarantee for the peace and security of the country. The prosperity which had attended and rewarded British rule in Lower Burma they wished to see extended to their neighbours in the upper country, to the mutual advantage of the people, the expansion of trade, and the spread of civilisation. His Excellency would not be in Burma many days without perceiving that the country deserved, and would well repay, a liberal expenditure on its administration and development. Even in Lower Burma there were some matters which called for reform and improvement, but it would be out of place to advert to these matters, more particularly on the present occasion. They trusted, however, that His Excellency would condescend to listen to the representations which they hoped to make concerning the affairs of the province at a more convenient opportunity during his stay. The address then concluded with a heart-felt prayer for the health and happiness of Lord and Lady Dufferin.

His Excellency replied as follows :—

Mr. CHAIRMAN AND GENTLEMEN,—I thank you most heartily for the kind reception you have prepared for me. I little imagined that in order to reach Rangoon I should have to pass through the gatehouse of the ancient castle of Killyleagh, and I need not say that both Lady Dufferin and myself are very much touched by the delicacy of the attention thus prepared for us. Although for some time past the affairs of Burma have been occupying the attention of the Indian Government, you can hardly expect me immediately after my arrival to say anything in regard to them. After my return from Mandalay I may perhaps have an opportunity of saying a few words to you in regard to the future prospects of the country. In the meantime I shall be only too happy to profit by any information which such old and experienced residents as yourselves may be good enough to place at my disposal. I again thank you most heartily and warmly for your magnificent reception.

A procession was then formed and the Viceroy proceeded towards Government House. In recognition of the services rendered by the local volunteers, the Viceroy's guard of honour consisted of mounted volunteers. A great portion of the route from the wharf to Government House was an unbroken line of triumphal arches and other decorations. The Burmese community had erected six arches, being the greatest number erected by any one nationality. The arches along the route were generally covered arcades, crowded with representatives of the various nationalities by whom they had been erected. By special permission of the Chief Commissioner, an address was presented to the Viceroy on behalf of the Burmese population of the province under the arch erected by that community; and the Viceroy received the address with a few words of thanks. In the evening His Excellency held a reception at Government House, which was very numerously attended.

ADDRESS FROM THE EUROPEAN COMMUNITY AT MANDALAY.

Their Excellencies the Viceroy and Lady Dufferin and Sir Frederick Roberts, with their respective staffs, left Rangoon for Mandalay on Monday, the 8th February. The first portion of the journey was made by railway to Prome, and occupied a few hours only. Here one of the steamers of the

Irrawaddy Flotilla Company, the *Mindoon*, was in waiting to convey Their Excellencies to Mandalay, which was reached at 10.30 P.M. On the same day the Viceroy made his public entry into the city. He was received, on landing at the wharf erected for the occasion, by Lieutenant-General Prendergast (Commanding the Burma Field Force), and the principal military officers in Mandalay. His Excellency, who was accompanied by Lady Dufferin, then proceeded to a reception room, constructed of canvas and wood, which had been erected opposite the landing-stage where the steamer was moored. At the end of the room were placed two state chairs from the royal palace. On the right of the chairs were seats for the military officers and the Burmese ministers; on the left for the civil officers and the local community. A guard of honour of the Hampshire Regiment was stationed outside.

Their Excellencies having taken their seats, Colonel Sladen introduced the representatives of the English and foreign communities at Mandalay, who presented His Excellency with the following address:—

YOUR EXCELLENCY,—We, the undersigned clergy, merchants, traders, and residents in Mandalay, desire to approach Your Excellency on the occasion of your first visit to the city, for the purpose of offering a cordial and respectful welcome to the Countess of Dufferin and yourself. We rejoice to receive you as the representative of the Queen-Empress, as Viceroy of India, and as a statesman who has made himself beloved in every country over which he has ruled, and as one who has always increased the happiness and welfare of those whom he has governed.

In Upper Burma there exists a wide field for improvement by developing the vast but hitherto neglected resources of the country, by restoring peace and order, by confirming to all a just and impartial administration of the laws, and by securing to the people all those blessings which flow from English rule. We feel confident that the interests of Upper Burma will receive Your Excellency's careful consideration, whilst the marvellous progress which the adjoining and kindred province has made since it became a portion of the British Empire demonstrates what beneficent changes may be effected in this the latest addition to Her Majesty's dominions, and we would assure Your Excellency of our loyalty and anxious desire to support and co-operate with the Government by all the means in our power in advancing the moral and material welfare of the country.

It affords us special pleasure to find that you are accompanied by the Countess of Dufferin, a lady who has used the influence pertaining to her exalted station for the purpose of ameliorating and raising the condition of her sex in British India, and who has thereby secured for herself the gratitude and affection of all.

In conclusion, we respectfully hope that both Your Excellencies may be spared to maintain the high position you at present occupy, and that in future years your visit to Burma may serve as one of the pleasantest reminiscences of your Eastern Administration.

The Viceroy replied as follows:—

GENTLEMEN,—I beg to return you, on behalf of Lady Dufferin and myself, our cordial thanks for the kind terms in which you have welcomed us to Mandalay. It is needless for me to assure you that the subjects to which you have referred have for some time past been occupying the close attention of the Government of India, and no effort will be spared to secure the desirable objects you have enumerated. Unfortunately the maladministration of the late King of Upper Burma has rendered lawlessness and dakoity so general throughout the land that it may require some perseverance and patience before perfect order is restored in outlying districts. But for these inevitable incidents of the situation we were quite prepared. Already some of the chief centres of disturbance have been tranquillised, and I have no doubt that our remaining efforts will be attended with similar success. In the meantime, it is the earnest desire of Her Majesty the Queen-Empress to establish at once such an order of things in Upper Burma as shall secure the permanent happiness and prosperity of its inhabitants. It is by this means that the interests of those who, like yourselves, are engaged in prosecuting commercial enterprises amongst them will be best promoted. I must not forget to express my personal thanks for the kind reference you have been pleased to make to Lady Dufferin in the concluding portion of your address. (Cheers.)

ADDRESS FROM THE BURMESE COMMUNITY, MANDALAY.

The Burmese community then presented an address of welcome, which the Viceroy, through Colonel Sladen, acknowledged briefly, and to which His Excellency subsequently sent the following reply in writing:—

GENTLEMEN,—I beg to thank you for the friendly welcome with which you have greeted me on my arrival at Mandalay, and I need not say how glad I am to find that you and your fellow-citizens should have accepted in so heartily and cheerful a manner the new order of things which has been established amongst you. Upper Burma has now been permanently in-

corporated with the British Empire, and you yourselves have
definitely become the subjects of the Queen-Empress and of
the British Crown. As a consequence, I am charged by Her
Majesty, and by her government, to assure you that your
prosperity, welfare, and interests will remain a constant object
of solicitude to her and to her ministers. No efforts will be
spared to improve your condition, to develop the resources of
your country, and to afford to each one of you opportunities of
employing his industry and his faculties to the best advantage.
Nor is it necessary for me again to repeat the promises already
made to you by my officers, that your religion will be respected,
that the property of your ecclesiastical establishments will be
placed under the protection of the laws, and that absolute
freedom of worship will be extended equally to all classes. I
may also take this opportunity of adding that the exertions of
the Government will be indefatigably directed to the suppression of disorder and to the creation of absolute security for
life and property from one end of the country to the other.
For many years past British administration has spread prosperity and contentment throughout the entire region of Lower
Burma, and you may rest assured that, having now become
indissolubly united with the other subjects of Her Majesty the
Queen, you will not fail to share with them the benefits
accruing from a just and temperate government administered
under the auspices of a powerful and beneficent Sovereign.

ADDRESS FROM THE MAHOMEDAN COMMUNITY OF MANDALAY.

To an address of welcome from the Mahomedan community of Mandalay, His Excellency, on the 18th February, sent the following reply:—

GENTLEMEN,—It has given me very great pleasure to receive
such a cordial welcome from the Mahomedan residents of
Mandalay. Her Majesty the Queen-Empress has at all times
taken a special interest in the well-being and advancement of
her Mahomedan subjects, and the Government of India has

very recently given public demonstration of its own anxiety to see the Mahomedan community of India marching fairly abreast of the other races of the Empire. You may rest assured that in Upper Burma, under the impartial administration of British officers, you will not only have full protection in the exercise of your religious rites, but every encouragement to improve your position and extend your commercial operations. I am glad to receive your testimony as to the success of the measures taken by my officers to prevent outrages at the time of the capture of the city and to restore order after the fall of the native government. I trust that you will continue to give them your loyal and constant support, and co-operate with them heartily in those measures of sanitation and improvement which it will shortly be necessary to inaugurate in Mandalay.

His Excellency, with Lady Dufferin, Sir F. Roberts, Mr. Bernard, and other officers, then drove in procession to the Palace. The route was lined with troops, only a comparatively small number of Burmese being assembled in the streets. There were two triumphal arches erected, and Venetian masts marked the route. Their Excellencies and party were shown over the Palace, and remained for a short time to see the Burmese drama of "Ramazat" performed.

MILITARY OPERATIONS IN UPPER BURMA.

On the evening of the 17th February, the Viceroy entertained at dinner Sir Frederick Roberts (Commander-in-Chief in India), Lieutenant-General Prendergast (Commanding the Forces in Upper Burma), Mr. C. E. Bernard (Chief Commissioner of British Burma), and a large number of military officers. After dinner His Excellency addressed the assembly as follows :—

SIR FREDERICK ROBERTS AND GENTLEMEN,—As this is the first time I have found myself in the presence of the Commander and chief officers of the army serving in the field in Upper Burma, I desire to take the opportunity of proposing to you the health of Sir Harry Prendergast and of all those, both officers and men, British and native, who have served under him during the recent successful campaign, and with the toast

I will couple the names of the officers and men of the naval brigade, as well as of the officers and men of the Burmese volunteer corps. It is needless for me to repeat what is known to all, that the invasion of Upper Burma was undertaken with regret by the Indian Government. We had no quarrel with its inhabitants, and the prospect of its conquest, whatever might be the ultimate advantage, was certain to be fraught with immediate expense, anxiety, and embarrassment. On the other hand, the existing relations between ourselves and the Burmese Court had become intolerable, inasmuch as they were fast tending to jeopardise the security and most vital interests of our own territories. We therefore chose the lesser of two evils, and determined to put an end to the disastrous rule of a prince who was a curse to his own subjects and an impossible neighbour. But in directing General Prendergast's advance upon Mandalay, the Government of India reminded him that it would be his duty to come as little as possible into collision with the people of the country, who are kindred in blood, in religion, and in all their material interests with our own subjects in Lower Burma. How admirably General Prendergast and those serving with him have executed those directions it is impossible to overstate. By rapidity of movement, by skilful strategy, by the exercise of humane forbearance, and by the assumption, whenever possible, of a conciliatory attitude, General Prendergast succeeded, with comparatively little loss upon our side, and, what was greatly desirable, with the infliction of a minimum of punishment upon those who were opposed to us, in occupying Mandalay, in capturing its king, and in taking possession of the country.

And believe me, gentlemen, that to have led a British army into an enemy's capital in such a manner is, under the circumstances, far more creditable to him and to those associated with him than would have been a costly victory, however glorious, on a fiercely-contested field of battle. Nor will his countrymen fail to appreciate the sense of duty which has enabled him and his army to win their stainless laurels. The annals of continental warfare show how a ruthless general may wilfully trace his name in letters of blood on the pages of history. General

Prendergast has chosen the better part, and, as a consequence, has enabled me to ascend the river, pass along the streets of the town, and enter the palace amidst the ranks of a smiling, trustful, and reconciled population. Again, it is a quality of success to conceal from public notice the many chances of failure which have beset, on all sides, the enterprise which it has crowned; but those who may hereafter study the nature of our recent operations will not fail to appreciate what disastrous consequences might have ensued had slackness or indecision on the one hand, or recklessness on the other, directed the movements of our troops. In the name, then, of his Queen and country, and in the name of the Government of India, I beg to tender to General Prendergast, his officers and his men, my warmest thanks, and in doing so I would desire to extend my expressions of gratitude to all those civil officers who so ably seconded his endeavours; to Mr. Bernard and to Colonel Sladen, to whose courage and knowledge of the people and of their language we are so much indebted for the surrender of the king, as well as to their various assistants. This, however, is neither the time nor the occasion for me to particularise individuals. In due course an official report of all the recent occurrences will be forwarded to the Government of India, which will then have an opportunity of bringing to the notice of the Sovereign the names of those who may have specially distinguished themselves. In the meantime there is one announcement I am authorised to make, which, I hope, will not be received with displeasure at this table, namely, that Her Most Gracious Majesty, with the advice of her ministers, has been pleased to grant a gratuity of three lakhs of rupees to the field force serving in Upper Burma.

And now, gentlemen, it only remains for me to hope that the work of pacification, under the auspices of the civil officers, will meet with the same success as has crowned our military efforts. For some time, indeed, they will still need the support and assistance of the troops, who have already shown with what patience and energy they can discharge the peculiarly harassing duties imposed upon them by the necessity of the suppression of dakoity—duties far more distasteful to regular troops than the hardships of open warfare. We were well aware, however, from previous experience, that it might take a considerable time, even after the constituted authorities of the country had made their submission, before absolute tranquillity would be restored. It took some years before Lower Burma settled down after the conquest of Pegu. As we all know, from time immemorial, dakoity has been the traditional weakness of the Burmese people. Unfortunately, under the weak and disastrous rule of King Theebaw, gang robbery became rife from one end of the country to the other, and this unhappy state of things has, of course, been still further stimulated by the disbandment of his army, and the confusion and disturbance in men's minds which the war and the sudden change of government were bound to entail. But I am glad to learn, on all hands, that district after district, under the supervision of our British officers, is being reclaimed from the reign of terror by which it was dominated. Above all things I rejoice to see that there is not the slightest sign of anything approaching to partizan warfare against ourselves, and that whenever a collision takes place between our troops and any native combatants, it is not that the English posts have been attacked, but that our soldiers have succeeded in overtaking various bands of marauders, acting without concert, who have been burning and pillaging harmless and unprotected villages. These excesses the Government of Her Majesty has decided to terminate at every risk and cost. With this view, and in order to give full effect to the proclamation issued on the 1st of January, by which Upper Burma was declared for ever annexed to the British Empire, the country will be at once placed under the supreme and direct administrative control of British officers, whose experience and energy will enable them, I trust, to repair in a few years the loss and injury entailed upon it by the misgovernment of its former ruler, to restore the security of life and property, and to raise it to the same high level of individual comfort and commercial prosperity as is enjoyed by the inhabitants of Lower Burma under an analogous *régime*. Though some months, or perhaps years, may elapse before we have seen the realisation of all our hopes, I have no doubt that ere a decade has passed away, we shall be able to reckon the inhabitants of Upper Burma amongst the most contented and prosperous of Her Majesty's subjects; and, when the pen of history shall eventually trace the causes and the results of the conquest of Burma, the good service which Sir Harry Prendergast and his gallant companions in arms have rendered their Queen and country at the most momentous period of the recent crisis, will be honourably recorded.

GENERAL ROBERTS AND GENTLEMEN,—I beg to propose to you the health of General Prendergast and of the officers and men of the three services who have acted under his command, and with that toast I would desire to couple the health of Mr. Bernard and the civil officers who so ably seconded their endeavours. (Loud and continued cheering.)

General Prendergast, in returning thanks to His Excellency the Viceroy, expressed the great obligations under which he lay to the officers and men of his force for the successful result of the campaign.

Mr. Bernard remarked that his difficulties had been much lightened by the excellent preparations for the campaign that had been made by the Government of India. He expressed his conviction that Upper Burma would quickly settle down to order, and that the country gave promise of a prosperous financial future.

ADDRESS TO THE HLUTDAW.

Before going on board the *Mindoon* steamer, previous to his departure from Mandalay, the Viceroy addressed the members of the HlutDaw or Great Council in the following short speech, which was read by Mr. Mackenzie Wallace, and translated sentence by sentence by an interpreter:—

GENTLEMEN,—I bid you good-bye. I thank you heartily for the friendly feeling you have shown me, and I have been very glad to make your personal acquaintance. You have now become British subjects under the rule of Her Most Gracious Majesty the Queen-Empress, and I have no doubt you will serve her with loyalty and fidelity. The country having passed under the direct administration of British officers, I must call upon you to give them your hearty support. Their highest desires and endeavours will be to promote the well-being of Her Majesty's Burmese subjects; to restore tranquillity amongst them; to develop the resources of the country; to respect its customs; to place its religious property and establishments under the protection of the law; and to advance the well-being of all classes. As good citizens, these objects cannot fail to be as dear to you as to them. It is the intention of the Government to make as much use as possible of native officers and of native assistants in carrying on the work of the administration, and to treat native gentlemen of dignity and position like yourselves with all the consideration that is your due. Your experience and your acquaintance with affairs will enable you to render considerable service to the British Government in the new positions which will be offered to as many among you as can be employed with advantage. In return for whatever favours may be conferred upon you I am sure I shall be able to count upon your rendering faithful and effective service to your new Sovereign.

ADDRESS FROM THE CHAMBER OF COMMERCE, RANGOON.

On Tuesday morning, the 23rd February, a deputation from the Chamber of Commerce of Rangoon waited upon the Viceroy at Government House, and presented him with an address. The address, on account of its length, was taken as read. It touched upon a large number of subjects affecting Burma, which, in the opinion of the memorialists, required reform.

LORD DUFFERIN, in replying, observed that the important questions referred to were deserving of the attention rather of the Viceroy in Council than of the Viceroy on tour. Alluding to a statement made in the address, to the effect that Lower Burma paid over to the Indian exchequer a net sum of one million yearly, the Viceroy said that though he could not accept that statement as representing the whole case, yet it was undoubtedly true that Lower Burma was a very rich province, and for many years past had been in a position to transmit large contributions to the revenues of India.

But, on the other hand, she was allowed to retain in her own possession a larger proportion of her income than most other provinces; consequently, though the Indian tax-payer had largely benefited, it might fairly be contended that Burma herself had not been wronged. She was as much an integral portion of the Indian Empire as the Central Provinces, and was consequently bound with them to contribute her quota to the general fund. Moreover, the expenses which the late war would entail, and which would be a charge on the Indian budget, might very well be regarded as a set-off to the alleged overplus of revenue which Lower Burma seemed inclined to complain of paying for Imperial purposes. In conclusion, Lord Dufferin said : I think it right to mention a circumstance which will probably interest you. You are aware that by the Queen's proclamation of the 1st of January, Upper Burma was annexed to Her Majesty's possessions and placed under the personal administration of the Viceroy. Of course it was obvious that the latter part of this arrangement could only be of a provisional character. This fact, together with other circumstances, seems to have cast a certain amount of ambiguity over the character of the proclamation itself. In order, therefore, to remove any doubt as to the nature of the government to be established in Upper Burma, I may at once tell you that that province will be placed under the direct and immediate control of British officers. The largest possible use, of course, will be made of native assistance, but the Supreme Government of the country will be in the hands of Her Majesty's British officials. I trust the conclusions arrived at by Her Majesty's Government will prove as conducive to the benefit of this province as I have no doubt they will be to the welfare and happiness of Her Majesty's subjects in Upper Burma.

DECORATION OF BURMESE GENTLEMEN.

On Wednesday afternoon, the 24th February, the Viceroy held a durbar at Government House, Rangoon, for the purpose of decorating with badges of honour three Burmese gentlemen and for the reception of various memorials. The latter were twelve in number, and consisted of addresses from the Municipality, the Educational Syndicate, the Volunteers, the Rangoon Bar, the Burmese inhabitants of Rangoon, the Persian traders, sundry merchants, the Tamil and Telegu Christians, the Gee Heng section of the Chinese community, the Shans, the Burmese Elders, and the Hokkien Chinese community. Most of the memorials referred to questions of purely local interest, Lord Dufferin replying more or less briefly to them.

In presenting the chains of honour to the Burmese gentlemen the Viceroy prefaced the gift with the following remarks :—

Amongst the many duties incumbent upon a Viceroy of India there is certainly none which gives him greater personal pleasure than that of conferring honour in the Queen's name upon such of Her Majesty's subjects as have merited their Sovereign's favour, and this pleasure is always enhanced when the recipient of such a mark of Imperial approbation is a native. Her Majesty's English subjects, living near her presence, have continual proofs of her beneficent regard, but those who, like our fellow-subjects here in the East, live remote from the footsteps of the throne, can scarcely form an adequate notion of the unceasing solicitude with which she watches over them. Such an act, however, as that which I am now performing will, I trust, be a sufficient proof of her readiness to recognise and reward merit, as well as of the deep interest which the Queen-Empress takes in the welfare of the inhabitants of her most distant provinces.

ADDRESS FROM SUNDRY MERCHANTS ON THE TIMBER TRADE.

An address on the subject of the management of the forests of Upper Burma was presented to the Viceroy by certain members of the mercantile community of Lower Burma, and on behalf of others carrying on business elsewhere in British India. The memorial urged that a monopoly in the trade in timber was inconsistent with English constitutional principles.

Mr. Egerton Allen, who acted as spokesman for the memorialists, also emphasised the same point, explaining that the views which he expressed were also those of the merchants of Calcutta, Madras, and Bombay. The Viceroy in replying said :—

GENTLEMEN,—The memorial undoubtedly deals with a very difficult, very thorny, and a very burning question. It is one of those subjects which it would be almost disrespectful for me to attempt to examine on the present occasion. The private interests at stake on the one hand are very considerable. The interests of the public at the same time require most careful protection at the hands of the Government of India. All I can say at present is, that we will go into the question with the assistance of those who are best competent to deal with it, and that we shall make a conscientious endeavour to act fairly in regard to existing interests, to protect the rights of the public at large, as well as to do whatever may be necessary to render the forest tracts of Burma as profitable as possible to the Government.

ADDRESS FROM THE RANGOON BAR.

In reply to an address from the Rangoon Bar, advocating certain reforms in the Superior Courts of the Province, His Excellency said :—

GENTLEMEN,—It is always with the greatest trepidation I venture to address a body of barristers. They are so skilful in dialectics, so practised in placing whatever case they have to advocate in a convincing light, that no one, except those who are endowed with an exceptional courage, would ever willingly enter into an argument with them. Unfortunately, at this moment I am unprotected by the presence of my responsible legal advisers, and as one of the most unlearned members of the Government of India, I scarcely feel myself competent to deal, during my casual visit to Rangoon, with the somewhat complicated and difficult questions that you have raised in relation to the composition of courts and their operation in Lower Burma. All I can say is, that I will carry your memorial to Calcutta, and will specially recommend it to those of my colleagues who are charged with the duty of advising the Government in such matters; and I further promise that I will not fail myself to take an intelligent interest in such recommendations as they may submit to me. The Government of India is a composite body, but its responsibilities are one and undivided. Our joint consideration—I dare not say our united wisdom—will be brought to bear on the question, and I shall then have the pleasure of communicating to you the decision at which we have arrived. In conclusion, allow me to express my very great pleasure at seeing you as a body, as well as the satisfaction with which I perceive that the Bar of Rangoon is recruited from various nationalities. Allow me also to thank you for the courteous, clear, and able manner in which you have brought your views to my notice, and again to assure you that they will receive our most earnest and respectful attention.

BURMESE COMMUNITY OF RANGOON.

In replying to the address from the Burmese community of Rangoon, His Excellency spoke as follows:—

GENTLEMEN,—I have great pleasure in observing that one common sentiment unites you with all your English fellow-citizens, and that is your great impatience of taxation, which seems to be a sentiment almost universal throughout the world. On coming to Rangoon, however, and observing the very prosperous appearance of the town and its inhabitants, I had hoped that taxation had probably pressed lighter upon you than, perhaps, on residents in other parts of India. When I go back to Calcutta, the inhabitants of Calcutta will certainly wish that they were Rangoon citizens when I inform them that the municipal taxes of Rangoon only amount to one half of the municipal taxation of Calcutta. At all events, whether the taxation is too high or too low, you have the consolation of knowing that you get something for your money in the shape of an excellent supply of water, a commodity which can hardly be too dearly purchased.

In conclusion, and passing from the immediate subject of your memorial, I desire to congratulate you on the admirable manner in which you and your fellow-citizens behaved during the recent crisis, and now you have the satisfaction of knowing that you are not citizens of the mere province of Lower Burma, but of united Burma, and, unlike what it was in past years, whenever your business shall call you to Mandalay or to any other place in Upper Burma, you will be protected by the same just laws, and will be under the same effective administration which has raised Lower Burma to its present pitch of prosperity. Her Majesty's Government counts upon your aid in assisting to make it known to your fellow-countrymen in Upper Burma that there is nothing which the Government more desires than to receive the Upper Burmese into the British system with the same cordiality, good-will, and affectionate regard, as you yourselves have enjoyed, to respect their privileges and customs, to place their ecclesiastical establishment under the protection of the laws, and to do everything that human ingenuity can do to make them a happy, prosperous, and contented people.

GEE HENG CHINESE COMMUNITY.

In replying to the address from the Gee Heng section of the Chinese community, the Viceroy said :—

GENTLEMEN,—In the first place I must tell you how delighted I am to see you. This is by no means the first occasion on which, as Her Majesty's representative, I have been called upon to examine into the claims, and, when those claims were proved, to protect the rights of Chinese residents. When I was Governor-General of Canada and came to British Columbia, I found that a large Chinese colony had settled there under the protection of British laws; and on entering the town of Victoria the Chinese of that city were good enough to erect in my honour almost as beautiful an arch as that prepared for me in Rangoon. With regard to the subject of your memorial, I understand that a question has arisen as to whether a certain building is a temple or not. That, of course, is a question of fact upon which I myself cannot pronounce, but I have no hesitation in telling you that if it is decided by the proper authorities that the building in question is a temple, it will be exempted from municipal taxation.

THE SHAN COMMUNITY.

In reply to an address from the Shan community of Rangoon, His Excellency said :—

I am very much interested in the Shan nationality. Her Majesty's Government is most anxious to make you, and not only you, but all the inhabitants of the Shan States, feel how desirous we are to gain their confidence, to cultivate their good-will, and to do everything in our power to promote their trade and advance their general interests. You will be doing the Government a real service, if you take any opportunity which you may have through your relations with the Shan States, of making the rulers and the inhabitants of those States understand that the British Government is fully determined to respect their independence, to abstain from all interference with their internal affairs, and to maintain the same friendly relations which existed between them and the late Burmese Government.

ADDRESS FROM THE BURMESE ELDERS.

Replying to an address from the Burmese Elders at Rangoon regarding the maintenance of the Buddhist religion, the Viceroy spoke as follows :—

As you must have already heard, the guiding principle of the Government of India is to respect the religious rights, privileges, and property of the various ecclesiastical communities which are located within the Indian Empire: its attitude to all religions is the attitude of benevolence and neutrality. At the same time I have no hesitation in saying that among the many questions which have preoccupied the Government of India in relation to the new condition of things, nothing has weighed so heavily upon the mind and conscience of the administration as the consideration of the degree to which the interests and stability of the national and religious institutions in Burma may have been influenced by the recent changes. The Queen now being the Sovereign of Burma is called upon to regulate, to a certain extent, the relations of the Buddhistic Church to the Government. Arrangements, therefore, will probably have to be made in order that the Burmese Buddhists may find themselves in as advantageous a position in regard to the headship and the discipline of their Church as they were before. The Chief Commissioner has received instructions to put himself in communication with the principal authorities of the ecclesiastical community for the purpose of hearing what their wishes may be regarding these arrangements, and of assisting them in the name of the Government of India; and every means will be taken to facilitate whatever system of Church government it may be their wish to see established amongst them. In conclusion, allow me to assure you that, irrespective of this particular question, I am only too happy to repeat what I have already said to the chief ecclesiastic of Upper Burma, namely, that the British Government gives you its most solemn pledge to respect your religion, to recognise the dignitaries of your Church, to protect your ecclesiastical property, to afford you full liberty of worship, and to place you upon an absolutely equal footing with all other religious communities of the empire. Furthermore, I must ask you to convey from me to your religious dignitaries and to the wearers of the priestly robe the assurance that the Government fully appreciate the good work the religious community are discharging in educating the young and in exhibiting an example of self-abnegation and purity of life and morals.

HOKKIEN CHINESE OF RANGOON.

In replying to an address from the Hokkien Chinese community of Rangoon, the Viceroy spoke as follows:—

GENTLEMEN,—I am very grateful to you for the kind expressions towards myself and Lady Dufferin, which are contained in your address. I assure you I fully recognise that wherever the Chinese come they make excellent citizens, are admirable examples of thrift, industry, and good conduct, and greatly assist in advancing the general good of the community. When in British Columbia, which is, as you know, a possession of Her Majesty on the Pacific opposite to China, I found many Chinese, and Her Majesty's Canadian Government never found it necessary to impose upon Chinese emigration those restrictions which have been imposed upon it in America. Finally, I assure you that now that we have become the immediate neighbours of the great Empire of China, the British Government as well as the Government of India will be anxious to draw still more close together those bonds of amity and good-will which so happily unite the two Empires. I trust that ere long the Irrawaddy will become a great highway between China and the rest of the world, and that the events which have recently occurred will be a mutual benefit to England and to China. The only further remark which I have to make, is to express my personal gratitude to you for the friendly expressions contained in your address, and to say that I have had much pleasure in making your acquaintance.

ADDRESS FROM THE TAMIL AND TELEGU CHRISTIANS OF RANGOON.

In reply to an address from the Tamil and Telegu Christians of Rangoon the Viceroy spoke as follows:—

GENTLEMEN,—I have the very greatest pleasure in receiving the very beautifully prepared address with which you have presented me. It is needless for me to assure you that everything that concerns the Christian communities in India will always be a matter of infinite solicitude to me. Although as Viceroy and representative of the Queen and as head of the Government I am bound to exercise the utmost impartiality in dealing with the religious interests of the various communities which co-exist and are intermixed with one another in India, there is no obligation incumbent upon me to refrain from expressing, as a humble member of the Church of England and as a Christian, my earnest and hearty sympathy with the Christian cause. I am glad to learn that your progress as citizens exemplifies in a satisfactory manner the principles and tenets of the religion you profess, and I trust you will always remember that others will judge of the merits and claims of your faith by the manner in which you practise its precepts.

I again thank you, gentlemen, most heartily for the friendly words in which you have addressed me.

THE COUNTESS OF DUFFERIN'S FUND.

At twelve o'clock on the 24th February, a meeting was held at Government House, Rangoon, under the presidency of Lady Dufferin, to receive a deputation of the committee of the Burma branch of the Countess of Dufferin's Fund. The gathering was of a very representative character, including Burmese, Chinese, Hindus, and Mahomedans, besides the European members of the committee, among whom were Mrs. Bernard, Mrs. Strachan, Mrs. Rowett, Mrs. Holdern, Dr. and Mrs. Douglas, and Dr. Pedley. The secretary to the committee read an address, thanking Lady Dufferin for meeting the deputation and giving various details regarding the working of the local branch of the fund, and plans for the future on various points were then made the subject of conversation. Dr. Pedley expressed the opinion that trained Burmese women would easily be able to gain their livelihood in Burma as midwives. The money of the fund would therefore be needed more for training than for their subsequent maintenance. Lady Dufferin informed those present that it was proposed in India to issue health primers and other books under the auspices of the fund, and enquired if a similar course would be suitable in Burma. The Bishop of Rangoon said that the Education Syndicate would give every assistance in the matter. Major Cooper, secretary to the central committee, stated that a letter on the question would be issued shortly to all the local branches. At the conclusion of the meeting, Mr. Mackenzie, Home Secretary to the Government of India, drew the attention of those present to the fact that what was required to place the fund on a sound financial basis, were not so much donations as the annual subscriptions.

At 3 P.M. on Thursday, the 25th February, the Viceroy and Lady Dufferin, with Sir F. Roberts, left Rangoon for Madras.

ADDRESSES AT MADRAS.

On 1st March, 1886, the *Clive*, with the Viceregal party on board, arrived in Madras harbour. Long before the hour arranged for the Viceroy's landing, the people began to stream down to the beach until many thousand natives had assembled all along the sea face and in the streets facing the harbour. Various deputations, with most of the local officials, military and civil, were assembled in a large *shamiana* which had been erected close to the pier. On Their Excellencies' arrival they were met by the Governor of Madras and Mrs. Grant Duff, Sir Herbert Macpherson (Commander-in-Chief of Madras), and the Hon. Mr. Sullivan (Member of the Madras Council). The first address presented to His Excellency was that of the Municipal Commissioners of Madras. The address stated that Madras was the oldest of the presidency capitals of the Indian Empire, and had always maintained its pre-eminence in loyalty to the Crown and in that enlightenment which sought to educate citizens so as to fit them to take their part in public affairs. It represented that the resources at the command of the Commissioners were by no means sufficient to carry out to completion the drainage schemes and the very necessary improvements in the water-supply which were required for the well-being of 400,000 inhabitants. The Commissioners had consented to the imposition of taxes upon the people, which they believed to be the utmost they could bear, and a hope was expressed that if in future any proposals were made, the State would assist the municipality.

The next address presented was from the native community. While giving His Excellency a hearty welcome, the opportunity was taken to draw his attention to various matters. There was generally an earnest desire that His Excellency should maintain and develop the just and liberal policy of his predecessor; the strict enforcement of economy in all branches of the administration was a matter which deserved serious consideration; satisfaction was felt at the appointment of the financial committee, as showing the Viceroy's desire to effect retrenchment, and it was hoped that His Excellency would see that the non-official and native element was properly represented on the committee. The apportionment of expenditure between India and England on a fair basis was also a matter to which His Excellency's attention was directed. Considering the progress education had made throughout India, it was hoped that the Viceroy would see the advisability of giving more consideration to the views and wishes of the people of India than heretofore, and of utilising the indigenous talent of the country more largely in the conduct of public affairs. A hope was expressed also that greater confidence would be reposed in the people by enlisting their voluntary services in the defence of the country, and by removing the restrictions on carrying arms for defensive purposes. Allusion was made to the severity of the salt and forest laws, to the need for the promotion of useful industries and of technical education; to the condition of the agricultural classes; and to the necessity which had arisen for putting the Legislative Councils on a representative basis and enlarging their powers.

An address from the Mahomedan community was next presented; then one from the Chamber of Commerce; and this was followed by a long address from the Mahajana Sabha, which dealt with various so-called native grievances. The Chamber of Commerce commenced its address by welcoming His Excellency on his return from the newest addition to Her Majesty's Indian Empire. The Chamber was confident that whatever might be the form of government which was ultimately adopted for Upper Burma, its inhabitants would have every cause to rejoice that they had been brought under the influences of western civilisation. Alluding to the bold, yet prudent, manner in which His Excellency had guided the ship of State during the many anxious months of last year, the Chamber said it was persuaded that, having by his skill and judgment secured for India the blessings of peace, His Excellency would now guide her in those paths of development and progress which lead to victories no less renowned than those of war. The Chamber expressed its special obligations to His Excellency for the courteous hearing which he had at all times extended to its representations; and they hoped that such representations, while laying no claim to infallibility, were not without their value to those entrusted with the great and honourable task of governing India. The Chamber explained that as the present visit of the Viceroy partook more of a private than of an official character, it had limited itself to a few short words of welcome, and they concluded by expressing a hope that in the future, as in the past, His Excellency might be enabled to justify the pride which his countrymen all over the globe felt in claiming him as one of themselves.

Mr. D. S. White, President of the Eurasian Society of Southern India, then presented an address of welcome from the Eurasian community. All these addresses, with the exception of the municipal address, were taken as read. The Viceroy replied to them, collectively, in the following terms:—

GENTLEMEN,—I beg to thank you most heartily for your kind welcome and for the various addresses which the important bodies and communities, whose representatives I see around me, have been good enough to present. I fully appreciate the loyal feeling which has prompted you to prepare so brilliant a reception for the representative of the Queen-Empress, and I am personally grateful for the friendly expressions of goodwill which you have made use of in regard to Lady Dufferin and myself. In reply, I cannot help, in the first place, observing how much I have been struck by the appearance presented by Madras from the sea, which is far superior to what I had anticipated. Some of its public buildings are of great architectural beauty, and what, perhaps, is a greater matter of pride to all its patriotic citizens, the eye of the stranger is at once attracted to many spots of historical interest. It was from this centre that the spread of the British Empire in India received its original impulse, and I am glad to think that the heart of your fine old city should still throb vigorously with such generous and patriotic sentiments as those with which your addresses are replete.

You can hardly expect me, on the present occasion, to touch on the various important topics to which you have very properly taken the opportunity of calling my attention. With some of the suggestions you have made I can cordially agree. Others, though of great local interest, possess a technical character, and no Viceroy could be expected to give an immediate answer with regard to them in the absence of his colleagues. Others again are of a very complicated and momentous nature, touching as they do upon various fundamental points connected with the government of India. Even upon these, however, I might have been disposed not to remain altogether silent were it not for a special circumstance, namely, that both the present Government and their predecessors have expressed their determination to institute an enquiry into the whole question of Indian administration. There is no doubt that the strongest men in England will be nominated to undertake this important duty, and you can rest assured that the points to which you specially referred will be certain to attract their attention. No one, I assure you, is better pleased than myself that such a body should thus take account and stock of the past, and consider with themselves in what way the result may be made the forerunner of a still more prosperous and satisfactory future. Every one must admit that the India of to-day is not the India of 1858, nor is it desirable to give any régime a cast-iron character. The wants and aspirations of one generation are different from those of another, and a wise government should endeavour to recognise the signs of the times, and adapt itself to their new requirements. As I make it a rule never to excite hopes which I cannot be certain of fulfilling, or to allow my views upon most questions to become prematurely known, I will content myself with saying that, if my opinions are called for, it is probable they will not be found to be out of harmony upon some important points with those of many wise, intelligent, and patriotic native gentlemen with whom I have come into contact.

And now, gentlemen, perhaps I could not find a better opportunity than the present of acquainting the united associations of Bengal, Madras, and Bombay, who have addressed Mr. Gladstone on the subject of the forthcoming enquiry, that Her Majesty's Government have not failed to consider the merits of a Royal Commission as distinguished from a Parliamentary Committee, but that in their opinion the second method, which is in conformity with precedent, would be most effective. They have, therefore, already made the announcement that they intend proposing a joint committee of both Houses for the purpose. And here I will take the liberty of correcting a misapprehension which has got abroad that some deep significance is to be attached to the fact that, while in my speech in the Legislative Council on the income tax I referred to the body appointed for the examination of our expenditure as a commission, it has subsequently been called a committee. As I myself originated the change, I may observe that my only motive was to prevent confusion between our own committee and what I then imagined would be called the Indian Commission sitting at home. Whether our body was termed a "commission" or a "committee" would have made no change in its powers or its constitution; and, now that the English enquiry is to be undertaken by a committee, it may possibly be desirable to denominate ours a commission. This, however, is a very small point which I cannot determine until I return to Calcutta. With regard to the suggestion that its numbers should be enlarged, I must at once frankly tell you that I do not think it would be desirable to do so, but I may mention that it is by no means intended that its members should remain closeted at Simla. On the contrary, they will visit the various centres of administration, and they will associate with themselves other persons of knowledge and authority to examine special points and questions affecting local interests.

There is but one other point to which I need specially refer. As has been remarked in one of the addresses, a very noble and generous offer was made both by the princes and by the people of India, at a time when war with a foreign power seemed imminent, by the one to place the resources of their States at the disposal of the Government, and by the other to form themselves into volunteer corps. The latter proposal was commented on by the Government of India in a very exhaustive and sympathetic despatch addressed to the Secretary of State. In this despatch due acknowledgment was paid to the generous and loyal sentiments evinced by such an offer, and everything that could be said on either side of the proposal was duly set forth. On the whole, however, we expressed an opinion that the accession to the military strength of India by the enrolment of a large number of native volunteer regiments, would not, perhaps, prove commensurate with the impediments in the way of the satisfactory establishment of such an organisation. Although we have had an intimation that Her Majesty's Government agrees generally in the view we have taken, the despatch in which their own opinion upon the question is embodied has not yet been received. It is for this reason, and in no way from any want of respect to those who have addressed the Government on the subject or from any failure to appreciate the patriotic motives which inspired the offers of service, that, to my very great regret, a proper reply to the various communications which have been received by the Government has been so long delayed.

In conclusion, gentlemen, allow me again to thank you for your friendly greetings, and to add that, although I am perforce precluded from discussing with you all the points you have brought to my attention, I will be careful to communicate to my colleagues the substance of such of them as affect your local interests, or are of immediate and practical moment and within the competence of the Government, and when the proper time comes, I shall carefully consider how far and by what means we may best meet the wishes of those whose recommendations are, upon many points at all events, entitled to the greatest respect.

INFANT MARRIAGES AMONG HINDUS.

At Madras on 2nd March, 1886, a deputation of native gentlemen, consisting of Brahmins and non-Brahmins, waited on the Viceroy to make a representation on the subject of infant marriages among the Hindus. The deputation was headed by Raja Sir T. Madhava Rao, who read an address on the subject.

The Viceroy replied that he was very glad to meet the deputation. The subject which they had brought to his notice was a very important one. There was nothing so well engrained in the British system of government as the fixed determination, as far as possible, not to interfere in the established national customs of the people. That was the policy of his predecessors, and to it he meant strictly to adhere; but it did not follow that there should be no departure from that policy, nor were the present Viceroy and the members of his Government precluded from watching with sympathy and approval any movement that had for its object the reformation of social customs. Personally, he thought that no custom could be more deleterious to morality and fraught with greater evils than that mentioned in the address. Every European nation would look upon it with horror. For his own part he would not like his child to enter into so momentous a contract under such conditions. If native opinion was not absolutely unanimous, there should at least be a general consensus of native opinion in favour of the movement. He had not yet been sufficiently long in the country to gauge the character, force, and extent of native opinion on the question. More than that he was not disposed to say at present, and they would not expect him to say more. At all events, they might go away satisfied that the movement had his sympathy and approval.

The *Clive* left Madras on Friday morning, the 4th March, and arrived on the following Monday afternoon at Calcutta, where His Excellency met with an enthusiastic reception from all classes of the community.

THE OUDH RENT BILL.

At a meeting of the Legislative Council which was held at Simla on the 9th of June, 1886, the Hon. Mr. Quinton moved that the Bill to consolidate and amend the law relating to rent in Oudh be referred to a select committee. Mr. Quinton spoke at some length on the necessity for legislation and on the objections urged by the Talukdars against the measure. The Hon. Rana Shankar Baksh (the representative of the Talukdars), while supporting the motion and accepting the two main principles of the Bill, pointed out those provisions which in his opinion were open to objection, and urged that the Talukdars might be allowed sufficient time for stating their objections and making suggestions. Sir Steuart Bayley having addressed the Council, His Excellency the President spoke as follows:—

I shall only trouble the Council with a very few observations, and I cannot preface them in a manner more consonant to my own feelings and to the sentiments which I know to prevail amongst my colleagues than by congratulating them and myself upon the acquisition of our new member,* who has already shown by the ability with which he has expressed his views what a useful and worthy accession he is likely to prove to the Legislative Council of the Government of India.

At our last meeting in Calcutta I explained that the reason why we did not then proceed with the Bill was the unavoidable absence of our colleague the Honourable Raja Amir Hassan, who was prevented from taking his place among us by severe illness. I added, however, that the Local Government, in order to save time, intended to publish a draft of the Bill and to collect the opinions of competent authorities upon it. Raja Amir Hassan is to our great regret still disabled from attending here, but a very well-qualified representative of the Talukdars, the vice-president of their association, has been appointed to assist us by his advice. The Bill has now been examined by the Talukdars, and we are in possession of their views, and I am glad to learn that in the main principles of the Bill they have expressed their acquiescence. I myself am fully convinced of the expediency of legislation on the lines of this Bill, and, while congratulating the Talukdars on the moderation they have shown, I am glad to understand from the previous speakers that there is a disposition to meet, as far as possible, the wishes of the association on minor points.

There is one special matter, however, upon which I should like to say a word in reply to what has fallen from my honourable colleague Rana Shankar Baksh Singh, and that is the question of compensation for disturbance. I understand that the Talukdars are inclined to consider that, were a claim of this sort to be conceded to the tenants, it would be tantamount to an acknowledgment of a right of permanent occupancy in their favour. Now this is a matter which has for many years past occupied my attention, and I must confess that in my opinion no such consequences can be held to flow from it. When a yearly tenant is unexpectedly evicted from his holding, the injury he sustains is not limited to the loss of his

---

* The Hon. Rana Shankar Baksh Singh, Bahadur.

improvements, but it entails a further loss occasioned by the disturbance introduced into his plan of life and his industrial undertakings. As a landlord I have myself always recognised the equitable claim of the tenant-at-will to compensation on this account, especially under a system of agriculture such as that which prevails in Oudh and in my own country, but I never held nor admitted that it implied either a proprietary or an occupancy right. When, moreover, we remember that this claim only amounts to one year's rent (in Ireland it was assessed at between four and seven years), and that it can be neutralised by the grant of an eight years' lease, I do not think that its recognition by the Legislature can be complained of by any one. I admit, however, that the interests of the landlord in regard to the tenant's disturbance claim should be safeguarded by allowing him to plead certain considerations as an offset or justification. However, I will not dilate further on this particular point, because it falls more properly within the competence of the committee to which this Bill has been referred. I will only conclude by saying that there is now no reason for further delay, and the Bill will proceed in due course through the regular stages. Between this and the time when the select committee will meet, the criticisms of the public on the Bill will be invited, and it will be examined anew by the association of the Talukdars and discussed with His Honour the Lieutenant-Governor and Chief Commissioner, who will visit Lucknow for the purpose.

The motion was put to the Council and agreed to.

SIR HERBERT MACPHERSON'S DEATH.

The Legislative Council assembled at Viceregal Lodge, Simla, on Thursday morning, the 21st October, 1886. Before proceeding with the ordinary business on the notice paper, His Excellency made the following remarks regarding the recent and unexpected death of Sir Herbert Macpherson, commanding the troops in Burma:—

Before the Council proceeds to its ordinary business, I desire to take this opportunity of expressing, in the name of the

Government of India, the deep sorrow and concern with which we have heard of the death of one of our most distinguished generals—Sir Herbert Macpherson. Until yesterday morning we had received no intimation even of his being unwell. On first reaching Mandalay, indeed, he noted in one of his letters to the Commander-in-Chief that he had suffered from a slight touch of the sun, but he spoke lightly of the matter, and from his subsequent correspondence there was no appearance of its having produced any inconvenient effects.

During the short time that he has remained in command in Burma, he devoted himself unremittingly to the arduous duties which he had undertaken, and after travelling about the country in various directions, he eventually went up to Bhamo. It is to be presumed that on his return he must have contracted the fatal fever of which he died. It was on his way out to sea, whither he was being taken in the hope of the sea air proving beneficial to him, that he expired.

In Sir Herbert Macpherson both India and England have lost a most talented and trustworthy officer, as well as a gallant and noble soldier. He has died in the discharge of his duty, and I have taken upon myself to communicate to his family in the name of my colleagues our deep sympathy and regret. I have received a telegram from Her Majesty the Queen in which she also expresses her deep sorrow at the calamity—for it is no less—which has thus suddenly overtaken herself and the country.

LAYING THE FOUNDATION STONE OF THE PUNJAB CHIEFS' COLLEGE.

The Viceroy left Bahawalpur early on the morning of the 1st of November, 1886, and arrived at Lahore the same evening. On the afternoon of the 3rd November His Excellency laid the foundation stone of the Punjab Chiefs' College. The ground plan of the college had been previously marked out, and on it was pitched a large, open shamiana, supported on silver poles, for spectators. In the centre of the shamiana, on an embroidered gold and red carpet, was the Viceroy's silver State chair, having on its right another silver chair for the Duke of Connaught, and on its left a chair for the Lieutenant-Governor. The seats for members of the College Council and for European spectators were on the left of the Viceregal dais, and those for native Chiefs and native gentlemen were on the right. Behind the Viceregal party sat the Duchess of Connaught, Lady Aitchison, Lady Helen Blackwood, Miss Thynne, and a few other ladies. In the roadway immediately in front of the shamiana and following its contour, were ranged, at open intervals, a detachment of the Northumberland Fusiliers, which corps also furnished a guard of honour. The route from the Durbar tent to the Government House was lined with troops. The Chiefs who were received with a salute were the Rajas of Chamba, Faridkot, Nahan, Mandi, Kapurthala, Nabha, and Jhind, the Nawab of Bahawalpur, and the Maharaja of Kashmir. Sir Charles Aitchison, the Duke and Duchess of Connaught, and the Viceroy arrived after the Chiefs, in the order named, and were received with the customary ceremonies.

As soon as the Viceroy had taken his seat, Sir Charles Aitchison read a statement explanatory of the establishment of the college. That institution, he said, was the outcome of proposals which had been under consideration since 1864, and which had been partially realised by the establishment of the Wards' School at Ambala. The school had not been so popular or so useful as to justify its continuance. It had, therefore, been determined to transfer the establishment under improved conditions to Lahore in the form of the Punjab Chiefs' College, which owed its inception primarily to the liberality of the Chiefs and Princes of the Punjab. The Lieutenant-Governor regretted that the principal subscriber, the Maharaja of Pattiala, who contributed half a lakh of rupees to the scheme, had not been able to be present, owing to illness. Sir Charles Aitchison confidently predicted for the college a large amount of success, and said that it would become a source of strength to the Government and a centre of good influence in the administration of the Punjab.

At the conclusion of the address the Viceroy formally laid the foundation stone, after which His Excellency addressed the assembly as follows :—

LADIES, YOUR HONOUR, YOUR ROYAL HIGHNESS, PRINCES, CHIEFS AND SIRDARS,—After Sir Charles Aitchison's full and eloquent description of the circumstances under which the establishment of the Punjab Chiefs' College was originally conceived and is now being so auspiciously inaugurated, it is not for me to say much. I have already had the opportunity, a year ago at the opening of the Mayo College, of explaining the grounds upon which my warmest sympathies were enlisted on behalf of institutions of this kind ; and probably in no part of India will adequate provision for the education of the young nobility and gentry of the land be more appreciated or more likely to be productive of good result than in this province. The great historical houses of the Punjab yield to none either in their antiquity, the traditions of high principles of valour and of honour by which they have been animated; or, what is better still, in their close intimacy and association with the people among whom they are established. But, as I have already said elsewhere, in these days of extensive education and of eager competition among all classes of the community, neither high descent, nor wealth, nor other adventitious circumstances will command the influence which otherwise might be their due, unless enhanced and dignified by intellectual attainments and mental cultivation. When, however, these are found to reinforce the social prestige derived from more material and accidental gifts, whether of birth, breeding, or riches, they endow the representatives of the ancient and renowned families of a country with a degree of importance and with opportunities of doing good, which, even in these democratic days, every one would probably acknowledge to be eminently beneficial. The people must have leaders and pioneers in the path both of moral and material progress, and a landed aristocracy such as has existed for ages amongst you is already pledged by its antecedents, by its material interests, and by the renown which it has inherited, to work for the common weal and to exhibit an honourable example of patriotic and unselfish exertion on behalf of the country at large.

It only remains for me to congratulate the Lieutenant-Governor on having been able to illustrate and adorn the close of his useful and honourable career as ruler of this province by the foundation of so useful an institution, an institution destined, I trust, to flourish from generation to generation to the end of time; and I am sure that I shall be only consulting the wish of those liberal-minded native princes, nobles, and gentlemen who have aided him in the accomplishment of the task he had set himself, if I suggest that his name should be attached to the building, and that from henceforth it should be known as the "Aitchison College."

At the conclusion of the Viceroy's speech the subscribers to the funds of the college as also a number of students were presented to His Excellency. This terminated the proceedings.

CONVOCATION OF THE PUNJAB UNIVERSITY.

On the morning of the 4th November, 1886, a Convocation of the Punjab University for the purpose of conferring degrees was held in the Montgomery Hall at Lahore. The Hall was thronged with the undergraduates of the University and other spectators, principally Rajas and native gentlemen of the Punjab. The Viceroy and the Duke and Duchess of Connaught were present. The business of the Convocation commenced with the reading of an abstract of the annual report by the Assistant Registrar. Then Sir Charles Aitchison, as Chancellor, conferred upon the Viceroy the degree of Doctor of Oriental Learning by virtue of the decree of the Senate declaring His Excellency, by reason of his eminent position and attainments, a fit and proper person for the said degree; and by virtue of a similar decree, the degree of Doctor of Literature was conferred upon the Duke of Connaught. The graduates and undergraduates having been presented to the Chancellor and having received at his hands the honours to which they were entitled, the Viceroy rose and addressed the Convocation as follows:—

Mr. CHANCELLOR, RAJAS, AND GENTLEMEN,—In the first place, I am sure you will not think it unnatural that I should take the earliest opportunity open to me to express the very great satisfaction I have experienced at having had the honour of a degree conferred upon me by the Senate of this University. It is a distinction of which any one might be proud, and I only wish I could think that my progress in the paths of oriental learning had begun earlier, and had been more successfully prosecuted. Still I am entitled to call myself, if not a very advanced, at all events a very earnest student of at least one branch of the special literature which you cultivate. On that account the University of Lahore will always possess for me the attributes of an *Alma Mater*, and I trust ere I leave India to have proved myself not altogether unworthy of her tutelage. (Cheers.)

And now I suppose that, following the example of my predecessors, I am expected to say something in reference to the ends and objects of this institution, its claims to public confidence, and the functions it is destined to discharge as one of the most powerful and important adjuncts of our educational system; but I must frankly say there is nothing I dislike more than talking of matters about which I am aware I know very little, and of which the rest of the world not unnaturally assumes I can understand nothing. At the same time there are certain characteristics attaching to the establishment and expansion of the Lahore University which fully come within the apprehension of all outsiders, and those are, on the one hand, the public spirit, liberality, and wisdom exhibited by the Chiefs and the inhabitants of the Punjab, to whom it owes its existence, and, on the other, the obvious advantage of the introduction into the very heart of the province of a seat of learning so essentially popular and national, and so responsive to the needs, wishes, tastes, and intellectual sympathies of the communities amidst which it is enthroned. One of the great dangers attending the setting up of an elaborate and brand-new educational system from one end to the other of a country which has only recently awoke to the consciousness of its needs in this respect, is that of stamping its products with a monotonously sterile uniformity, devoid of local colour, indigenous spontaneity, and discursive originality and ambition. (Applause.) It is on this account, if on no other, that I should hail with pleasure the existence of a home of education endowed with such distinctive characteristics as yours; and fitting it is that, while in other parts of India, to Western science and the products of Western literature should be assigned the pre-eminence and importance they undoubtedly deserve, here at least we should be reminded that treasures of wisdom and of a high morality, the pleasant fields of a rich poetical literature, and deep mines of philological, antiquarian, and historical lore, are to be found in regions which lie altogether apart and separate from Western observation and experience. In what manner your labours in the one hemisphere may most effectually supplement and commingle with the achievements of your fellow-workers in the other; how you may best apply the products of your own past, so rich in everything that can warm the fancy, excite the imagination, or exercise the speculative and metaphysical faculty, to the practical requirements of your future and the exigencies of our present hard and exacting age, is one of the principal problems with which you have to deal, and for which I have no doubt you will find a satisfactory solution. (Cheers.)

If, however, turning aside from this main question, I permitted myself to offer a practical suggestion which, though lying perhaps a little on one side of the direct route you are called upon to follow, nevertheless clearly comes within the scope of your natural functions, it would be, in the first place, that you should undertake a persistent and well-considered search throughout the Punjab for Arabic and Persian manuscripts, resembling that which for many years has been carried on, with the assistance of the Government of India, by the Asiatic Society of Bengal for Sanscrit manuscripts. Already, as far as Sanscrit is concerned, great progress has been made in the direction I have indicated by various learned gentlemen, both European and native; but, as yet, no similar endeavours have been made to register or catalogue what are probably equally valuable stores of the Arabic and Persian books and writings which must exist in private hands all over Northern India. When we remember for how long a period this part of the Peninsula remained under Mahomedan rule, it cannot but be that a very suggestive and instructive literature of the nature I have described must exist from one end of this province to the other. At present European scholars who deal with Arabic and Persian have to depend for their materials upon the manuscripts treasured in the great libraries of Europe, but the materials at their disposal are both sparse and incomplete. If, however, such of the literature of these two languages as is to be found in Europe were to be supplemented and enlarged by whatever of the same sort has been preserved in this country, and if it were properly catalogued and displayed, there is no doubt a considerable impulse would be given to the critical and speculative advancement of those very studies which it is your special aim to promote, while you would gain the not unimportant collateral advantage to be derived from visits to India of our most accomplished European scholars. Probably amongst those whom I am addressing, there are many gentlemen who themselves possess Persian and Arabic libraries, and, as a member of a Philobiblon Society, I am well aware that nothing would give them greater pleasure than that the contents of their bookshelves should be known and appreciated. (Cheers.)

Another point which I would venture to recommend to the attention of the members of the Lahore University would be a detailed survey of the numerous vernacular dialects of the Punjab, the collection of such monuments of their literature as exist, and the recording of the legends and other descriptions of folk-lore which are so rife in all these surrounding districts. You must remember, gentlemen, that your jurisdiction extends into those mysterious regions which witnessed in bygone ages the confluence and the dispersion of those shadowy generations whose movements indeed we cannot trace, but the disseverance of whose destinies has stamped the face of the world both in the East and in the West with their characteristic features for all eternity. In your hands perhaps may lie the key to one of the most interesting problems that has ever occupied the attention either of the philologist or the historian; and even though the primeval secret of all may elude your search, there is no doubt that a careful study of the dialects, folk-lore and traditions, which have been deposited by the various races and tribes, whether Aryan or Mongolian, Greek, Syrian, Turk, or Pathan, that have passed through the folds of the mountains forming your northwestern boundary, cannot fail to furnish you with a mine of material for ethnological and sociological study which as yet has been hardly worked at all, and which, if properly cultivated, will be productive of the most important results. (Applause.)

I have only to conclude, Mr. Chancellor and gentlemen, by thanking you for the kind attention with which you have listened to the few imperfect observations which I have addressed to you; and I wish to take this opportunity of stating that, as long as I remain in India, I shall esteem it a pleasure and a privilege if I may be permitted to place annually at the disposal of the authorities of this University a gold medal, to be competed for under whatever conditions the Senate itself may determine. (Loud applause.)

His Excellency's address terminated the proceedings.

INVESTITURE OF SIR WEST RIDGEWAY WITH THE K.C.S.I.

On the afternoon of 4th November, 1886, the Viceroy held a Chapter of the Order of the Star of India at Government House, Lahore, for the formal investiture of Sir West Ridgeway, Chief Commissioner with the Afghan Boundary Commission, with the K.C.S.I.

After the ceremony the officers of the Commission were presented to the Viceroy, who addressed the assembly as follows :—

GENTLEMEN,—Great has been my pleasure in conferring upon Sir West Ridgeway, the distinguished Chief of the Boundary Commission, the honour which has been so justly awarded to him by the gracious favour of Her Majesty. I feel that my satisfaction would not be complete unless I took this opportunity of welcoming back to India those other officers who have returned with him to Lahore, and who have so ably seconded his endeavours in carrying out the difficult and arduous duties imposed upon him. There are, indeed, few tasks more ungrateful, or more exposed to mortification, than that of delimiting a frontier in the interest of an ally. In matters of the kind there are always disputable points which it is almost impossible to settle without exciting a certain amount of discontent in the minds of those on whose behalf we are mediating; and it is difficult to make them understand that there must be a certain amount of "give and take," and that the right is not always on one side. I am happy to think, however, that, thanks to the good sense and intelligence of the ruler of Afghanistan, we have already been able to settle more than one controverted matter in a pacific manner, and I am certainly of opinion that the moderation and the conciliatory spirit shown by His Highness in regard to the demarcation of the western portion of his frontier ought to facilitate the arrangement of the only remaining point in dispute in a manner consonant to his interests, and, as I believe, to his rights. Be that, however, as it may, I desire to assure Sir West Ridgeway and all his associates that their countrymen and the whole Indian community, whether European or native, are heartily glad to see them back amongst us. From their first departure to the present moment we have watched their proceedings with the deepest interest and sympathy. We are fully aware of the arduous and trying circumstances which have attended the execution of their mission, that they have been exposed to great privations, hardships, and sickness, and that on more than one occasion they have occupied a situation of considerable peril. From first to last, however, their conduct has been deserving of the highest praise, and has been conspicuously characterised both by fortitude and patience; nor is it inappropriate to remember that, apart from the diplomatic work upon which they have been engaged, they are also able to show, thanks to the energy and industry of their scientific colleagues, geographical and scientific results of the most interesting and valuable character. Last, not least, however, I would desire to congratulate them on the auspicious circumstances under which they visited Cabul, as well as on the rapidity of their march from the capital of Afghanistan to the British frontier. That an English mission so constituted should be received as honoured guests by the Amir, and with the most hearty and friendly welcome at the hands of his subjects along their entire route, is in itself a remarkable and significant circumstance which cannot fail to have a most beneficial effect upon the future relations between the Governments of India and Afghanistan.

In conclusion, gentlemen, allow me to hope that, however disagreeable and irksome may have been a great portion of the period you spent on the Afghan frontier, at all events hereafter it may suggest none but the pleasantest reminiscences, for I am happy to think that the one thing necessary to make a retrospect agreeable to all the servants of Her Majesty, whether European or native, civil or military, is the consciousness that they have successfully and faithfully done their duty.

STATE DINNER AT BARODA.

On the evening of November 9, 1886, the Gackwar gave a State dinner at the Nazar Bagh, in honour of the Viceroy, about ninety guests being present. The Gaekwar entered before the cloth was removed, and proposed the health of the Queen and of the Viceroy. In proposing the latter, His Highness said:—

"I am proud to be able at last to welcome His Excellency as my guest. Never before has a Viceroy of India visited our country; never before have we had the opportunity of receiving with all possible honour the representative of our gracious Empress, the revered Lady and Sovereign, whose reign is soon to be solemnised as one of the most fortunate, the most glorious, and most beneficent the world has ever seen.

"It is to-day, in proposing the health of His Excellency, that I may give what expression I can to the feelings of profound satisfaction which move my family, when we realise the position we hold in Imperial India. The greatness and unity of the British Empire have just been signalised in London through the exertions of His Royal Highness the Prince of Wales; and I wish to-day to recall with gratitude the name of the Prince who visited Baroda when I was still a boy.

"I beg His Excellency to receive my heartiest thanks for his visit, and to believe that it will long be remembered among us as a signal honour and a token of his regard and friendship for the State of Baroda. Ladies and Gentlemen, the health of His Excellency!" (Applause).

The Viceroy replied as follows:—

YOUR HIGHNESS, LADIES AND GENTLEMEN,—In rising to acknowledge the toast which you have been good enough to propose in such kind and cordial terms, I naturally desire to take this opportunity of expressing the extreme satisfaction I have had in making your Highness's personal acquaintance. That satisfaction has been very much enhanced by finding you in the midst of your State and of your capital, discharging those great and responsible duties pertaining to your station with an intelligence and a conscientiousness which are beyond all praise. There is nothing which can be so entirely satisfactory to the representative of Her Majesty in this country, as to find the Princes of India, upon whose friendship and allegiance Her Majesty so implicitly relies, in such complete possession as is your Highness of the respect alike both of his English and native fellow-subjects. When I came to Baroda and saw on every side so many signs of improvement and of progress—magnificent buildings of great public utility rising in every direction, with every provision made for the health, as well as for the gratification, of the people—when I found your Highness surrounded by a contented population whose prosperity and personal affection for your Highness it was impossible to mistake or misapprehend, I then indeed felt fully confirmed in that opinion which I had already been led to entertain of your Highness; and I go away convinced that, in your Highness, India is blessed with one of those wise, high-minded, and conscientious rulers whose life is a blessing to their people, and whose co-operation with the Government of India is more calculated than anything else to assist us in the performance of our own onerous and important duties.

I have noted with much satisfaction the loyal and affectionate terms in which you have been good enough to allude to Her Majesty the Queen-Empress; and it will be my pleasant duty, on the very first occasion, to make Her Majesty acquainted with the expressions which have fallen from your Highness's lips. I am also pleased to acknowledge the friendly manner in which you have referred to the Prince of Wales, and I may mention that before leaving England His Royal Highness laid upon me his command to remember him to all those Princes of whose hospitality he had partaken, and of whose friendship he was so proud.

In conclusion, I would desire, not only in my own name, but on behalf of all those who are here present—and I am sure I am expressing what they feel very deeply—to return our warmest thanks for the spectacle which you have offered to our admiring gaze—a spectacle which has not consisted in useless and meretricious pageantry, but which presents the far more solid and agreeable sight of a prosperous and flourishing country with every sign of improvement and progress, educational establishments, hospitals, a magnificent park for the delectation of the people; and last, but not least, a semicircle of 4000 children assembled under the auspices of your Educational Department. I do not think it has ever fallen to me, or to any of us in a single day, to see so many sights which have occasioned us such real or such legitimate pleasure. And now, ladies and gentlemen, in conclusion, it only remains for me to propose the health of the Maharajah. (Loud applause.)

The Viceroy left for Bombay on the 10th inst.

ADDRESS FROM THE BOMBAY CORPORATION.

The Viceroy, accompanied by his staff, arrived at Bombay from Baroda on the 10th November, and on the same day embarked on the Indian Government steamer *Clive* for a visit to Viziadroog, a port some distance down the coast, in the Ratnagiri District, where there is an interesting old fort which was held by the pirate Angria in the beginning of the eighteenth century, and was captured by Clive and Watson in 1756. His Excellency returned to Bombay on the 13th November, and was received on landing by all the principal civil and military officials and by a number of native Princes (the chief being Maharajah Holkar of Indore), who had come to Bombay to meet His Excellency. On landing, the Viceroy was met by a deputation from the Bombay Corporation, who presented him with an address of welcome, to which His Excellency replied as follows :—

Mr. CHAIRMAN AND GENTLEMEN,—It is now, as you have just reminded me, nearly two years since I first landed here, and I need scarcely say that the splendid and cordial reception with which I was then honoured has remained deeply graven on my memory. To meet with such cordiality and confidence when setting foot in a new country, for the prosperity of which I could not but feel myself in a great measure responsible, was peculiarly encouraging, and it is now, if possible, still more gratifying to find that the experience of two eventful years, during which the Government of India, besides fulfilling its ordinary duties to the people, has had to deal with several most intricate, most delicate, and most important problems, has in no way diminished the confidence with which Bombay greeted me on my arrival.

Since first making your acquaintance, I have visited, as you have said, many parts of this great empire, and I have everywhere enquired into the vitality and progress exhibited by municipalities and other organs of local self-government; and, though it may be premature to draw general conclusions and invidious to make comparisons, I cannot help telling you that I know of no municipality imbued with a more enlightened, wisely progressive, and thoroughly practical spirit than the municipality of Bombay. I am well aware how much your efforts are hampered by the difficulty of raising capital at a reasonable rate of interest, and I have always regretted, when studying the papers connected with this subject, that we could not come to your aid in the way you desired. Nor can I hold out any immediate prospect of the Government of India abandoning the financial policy which it has adopted after very careful consideration. I have little doubt, however, that, if your present high reputation is maintained, the carrying out of the projected works will be little, if at all, delayed, for the increasing confidence in the wisdom and prudence of your administration will supply the guarantee which you require. The financial assistance granted by Government to the Port Commissioners to which you have referred in the course of your address, will indirectly help you by fostering the wealth and prosperity of the city as a whole. How much this wealth and prosperity are objects of solicitude to the Government is shown by the large amount of attention recently devoted to your harbour defences.

In conclusion, gentlemen, it remains for me simply to thank you very warmly, as the representatives of the city of Bombay, for this second cordial reception, and for the friendly sentiments which you have been good enough to express. May your beautiful city long continue to enjoy its well-merited prosperity!

ADDRESS FROM THE POONA MUNICIPALITY.

The Viceroy, accompanied by the Countess of Dufferin, arrived at Poona on the 19th November, 1886, and was received at the railway station by a large assemblage of civil and military officers and leading natives of the town. On leaving the station His Excellency drove direct to the Council Hall, where he received three addresses of welcome, viz., from the Poona Municipality, the Poona Sarvajanik Sabha, and the Deccan Education Society. The addresses touched upon various subjects of a local and general character. In replying to the deputation from the Poona Sarvajanik Sabha, His Excellency said :—

GENTLEMEN,—You will have already heard that pressure of business has prevented me from preparing a written reply to the loyal and friendly address you have been good enough to present to me, but the omission shall be supplied in due course. In the meantime, as in the case of the municipality, I will venture in a few unpremeditated words to touch upon one or two of the points which you have so properly brought to my notice. With regard to the first of them, namely, the Deccan College, and the probable action of the local government in reference to that institution, all I can say is, that until I arrived in Bombay I did not even know that a Deccan College question existed. The subject has not yet been brought to the notice of the Supreme Government, either by the finance committee, whose final report, indeed, has not yet been drawn up, or by the local government. It is consequently altogether impossible for me to discuss the merits of the question. My Government will be prepared to go into the whole matter as soon as it is brought to its notice through the proper channel; that is to say, in the shape of some recommendation from the Government of Bombay. Whatever may be the views of that Government, we shall be disposed to consult them with the greatest respect and attention, in connection with any observations or memorials by which they may be accompanied, whether emanating from yourselves or from any other parties.

I now come to the second subject upon which you have touched, namely, the commission which has lately been appointed for the purpose of examining the whole question of the Indian Civil Service. I note with pleasure that you have not only expressed yourselves content with the composition of that body, but that you have also gone out of your way to assure me that you do not share in those misgivings which have been expressed in other parts of India with regard to the good faith and intentions of the Government in reference to the appointment of that commission. Nothing has filled me with such astonishment, nothing has made me feel so deeply how great are the difficulties of Government in this country as the insinuations which have appeared in certain organs of the press with regard to this subject. When the Government of India has succeeded, after many years of persistent effort, in bringing about the re-examination of the conditions of the Indian Civil Service, it is indeed a matter of surprise that there should be found—I will not say amongst you, for I am happy to think that you have repudiated so unworthy an insinuation, but amongst some of those who represent themselves as guides and leaders of Indian public opinion—men so incapable of appreciating what has been the character of English rule and of its English representatives as to assert, in the face of their countrymen, that the only object of the Government of India in appointing the Civil Service Commission has been to deceive the people of India, and to resort to a base and abominable trick, for the purpose of restricting still further the privileges of those who are so justly anxious to serve our Sovereign in the civil service of their country. Gentlemen, I say again that nothing has more pained and surprised me than the discovery that men who profess to be representatives of educated opinion in India should have conceived the possibility of Her Majesty's Government at home and of the Indian Administration conspiring to pass a fraud upon her native subjects.

I now proceed, gentlemen, to examine the various suggestions which you have been good enough to make to me in regard to the composition of the commission. In the first place I must remind you that the commission is not like Parliament. In the commission, in order to obtain proper representation of those whose interests are likely to be affected, it is not necessary that it should consist of any fixed proportion of the representatives of those interests. The commission itself is in a certain sense a judicial body. It is desirable, of course, that it should contain men well acquainted with the subject, and consequently that it should be composed of persons drawn from various classes of the community; but the real representatives of the different views of those whose interests are likely to be affected by the results of the inquiry are the witnesses examined before it. Moreover, you must always remember that for practical purposes it is essential that the commission should be of manageable dimensions. The Government of India originally intended that it should only consist of twelve members, the usual number and the number best suited for carrying on the practical work of a commission, but on the other hand, there were other considerations which induced us to enlarge its number to sixteen. You, however, seem to wish that it should consist of twenty or twenty-two members. I tell you frankly that this proposal I cannot consent to. So large an increase in the numbers of the commission would certainly interfere with its practical utility. This consideration alone induced me to omit from the commission a representative of one of the most intelligent and loyal communities in the country—that is, of the Parsi community. Unfortunately there is no Parsi member on the commission—a fact which I much regret. Thus, gentlemen, I am sure you will see that we had good and sufficient reasons for not enlarging the commission. If you consider who are the members of the commission, you will find that it is constituted upon a very liberal basis. Does there exist in India a man who possesses more justly or more completely the confidence of the native inhabitants than Sir Charles Aitchison? Then, again, we were recommended by the Government at home to put upon the commission an English lawyer. I immediately suggested that Sir Charles Turner should be sent out to us, as I knew there was no man who more entirely possessed the goodwill, affection, and confidence of the natives of India. We then referred the nomination of the other members to the local governments, as was our duty. We appointed an East Indian, because East Indians are a community which for special reasons ought, I think, to be given an opportunity of having their claims heard. Further, the Secretary of State gave a pledge in Parliament that the Uncovenanted Civil Service should be represented, and a member of that body was accordingly added. When, therefore, you come to see the motives by which we were guided, and the conditions and restrictions under which the commission was instituted, I think you will admit that the interests of all concerned have been carefully considered.

It now, gentlemen, only remains for me to refer to the concluding paragraph of your address. When I was at Madras, in the early part of this year, it was my pleasing duty to announce to the gentlemen who were good enough to welcome me to the capital of that Presidency, that Her Majesty's Government had determined to appoint a commission for the purpose of re-examining the conditions and operations of some of our administrative machinery. In making that announcement, I expressed my deep satisfaction at the course pursued by the Home Government. Although the shortness of time which I had been amongst you had prevented me from studying, as fully as I could have wished, all the various important questions connected with the Indian administration, yet it was obvious to me, as I then stated, that since the time of Sir Charles Wood great changes had taken place in the condition of this country; that higher education had made considerable strides; that the intelligence of the educated classes had largely expanded; and that there was no lesson more forcibly taught to us by history than that institutions ought to keep pace with the progress of events and of a country's intellectual development. Further than this I said I would not go: first of all, because I did not think my limited experience entitled me to pronounce a more definite opinion, but principally for the obvious reason that, from the moment Her Majesty's Government has announced that an inquiry is about to take place on any important subject, it becomes out of the question for the Government of India to commit itself prematurely to any opinion or line of action in regard to it. To make, therefore, an announcement in regard to any of the questions to which you have referred would be not only inopportune, but, as I am sure you will understand, it would be absolutely and entirely impossible. However, I will say that, from first to last, I have been a strong advocate for the appointment of a committee or commission of this sort, and that when succeeding Governments in England changed, I have on each occasion warmly impressed upon the Secretary of State the necessity of persevering in the nomination of such a commission. In the meantime a Civil Service Commission has been set going, the door to inquiry has been opened, and it only remains for you, by the force and logic of your representations and of the evidence you may be able to submit, to make good your case; and if you succeed in doing so, all I can say is that nobody will be better pleased than myself.

BANQUET AT HYDERABAD.

On the evening of the 24th November, 1886, the Viceroy, accompanied by the Countess of Dufferin, arrived at Hyderabad and was received by the Nizam and the chief nobles with due ceremony. Mr. Cordery, the Resident, with all the officers commanding regiments and batteries at Hyderabad, took part in the reception of Their Excellencies. In the evening His Excellency held a Levée, and on the following day ceremonial visits were exchanged between the Viceroy and the Nizam. In the evening the Nizam entertained Their Excellencies at a banquet in the palace, and after dinner the Viceroy proposed the Nizam's health in the following speech :—

LADIES AND GENTLEMEN,—I now rise to propose to you the health of His Highness the Nizam. His Highness represents a dynasty and a State which, in former days, when India was the theatre of war and disturbances, were always the faithful allies and friends of the British crown, and I am happy to think that during the long and tranquil period which has since supervened, the extraneous forces which then united us have resulted in the creation of a still more complete identity of political and material interest between us. His Highness is a young man, standing on the threshold of what I trust will prove a most happy and fortunate career. Indeed I do not know in the world a more enviable position than that of our Indian Princes. Enjoying as they do, under the *ægis* of the British Imperium, an absolute immunity from those anxieties by which the chiefs of the European States are perpetually exercised, namely, the danger of invasion from without and the fear of revolution from within, they are able to give their whole time and attention to the most interesting and the noblest task which can occupy the human mind, the advancement of the States along the road of modern progress and the improvement of the material welfare and happiness of the millions entrusted to their charge. Such a field as this is amply sufficient to satisfy the widest ambition or the most soaring aspirations that ever entered into the heart of man. And not only so, but they have the additional satisfaction of knowing that Her Majesty and her Government have but one desire, and that is to extend to them on all occasions their heartiest sympathy and assistance, and to do everything in their power to augment their prestige, support their authority, and enhance their personal consideration. In return we ask for nothing but that they should administer their States wisely and beneficently, in accordance with their lights and the local requirements and characteristics of their situation; for long years of a traditional and unswerving loyalty exhibited through many a generation on their part render even the mention of such a requirement as fidelity to their Sovereign and Empress unnecessary upon ours.

LADIES AND GENTLEMEN,—I am happy to have this opportunity of assuring His Highness that there is no community in India in whose prosperity and happiness Queen Victoria, the people of England, or the Indian Government, take a deeper interest than of the great historical State over whose fortunes he has been called upon by Providence to preside, and most heartily do I trust that His Highness may long live to pursue the responsible and honourable career now opening before him.

LADIES AND GENTLEMEN,—I beg to propose the health of His Highness the Nizam.

The Nizam acknowledged the toast by drinking to the health of His Excellency.

BANQUET AT MYSORE.

On the evening of the 30th November, 1886, the Maharaja of Mysore entertained Their Excellencies Lord and Lady Dufferin at a banquet in the Residency, a large number of guests having been invited to meet them. After dinner the Maharaja entered and took his seat beside the Viceroy, and subsequently rising proposed, through his Dewan, the health of Their Excellencies. The Viceroy in responding to the toast said :—

LADIES AND GENTLEMEN,—In returning thanks for the great honour which has been done me by our distinguished host, I only wish I could express myself in terms as appropriate and graceful as those in which the toast has been submitted to your notice. But though that perhaps may be difficult, I can assure you that I fully appreciate the great kindness and the princely hospitality with which he has entertained the representative of the Queen-Empress and the friendly personal sentiments he has expressed towards myself. When I remember that, not many years ago, this State and neighbourhood were the centre of a cruel despotism, and the theatre of war and confusion, of race hatreds and religious animosities, I cannot help congratulating the Maharaja on the change which has intervened. Under the benevolent rule of himself and of his dynasty, good government, enlightened progress, universal peace, and the blessings of education are everywhere in the ascendant; and there is no state within the confines of the Indian Empire which has more fully justified the wise policy of the British Government in supplementing its own direct administration of its vast territories by the associated rule of our great feudatory princes. When I think that I myself was admitted to the familiarity of the heroic soldier, of whose early achievements Seringapatam and the surrounding country were the theatre and the witnesses, it is difficult to believe that the changes to which I have referred should have been the fruits of what I may call contemporary history. It has now been my good fortune to have passed through most of the native States of India, and to have come into personal, and I may say intimate, contact with their chiefs, and I have no hesitation in saying that though there may be differences between them, though some States may be more advanced than others, some rulers less sensitive than others to the weighty responsibilities imposed on them by Providence, on the whole my experiences have been eminently satisfactory and reassuring, and the Queen-Empress and the Government of Great Britain have the greatest reason to congratulate themselves on the general enlightenment, the desire to do their duty, and the conscientious application to affairs which is so generally prevalent amongst them.

In conclusion, I trust I may be permitted to add a few brief words of heartfelt thanks for the kind reference which His Highness has been pleased to make to Lady Dufferin's earnest desire to improve the medical treatment of the women of India. I believe that in bringing this subject to the notice of the community at large, Lady Dufferin has contributed to one of the greatest ameliorations which have ever been introduced into the country. I can assure you there is nothing which can so encourage her to persevere in her efforts as to feel that, alike by princes and by people, her humble efforts have been so generously appreciated.

Ladies and gentlemen, I will now call upon you to drink the health of His Highness the Maharaja.

ADDRESS FROM THE MYSORE REPRESENTATIVE ASSEMBLY.

In reply to the address from the Representative Assembly of Mysore, His Excellency spoke as follows:—

GENTLEMEN,—I have listened to your address with great pleasure and interest. It is always a fortunate circumstance when the Viceroy finds himself in the midst of a community who are able to bring to his notice such proofs of their general prosperity as those to which you have referred, and still more so when in the language with which he is approached he sees evidence of an equally wide-spread contentment with the administration under which they live. That you should use such terms does not surprise me, for your good fortune has placed you under the rule of one of the most intelligent, upright, and high-minded amongst the great princes of India, and, when I leave his territory, I shall have the satisfaction of knowing that, at all events as far as this part of the country is concerned, its welfare, its proper security, and its peace are amply provided for. I have noted what you have said about your Famine Railways, and I deeply sympathise with the natural anxiety which you express in regard to that subject. It is one which is constantly engaging the attention of the Supreme Government, and, as I have no doubt you are aware, during my illustrious predecessor's term of office, large and extensive schemes were originated, for the purpose, as far as possible, of safeguarding Mysore and other districts of India from the danger of famine. That scheme is being steadily prosecuted, but I regret to say that, in consequence of its great extent and cost, it is impossible that all parts of the country should be provided with the necessary railways at the same time. I think, however, you may be content with the reflection that your interests in this respect are in the hands of the Honourable Member of my Council representing the Public Works Department, who is as capable as any man I know of dealing effectively with the complicated problem before him.

I am very glad that you have touched upon the question of education, as it gives me an opportunity of expressing in as earnest and as strong language as I can command, the extraordinary pleasure I have experienced in seeing on every side such manifest signs of the deep interest with which that subject is regarded in this State as well as of the liberal and intelligent energy with which its development is being prosecuted. When I passed along what I imagine must have been a quarter of a mile of street, lined on either side, in rows eight or ten deep, with the youth of the country congregated under their respective teachers, I felt that you were laying broad and deep for all time to come the foundations of a prosperous future. But, great as has been my satisfaction at these proofs of the progress made in the matter of general education, I was still more pleased by a sight which I imagine is not to be seen in any other part of India, and that is the appearance of rows and rows of young ladies belonging to high-caste families assembled together under the same admirable system, and enjoying, as far I can understand, as extensive opportunities of acquiring knowledge, of enlarging their experiences, and of strengthening their understandings, as could be found in any of the most advanced cities of Europe; and those gentlemen who are the leaders of society, and who represent the aristocracy of the land, who have in so generous and liberal-minded a manner seconded the noble efforts of Her Highness the Maharani to establish the Mysore Female School, are entitled to the greatest credit for their exertions. I only wish that in all the other chief towns of India a similar degree of wisdom and of comprehension of the true interests of a nation were to be found. Believe me, gentlemen, if you wish to make the homes of India centres of domestic happiness and peace, as well as fountains of light and of every noble and holy aspiration, you will educate your daughters. It is by the mother that the child is properly furnished forth on his difficult and dangerous journey through life; it is from the mother that he receives his first impulse along the paths of virtue, and it is by educating the mother that a generous and powerful nation is most surely and most rapidly created.

In conclusion, gentlemen, allow me to thank you for the friendly welcome with which you have greeted me. I am glad to see you around me, and I am pleased to think that the Maharajah should have called to his councils men of such intelligence, influence, and authority. I am sure that both His Highness and the State will equally profit by your assistance.

VISIT TO PONDICHERRY.

The Viceroy arrived at Pondicherry on the afternoon of Friday, 10th December, 1886, and met with a very cordial welcome from the Governor and chief functionaries of State. His Excellency was received at the railway station by the Mayor of the city, the Director of the Interior, and the Commandant of the station, and was conducted to a pandal or canopy in which were assembled M. Manès (the Governor) and all the chief officers of State. M. Manès welcomed His Excellency to Pondicherry in the following speech:—

"La Ville de Pondichéry est aujourd'hui en fête toute heureuse d'accueillir Votre Excellence et de lui manifester ses respectueuses sympathies. Je me félicite à mon tour de saluer au nom de la République le digne Représentant de la grande nation britannique, certain que la visite dont Votre Excellence veut bien honorer le chief-lieu des Établissements Français dans l'Inde, ne pourra qu'être féconde en résultats heureux. Il m'est agréable surtout en cette occasion d'être l'interprète de la population entière accourue sur votre passage et de vous dire que Votre Excellence soit la bienvenue parmi nous."

The Viceroy replied as follows :—

EXCELLENCE,—Je suis très touché de l'accueil bienveillant que vous m'avez donné et de tous ces préparatifs que vous avez faits pour ma réception. C'est pour moi un grand plaisir de me trouver sur le sol français, et je peux vous assurer que je suis également animé de ces sentiments amicaux auxquels vous venez de donner une expression si éloquente en me souhaitant la bienvenue.

The following is a translation of the above :—

I am very much touched by the kind welcome which you have given me, and by all these preparations which you have made for my reception. It is a great pleasure to me to find myself on French soil, and I can assure you that I am equally animated with those friendly sentiments to which you have just given such eloquent expression in bidding me welcome.

In the evening there was a State dinner at Government House, at which M. Manès proposed the health of the Queen. In return His Excellency proposed the toast of the President of the French Republic in the following terms :—

MESSIEURS ET MESDAMES,—Son Excellence le Gouverneur a bien voulu porter un toast en termes éloquents et sympathiques à la santé de Sa Majesté la Reine-Impératrice. En revanche je demande la permission de porter un toast à la santé du Président de la République Française. Si malheureusement je ne dispose pas de ce don d'éloquence dont Son Excellence a fait preuve, je peux vous assurer que je suis animé de sentiments non moins sincères et tout aussi chaleureux quand je vous prie de boire avec moi à la santé de cet éminent citoyen français, qui a su gagner, par son caractère privé aussi bien que par ses qualités d'homme d'état, le respect et l'estime de l'Europe—ou plutôt du monde entier—et qui, selon l'avis de tous les partis politiques, a bien mérité de la patrie. Ici dans ce coin eloigné de cette grande patrie qui vous est si chère, je suis heureux de trouver une occasion de me faire l'interprète de ce respect et de cette estime dont il jouit universellement à si juste titre. Buvons, messieurs et mesdames, à la santé de Mons. Grévy, Président de la République.

The following is a translation of the above speech :—

LADIES AND GENTLEMEN,—His Excellency the Governor has been good enough to propose, in eloquent and sympathetic terms, the health of Her Majesty, the Queen-Empress. In return I ask permission to propose the toast of the President of the French Republic. If unfortunately I have not at my disposal that gift of eloquence which His Excellency has displayed, I can assure you that I am animated by sentiments not less warm and sincere when I ask you to drink to the health of the eminent French citizen, who, by his private character as well as by his qualities as a statesman, has earned the respect and esteem of Europe, and indeed of the world at large, and who by the testimony of all political parties has deserved well of the Fatherland. Here in a remote corner of that great Fatherland which is so dear to you, I am happy to find an opportunity of making myself the interpreter of the respect and esteem which he so universally and so justly enjoys. Ladies and gentlemen, let us drink to the health of Monsieur Grévy, the President of the French Republic.

At a later stage of the dinner, M. Manès proposed the health of the Viceroy in the following terms :—

"Tout en regrettant votre trop court passage parmi nous, je remercie Votre Excellence de sa sympathique visite, dont je garderai la plus durable impression, car à l'honneur qui m'a été réservé de vous saluer, l'un des représentants les plus éminents du Gouvernement Britannique, demeurera toujours attaché le souvenir d'avoir été le premier gouverneur des Établissements Français appelé à recevoir Son Excellence le Viceroi de l'Inde. J'aimerai à me rappeler aussi que votre visite aura, pour ainsi dire, inauguré la prise de possession des hautes fonctions que m'a confiées la République, présage heureux pour mon administration, en même temps qu'elle est une nouvelle preuve de la bonne entente de nos gouvernements."

His Excellency replied as follows :—

MESSIEURS ET MESDAMES,—En me levant pour remercier Son Excellence des bonnes paroles dans lesquelles il a bien voulu parler de ma visite à Pondichéry, j'espère que les personnes aimables que je vois autour de moi m'excuseront si je ne parviens pas à exprimer pleinement et dûment mes sentiments de reconnaissance, mais vous comprenez, messieurs et mesdames, que quand le cœur est plein d'émotion on se sent fort gêné si l'on doit se servir d'une langue qui n'est pas la langue maternelle. Depuis de longues années j'ai le bonheur de vivre en rapports plus ou moins intimes avec les

L

Français les plus distingués dans la carrière de la politique et de la diplomatie, des arts et de la littérature, et j'ai toujours rencontré auprès d'eux, ainsi qu'auprès de leurs compatriotes en général, beaucoup d'égards et de bonté. Ainsi, messieurs, tout naturellement, me trouvant dans le voisinage de votre ville si célèbre dans l'histoire de l'Inde Méridionale, j'ai voulu présenter mes respects à la République et à la nation françaises dans la personne de leur représentant. En même temps j'ai pensé que je pourrais peut-être apprendre quelque chose qui me serait utile dans l'exercice de mes fonctions officielles, en me faisant une idée de l'organisation administrative de votre colonie. Mais avant tout j'ai voulu accentuer, par une visite aux Établissements Français dans l'Inde, le désir de mon Gouvernement de maintenir avec mon hôte et collègue distingué des rapports d'amitié sincère et cordiale. Quelques-uns des noms les plus illustres dans l'histoire de France appartiennent à l'histoire de l'Inde, et tout Anglais qui se trouve dans ces parages doit éprouver le désir de témoigner son respect et son admiration pour des généraux comme de Bussy et pour de grands hommes d'état comme Dupleix.

Dans ces sentiments de respect et d'admiration le souvenir des anciennes rivalités s'éteignent et maintenant nous ne sommes heureusement des rivaux que sur le champ des progrès pacifiques.

À vous, Excellence, et aux Établissements que vous administrez avec tant de dévouement je souhaite ardemment toute sort de bonheur et de prospérité, et je peux vous donner l'assurance que rien ne manquera de mon côté pour consolider ces liens d'amitié et de cordialité qui unissent les Français et les Anglais aux Indes. Je regrette seulement que mon séjour à Pondichéry, sous votre toit si hospitalier, soit nécessairement de si courte durée, mais je suis obligé de partir demain matin afin de pouvoir passer quelques heures chez le nouveau Gouverneur de Madras, qui vient de prendre possession de son poste. Ce fonctionnaire distingué a probablement consacré, pendant son voyage sur mer, une partie de son loisir à parcourir l'histoire de la province qui lui est confiée, et comme il a sans doute appris qu'à une époque pas trop reculée, les habitants de Pondichéry avaient assiégé et pris sa capitale, il se sentira peut-être rassuré en apprenant de ma propre bouche que vous, messieurs, vous n'avez nulle intention de suivre sous ce rapport, l'exemple de vos aïeux.

Messieurs et Mesdames, je vous invite à boire avec moi à la santé de notre aimable hôte, Son Excellence le Gouverneur des Établissements Français dans l'Inde.

<small>The following is a translation of the above speech :—</small>

LADIES AND GENTLEMEN,—In rising to return thanks for the kind terms in which His Excellency has been good enough to refer to my visit, I trust that the amiable persons around me will excuse my shortcomings if I fail to express my gratitude in adequate and becoming terms; but you understand, ladies and gentlemen, that when the heart is very full a foreign language is always a difficult channel through which to convey its outpourings. I have had for many years the good fortune to live on more or less intimate terms with the Frenchmen most distinguished in the world of politics, diplomacy, art, and literature, and I have always received from them, as well as from their fellow-countrymen in general, much attention and kindness. I was therefore naturally anxious, when I found myself in the neighbourhood of your city, so celebrated in the history of Southern India, to pay my respects to the Republic and to the French nation in the person of its representative. I also thought it possible that I might learn something which might prove useful to myself in the discharge of my official functions by making myself acquainted with your administrative machinery. But above all things I was desirous of accentuating by my presence in French India the wish of my Government to maintain the most cordial and affectionate relations with my distinguished colleague and host. Some of the most illustrious names known in the history of France belong to the history of India, and no Englishman can find himself in this locality without involuntarily wishing to pay his passing homage to such a general as Bussy and to such a great statesman as Dupleix. In these sentiments of respect and admiration, the remembrance of ancient rivalries are extinguished, and now we are, happily, rivals only on the field of peaceful progress. That all good fortune and prosperity may attend you, sir, your state, and the honourable citizens whose affairs you so ably administer, is my most earnest auspication, and, believe me, nothing shall ever be wanting upon my part still further to consolidate those bonds of amity and mutual good fellowship which now characterize the relations of the French and English in India. I regret extremely that my stay in Pondicherry and under your hospitable roof should be so short, but I am forced to set out to-morrow morning, in order to meet the newly-arrived Governor of Madras. That distinguished officer has probably employed his leisure hours at sea in reading the history of his Presidency, and having thus acquainted himself with the fact that on a particular occasion you captured his capital, it may reassure him to learn from my own lips that you have no intention of repeating the achievement. Ladies and gentlemen, I invite you to drink with me the health of our amiable host, His Excellency Monsieur de Manès, the Governor-General of French India.

ADDRESS FROM THE INDIAN ASSOCIATION.

On the 30th of December, 1886, a deputation from the Indian Association waited upon the Viceroy at Government House with an address of welcome on His Excellency's return to Calcutta. Foremost among the topics which the association desired to bring to His Excellency's notice was the reconstitution of the Legislative Councils. Local self-government in Bengal had, on the whole, been a success, and the association ventured to hope it might be extended to the wider concerns of the province, feeling that the time had come for the recognition of the representative system in the government of the country. In 1885, when complications arose on the North-west frontier, the Indian population had offered to enlist themselves as volunteers, but no answer had been received to the numerous petitions addressed to Government on the subject. The association desired to call His Excellency's attention to the condition of the coolies in Assam. The disclosures which had been made in the newspapers and courts of law pointed to the necessity of reform in this direction. The time seemed to have come when both Act XIII. of 1859 and Act I. of 1882 might be repealed, and the importation of labour into Assam permitted to be regulated by the law of supply and demand. The association suggested the appointment of a Commission of Enquiry into the matter. The association noted with gratitude that the question of technical education had engaged the attention of the Viceroy, and recommended the establishment of a technical college in Calcutta. In conclusion, they hoped that it might be permitted to the people of India to associate His Excellency's name with a beneficent era of domestic reform.

The Viceroy replied in the following terms:—

GENTLEMEN,—I need not say that I am very grateful to you for the kind words with which you have welcomed my return to Calcutta, and that it is always a pleasure to me to enter into communication with persons of such intelligence and distinction as yourselves. I trust that my progress through a considerable portion of the south of India has not been altogether without profit. Though the acquaintance I have made with various important localities has been necessarily superficial, I have, at least, had an opportunity of coming into contact with a great number of gentlemen of standing and influence in their several districts. This in itself has been both a very great pleasure and an unspeakable advantage to me. There are few things that I more prize than the enjoyment of frank personal intercourse with the leading minds of India.

In your address you refer to certain questions connected with the administrative machinery of this country, which have more than once been brought to my notice, and you seem to expect that I should make some statement on behalf of the Government in regard to them. This is, I think, not altogether a reasonable demand. I have already stated on more than one occasion that the India of to-day is in many respects a different India from that which existed twenty years ago, when the constitution of the Government of India received its present shape. Since then a class of highly educated men has come into existence—gentlemen who, like yourselves, are well acquainted with the political and economic literature of Europe, who have assimilated Western ideas, and who naturally consider that it would be advantageous to the country if they had an opportunity of becoming more largely associated than has hitherto been the case with their British fellow-subjects in the task of administration. I fully recognise that this is a very legitimate and laudable ambition; and I must remind you, as I have reminded others, that successive Governments at home have admitted the desirability of re-examining the working of the Act of Parliament of 1858, with the view, it is to be presumed, of ascertaining whether its provisions ought not to be more closely adapted to the altered conditions of the present day. The matter may, therefore, be considered as being *sub judice,* and a moment's reflection will enable you to understand how impossible it is, under these circumstances, for the Government of India to make any declaration on the subject.

Another subject to which you have referred is the question of Volunteering in India; but I am a little surprised to find you state simply that the Government has not announced the view it takes of this matter. Nearly a year ago, at Madras, the moment I learned the decision of the Home Government —and you will remember that it was Mr. Gladstone's Government that was then in office—I took the opportunity of publicly announcing the regret I felt in not being able to accede to the wishes of the petitioners. I said that there was no doubt in my mind that their desire to enrol themselves as volunteers was prompted by the purest spirit of loyalty and patriotism; but when the Government of India came to consider the practical methods by which effect could be given to the movement, it very soon became apparent that the difficulties and disadvantages attending the elaboration of any plan for the embodiment of a volunteer army altogether outnumbered and outweighed the military and practical advantages to be derived from the realization of the scheme. Nor can I hold out to you any hope that either the Government at home or the Government of India will be likely to change its decision.

I am glad to see that you duly appreciate the desire of the Government, by the appointment of the Public Service Commission, to re-examine every question connected with the admission of natives to the Civil Service in a sense favourable to their interests, and the proceedings of that body are in themselves a proof of the thorough and energetic spirit in which the work has been undertaken.

It has been a real pleasure to me to learn that you attach due importance to the question of technical education. It is a matter of the utmost moment to this country, and nothing shall be wanting on my part to confirm and widen its basis, and to elevate its superstructure. I intend to spare no endeavours to promote its best interests; but let me assure you that nothing would be further from my thoughts than to allow whatever efforts it may be desired to make on behalf of technical education to retard or interfere with that higher education to which you very properly attach so much importance.

You have referred also to the subject of coolie labour in Assam. This is a matter to which the Government of India has recently devoted, and is still devoting, a considerable amount of attention. We have accepted in principle that special legislation should be maintained only as long as it is practically necessary for the protection of the two classes concerned, but I am not prepared to say when it will be safe to leave the coolies to the unfettered action of the harsh economic law of supply and demand without any special protection from the administration. The existing procedure may, however, I think, be improved, and for this purpose it is intended to amend the executive rules now in force. In view of the recent inquiries and of the Secretary of State's decision to give Act I. of 1882 a further brief trial, it would be premature at the moment to appoint a commission, but I may tell you that the working of Act XIII. of 1859 is now under the consideration of the local government, and that the representations which you have made to me will be carefully examined when the report of the local government is received.

CONVOCATION OF THE CALCUTTA UNIVERSITY.

A convocation of the University of Calcutta for conferring degrees was held on Saturday, the 8th of January, 1887, at the Senate House in the presence of a large gathering, composed of European and native ladies and gentlemen. The members of the Senate in academic costume assembled at 2.55, and at three o'clock the Vice-Chancellor and the Fellows proceeded to the entrance hall to receive His Excellency the Chancellor. On the arrival of His Excellency a procession was formed and entered the hall. The Registrar then conducted His Excellency to the dais, where the Lieutenant-Governor of Bengal, the Chief Justice, and the *ex-officio* Fellows and members of the syndicate occupied seats. The Vice-Chancellor, having declared the convocation opened, called upon the Registrar to read the names of the candidates for degrees. Among these were two native ladies from the Bethune School. After they had received their degrees of B.A. they were introduced to the Viceroy, who shook hands with them and congratulated them. When the ceremony of presenting diplomas was concluded His Excellency the Chancellor, in calling upon the Vice-Chancellor to address the Convocation, said :—

VICE-CHANCELLOR, LADIES AND GENTLEMEN,—Although I do not intend to detain you with any observations of my own before calling upon our Vice-Chancellor to address you, it is but natural that I should take this opportunity of congratulating the University upon the eminent position it holds among our Indian institutions. In 1882, when my illustrious predecessor addressed you as Chancellor, he called attention to the fact that this University had been in existence for a period of a quarter of a century, and he referred with satisfaction to the admirable results which had been produced in the provinces subject to its influence. Since then a good deal has occurred. A Government commission was appointed for the purpose of examining the position of education throughout all India, and it laid down the lines upon which, I believe, education is destined most successfully and safely to proceed. At the same time Lord Ripon expressed the hope that, side by side with the Government system of education, there should spring up through the medium of local effort, free and independent educational institutions characterized by greater variety and spontaneity. Before the commission had reported, various circumstances occurred to prove that the wise words of your late Chancellor had not fallen upon barren ground, and there is nothing which has given me greater pleasure than to observe with what remarkable energy and with what illimitable liberality independent and local efforts on behalf of education have been prosecuted throughout the country. (Cheers.) But the secret of all progress is untiring and unceasing effort, and I trust, therefore, that I shall not be considered to ignore or overlook the past if I express the hope that not only those efforts will be continued, but that this University will go still further afield, and will eventually proceed to cultivate ground which hitherto has been only imperfectly tilled. You, gentlemen, as representatives of the enlightenment of modern India, are not only bound to direct the efforts of your fellow-countrymen towards the study of literature, of law, and of medicine, but it is also incumbent upon you to turn your attention to the development of those scientific pursuits upon which the material prosperity of every nation so much depends, and which are such essential characteristics of that civilization which is being so rapidly assimilated by the people of this country. (Cheers.) I have learned with satisfaction that the changes, which after due deliberation have been introduced into the courses of this University, have amply fulfilled the expectations of those who inaugurated them. Those changes have all been in the direction of greater thoroughness. That is entirely as it should be. Thoroughness ought to be the watchword inscribed over the doors of every temple of learning, for believe me that, although pedantry may be excused in such an institution as this, anything approaching to dilettantism can only be regarded as the sign of irretrievable deterioration. Consequently I again repeat to you that, whatever else you do, be careful that your system is thorough. That it has now become so is, I believe, admitted, and it is a source of pride to all of us to know that those gentlemen who have passed before me to-day are able to go away with the conviction that they have received a sound and thorough education, and that they have won their diplomas by dint of untiring industry and application. (Cheers.) But however thorough may be your system, it is also desirable that it should extend over as wide an area as possible, and I am glad to think that, under the auspices of this convocation, favourable conditions have been created for the promotion of female education. (Cheers.) It must have given us all the greatest pleasure to see those two ladies approach the Vice-Chancellor and receive at his hands their diplomas, which they may justly regard as a source of honour to themselves and to everyone connected with them. (Cheers.) Gentlemen, I will not longer detain you. I will simply congratulate you upon the continued proofs which every year exhibits of the wholesome influence you exercise over the various collegiate and other educational establishments in India, while at the same time I express the hope that, from year to year, your efforts may be ever crowned with increasing and permanent success. I now call upon the Vice-Chancellor to address the Convocation. (Loud cheers.)

The Vice-Chancellor then addressed the convocation at great length, after which the proceedings terminated.

THE COUNTESS OF DUFFERIN'S FUND.

The second general meeting of the National Association for supplying Female Medical Aid to the women of India was held in the Town Hall, Calcutta, on Wednesday, the 26th January, 1887. The Viceroy occupied the chair, the Countess of Dufferin being seated at his left hand, and Lady Rivers Thompson at his right. The attendance was very large and represented all sections of the community. In opening the proceedings His Excellency made the following remarks :—

LADIES AND GENTLEMEN,—It is a great pleasure to me again to preside on this occasion, to see around me so many supporters of the movement in favour of the better medical education of the women of India, and to know that the principles which we are so earnestly advocating have taken such deep root in the convictions and the affections of the people of India. I congratulate all present heartily on the success which has attended their exertions, and I only trust that it will be a motive of encouragement to us to make still more energetic efforts.

The Hon. Mr. Peile then presented the report of the Central Committee and explained the work which had been done by the association during the year. His motion that the report should be accepted and confirmed was seconded by Mr. Cruickshank, President of the Chamber of Commerce. The Lieutenant-Governor also addressed the meeting on the motion to make certain additions to the articles of association, which was seconded by the Hon. Abdul Jubbar. Maharajah Narendra Krishna then proposed " that the grateful thanks of the people of the country be conveyed to Her Excellency the Countess of Dufferin for the establishment of the association named after her" and for her active sympathy in promoting the objects of it. The resolution was seconded by Nawab Abdul Latif, and the Viceroy returned thanks for Her Excellency in the following terms :—

LADIES AND GENTLEMEN,—I was quite unprepared, as was Lady Dufferin herself, for the kind manner in which two of your eminent citizens have been good enough to allude to her, and therefore I trust I shall be forgiven if I am only able to return our thanks in a very inadequate manner. This, however, I may be permitted to say, that the best reward which Lady Dufferin can receive, will be found in the hearty and cordial support which this movement is obtaining at the hands of all classes and of all communities in the country. Now, ladies and gentlemen, having said this much, perhaps as an humble outsider, uninitiated in the mysteries of the internal government of the fund, I may be permitted to address to those who superintend its operations, on the one hand a compliment, and on the other a criticism. In the first place, I desire to compliment them on their admirable State papers. India in all times has been celebrated for the admirable character of these documents, and I am glad to think that no matter from what source—whether from Bombay, from Madras, from Calcutta, or from the central committee—these documents emanate, they are all characterized by a laudable simplicity of expression and by the extreme lucidity with which they give a vast amount of complicated information. The criticism which I would desire to address to the managers and to the governing body of the fund is that they are a great deal too modest in their demands and in their requisitions. When I heard them simply talking of three more lakhs—of a maximum of five lakhs—as the utmost to which they dare aspire, I could not help thinking that it would have been more becoming the occasion, much more appropriate to the cause which they are so nobly advocating, and much more respectful to the constituencies to which they are authorized to appeal, that they should have talked of fifty lakhs. When we remember, on the one hand, what is the task that they have set themselves—the way in which they are bringing health and light and happiness into millions of Indian homes, and on the other hand, as I myself have had an opportunity of observing, that from one end of India to the other, every community in the land is full of sympathy with this movement—then I feel that if only they have the courage of their opinions and make a sufficiently peremptory and earnest appeal to their friends and admirers, they will obtain an infinitely larger sum than that to which their ambition seems at present restricted. (Cheers.) No one knows better than myself the difficulty of obtaining money in India. It is one of those disagreeable problems which I have had to face under very disheartening circumstances, but let me tell the Lady President of the fund that it will probably prove a far more graceful, as well as more successful method, to throw herself on the generosity of the Indian people than, as I have been obliged to do, to resort to those mechanical means by which alone the Government coffers can be replenished. (Laughter and loud cheers.)

On behalf of Lady Dufferin I beg to express to you my warmest and most hearty thanks for the kind manner in which you have been pleased to receive this expression of her thanks. (Cheers.)

Maharajah Sir Jotendro Mohun Tagore then moved a vote of thanks to the Viceroy for presiding, which was seconded by the Hon. Mr. Steel, and carried with acclamation. This concluded the proceedings.

CELEBRATION OF THE QUEEN'S JUBILEE.

The 16th and 17th February, 1887, were the days officially set apart by the Government of India for the simultaneous celebration throughout India of the fiftieth year of the reign of Her Majesty the Queen-Empress. Each Presidency, Province, and native State, each city, town, and centre of population, organised and carried out its own arrangements for the ceremonials and festivities which were observed on the occasion. In Calcutta, the winter headquarters of the Supreme Government, the Jubilee was ushered in by an imperial salute of 101 guns fired from the ramparts of Fort William at sunrise. This was followed at nine o'clock by a parade and march-past of the troops and volunteers on the Maidan in the presence of the Viceroy, the Commander-in-Chief, the Lieutenant-Governor of Bengal, and an immense concourse of people, European and native. After the parade the Viceroy, with the Countess of Dufferin, attended a special thanksgiving service at St. Paul's Cathedral, and in the afternoon, at five o'clock, His Excellency proceeded to the racecourse, where, in the presence of a large assembly of all classes of the community, he received about 300 deputations (representing the great commercial and landed interests of the Lower Provinces of Bengal, public and political bodies, literary and scientific associations, &c.), who came to wait on His Excellency with addresses of loyal congratulation to the Queen-Empress. On the arrival of the Viceroy and the Countess of Dufferin, Their Excellencies were greeted with loud and continued cheers from the spectators, and were received by the Lieutenant-Governor of Bengal, the Commander-in Chief in India, the members of the Viceroy's Council, the Bishop of Calcutta, the Chief Justice of Bengal, and the Headquarters and District Staff.

On the Viceroy taking his seat, Sir Rivers Thompson, in introducing the various delegates to His Excellency, delivered a brief address, after which His Excellency rose and spoke as follows :—

GENTLEMEN,—It is with equal pride and pleasure that I now come forward to thank the representatives of the various cities, associations, and communities who have gathered around me to-day for the purpose of presenting to Her Majesty their congratulations on her having entered the fiftieth year of her reign. A more prosperous reign, a more blameless ruler, or a more beloved Sovereign the world has never seen. (Cheers.) Wisdom, justice, piety, duty have been the guardians of her throne and the companions of her daily life, and though it has been impossible for a monarch, ruling dominions which comprise within their limits a fourth of the human race, to escape from those vicissitudes which the responsibilities of Empire entail, it may be said with truth that under her fortunate auspices her people have issued triumphant from every trial, and that, with each revolving year, the foundations of her realm have become more firmly established, and the loyalty and devotion of her subjects to her throne and person have grown more tender and intense. (Applause.) At this moment 200 millions of her Indian

subjects are giving expression to the feelings and sentiments
I have described, with a unanimity and spontaneity which I
believe it would be impossible to parallel in any other country
in the world. Of set purpose my Government has left the
initiative and the organization of those public rejoicings,
which are taking place in every capital city, town, and village
in India, to the unprompted impulses of the people. In a
land where official action is generally the prime mover,
officialism has for once stood upon one side, and has left the
nation face to face with its Empress. (Cheers.) In the simple
language which is native to their affectionate disposition,
there have gone up to-day from every shrine, from every place
of worship, from the tabernacle of every heart, prayers for her
happiness, blessings on her goodness, and the incense of an
honest and trustful devotion. The great princes in their
durbars, the municipalities in their city halls, the soldiers in
their barracks, the zemindars in their country houses, the
citizens in their pavilioned streets, and the ryots in their
humble homesteads feel, and justly feel, that the close of half
a century which has encompassed and endowed the land with
universal peace—which has brought justice to every cottage
door—which has bridged the floods and pierced the jungle—
which has converted millions of barren acres into well-watered
plains—which has sensibly diminished the risks both of
famine and of pestilence—which has lit a hundred lamps of
learning in every chief centre of population and placed within
the reach of the humblest Indian student the accumulated
wealth of Western learning, science, and experience—every
English and Indian subject of the Queen, I say, justly feels
that such a day of retrospect as this is indeed a fitting occasion
for commemoration and mutual congratulations. (Applause.)
But if we rejoice in the past, it is not merely on account of
the actual good it has brought us, but because the past is the
parent and creator of the future. Change and development
is the law of human existence; and great as have been the
achievements, both in England, in the colonies, and in this
country, which will ever render the Victorian era memorable in
the annals of history, they will prove, I trust, but the forecast

and preface to even greater and still happier times. (Cheers.) Wide and broad, indeed, are the new fields in which the Government of India is called upon to labour—but no longer, as of aforetime, need it labour alone. Within the period we are reviewing, education has done its work, and we are surrounded on all sides by native gentlemen of great attainments and intelligence, from whose hearty, loyal, and honest co-operation we may hope to derive the greatest benefit. In fact, to an administration so peculiarly situated as ours, their advice, assistance, and solidarity are essential to the successful exercise of its functions. Nor do I regard with any other feelings than those of approval and good-will their natural ambition to be more extensively associated with their English rulers in the administration of their own domestic affairs; and glad and happy should I be if during my sojourn amongst them circumstances permitted me to extend and to place upon a wider and more logical footing the political status which was so wisely given a generation ago by that great statesman Lord Halifax to such Indian gentlemen as by their influence, their acquirements, and the confidence they inspired in their fellow-countrymen, were marked out as useful adjuncts to our Legislative Councils. (Applause.) But while thus recognising in the fullest manner the legitimacy of such political aspirations as those to which I have referred, I hope that they will not divert our Indian fellow-subjects from those equally imperative duties which lie altogether outside the circle of political interests and administrative action, and upon which indeed far more than on anything which Government can do the prosperity of the country depends. Such, for instance, are the improvement of our agricultural systems—the reclamation of waste lands, and the planting upon them of the redundant populations at present inconveniently accumulated in congested districts—the opening up of fresh avenues of industry both to our urban and rural classes by the spread of technical education—the improvement of the sanitary conditions not merely of our great towns, but of our villages, of our hamlets, and of the dwellings of the poor—the wise and judicious diffusion of education and knowledge amongst the future mothers of the next generation—the ripening of public opinion in regard to some of those social questions which lie at the root of all domestic happiness and morality—the expansion and consolidation of that movement on behalf of the better medical treatment of Indian women in which our Sovereign takes so deep a personal interest—the development of our native industries, some of which, I am happy to think, are already competing on triumphant terms with their European rivals—the creation, or rather I should say the reintegration, of that artistic genius which in former days rendered India famous for her architecture, her decorative taste, her ornamental treatment of the precious metals, her portrait and miniature painting, and the illumination of her manuscripts—and, finally, the bringing into line of all the more backward populations of every race and creed, so that each may compete on equal terms with the others for whatever prizes this life has to offer, whether in the shape of honourable distinction or material advancement. (Applause.) These at least are a few of the objects which the past fifty years of Queen Victoria's reign have placed us in a favourable position for pursuing, and most heartily do I join with you in hoping that our loved Empress may live to witness their successful attainment. Believe me, I speak from personal knowledge when I say that, amongst her many pre-occupations and anxieties, there is no section of her subjects whose interests she watches with more loving or affectionate solicitude than your own. Moreover, in doing this, she most truly represents, as it is fit and right their Sovereign should, the feelings and instincts of the English people. Through the mysterious decrees of Providence, the British nation and its rulers have been called upon to undertake the Supreme Government of this mighty empire; to vindicate its honour, to defend its territories, and to maintain its authority inviolate; to rule justly and impartially a congeries of communities, many of them widely differing from each other in race, language, religion, social customs, and material interests; to preserve intact and unimpaired the dignity, rights, and privileges of a large number of feudatory princes; to provide for the welfare of a population nearly as numerous as that of Europe, and presenting every type of civilization known to history from the very highest to the very lowest; to safeguard and to develop the enormous moral and material British interests which have become inextricably implicated with those of the natives of the soil; to conduct its administration in a way to win the love, confidence, and sympathy of races as keenly sensitive to injustice and wrong as they are ready to recognise kindness and righteous dealing; and eventually to evolve from its present intricate and imperfectly adjusted mechanism a homogeneous community so well balanced and co-ordinated, so united in its material interests and in its moral convictions, as to form a loyal, patriotic, and compacted whole. Within what period this result is to be achieved is a secret hidden in the distant future, but of one thing you may be sure, that there is no determination more fixed and immoveable in the will of England, there is no wish dearer to the heart of Her Majesty and of the British people, than faithfully, firmly, and courageously to discharge the difficult and stupendous duties which I have thus rapidly enumerated, in the interests and for the benefit of our Indian fellow-subjects and brothers. (Loud and continued cheers.)

A brilliant display of fireworks brought the proceedings of the day to a close. The illumination of Calcutta took place on the following evening, and the Viceroy drove in procession through the principal streets of the city to witness it.

BURMA MILITARY POLICE.

At the Legislative Council, held at Simla on the 27th of July, 1887, the Bill for the Regulation of Military Police in Burma was taken into consideration and subsequently passed into law. Mr. Peilo explained that the object of the Bill was to repeal the Military Police Regulation which was introduced into Upper Burma in January last, and to put the Military Police under the same law in Upper and Lower Burma. Mr. Peilo also moved a number of amendments in the original Bill, which were merely additions or alterations to make the meaning clearer. In putting the motion the Viceroy spoke as follows:—

Before putting these amendments I should be glad to take the opportunity, which as yet I have not had, of expressing on behalf of my colleagues in the Government of India the great satisfaction afforded to us by the admirable manner in which the Indian Military Police of Burma have discharged their difficult and arduous duties from the date they were despatched to that country. Although from time to time the Government of India, through the Home Department, has conveyed to the officers, European and native, of that corps various indications of their approval, I do not think that any very formal recognition of their services has as yet been made. There is no doubt that the duties which have fallen to their share have been as arduous, as dangerous, and as trying to their health as those to which the military forces of Her Majesty in Burma have been exposed, and both in regard to the physical courage and patience which they have displayed, and to their discipline and obedience to command, they have in no degree fallen behind the other police forces of India. Indeed, on several occasions, the Military Police of Burma have distinguished themselves in a very remarkable manner, and, on more than one occasion, individual native officers have shown extraordinary bravery and enterprise.

I entirely agree with the observations which have fallen from my honourable colleague, Mr. Peile, that it is of the most essential importance that this force should be worked up to a very high level of military discipline. We must remember that it discharges its duties under very peculiar conditions. It is a force sent to Burma for the purpose of maintaining the domestic peace of the country, but at the same time it is composed of men who are alien in race, in religion, and in language to the population amongst whom they exercise their duties. Consequently, unless there is introduced into the force the bonds of a very strict military discipline, there might be a danger lest it should transgress the proper limits of police action. Thanks to the judicious and practical recommendations of the Commander-in-Chief, when he was in Burma and had an opportunity of observing both the defects as well as the good qualities of the force as it was then constituted, the Government of India, acting by his advice, was able to introduce into Upper Burma those improvements and those special arrangements which, in consequence of their successful operation, my honourable colleague is now anxious to extend to the force in Lower Burma. It is satisfactory to think that the alterations about to be applied to the organization and composition of the force in Lower Burma have successfully operated in the Upper Burma Police Force.

I do not think it will be necessary for me to re-read the various amendments proposed by my honourable colleague, and therefore I shall proceed to put them *en bloc*.

The motion was put and agreed to, after which the Bill was passed into law.

FRENCH TRAVELLERS AT SIMLA.

On Thursday, the 18th August, the Viceroy entertained at luncheon three French scientific travellers (Messrs. Bonvalot, Pepin, and Capus) who had crossed from Central Asia into India by the Baroghil Pass and Chitral, suffering much privation and hardship on the journey. After luncheon His Excellency proposed their health in the following terms :—

His Lordship on rising said he was desirous, both as the head of the Government of India and as an ex-President of the Royal Geographical Society of England, to congratulate his guests upon their safe arrival in Simla, and stated with what great pleasure he welcomed them to the dominions of Her Majesty. He then expressed in very warm terms his admiration of their tenacity, courage, and endurance in surmounting successfully the innumerable difficulties which had impeded their progress across the snowy ranges of the Himalayas. They had indeed suffered great hardships, but they had borne them with the gaiety and fortitude natural to the gallant nation to which they belonged. We should all profit by the experiences they had gone through, and he looked forward with great pleasure to the account of their adventures, which, in the interests of science, he hoped they would give to the world. He regretted extremely that their stay at Simla should be so short, as both his countrymen and his country-

women would have joined in trying to make them forget
the trials and sufferings they had lately endured. However,
he well understood their desire to get back to their own
country and to their friends, and he was quite sure that all
present, especially the members of the Indian Government,
would join him in wishing their guests a prosperous voyage
across the sea, and a happy return to France, where the
services they had rendered to geographical science would
be certain to meet a fitting reward at the hands of their
appreciative countrymen.

INVESTITURE OF THE COUNTESS OF DUFFERIN WITH THE PERSIAN ORDER OF THE SUN.

The following notification in the Foreign Department of the Government of India (No. 1804E., dated Simla, the 2nd September, 1887) appeared in the *Gazette of India* of 3rd September with reference to the above ceremony :—

"On the 27th of August, Haji Mirza Hoossein Goli Khan, Motamid-ul-Vizareh, Consul-General for Persia in India, arrived at Simla for the purpose of investing Her Excellency the Countess of Dufferin, C.I., G.C.S., by command of His Majesty the Shah of Persia, with the Imperial Order of the Aftab (Sun) of the Sublime Persian Empire, which Illustrious Order Her Majesty the Queen-Empress had graciously authorized Her Excellency to accept. The investiture took place on Monday, the 29th August, at a durbar held in Simla by His Excellency the Viceroy and Governor-General."

On the following day (the 30th August) the Viceroy, accompanied by the Countess of Dufferin, received the Persian Consul again in Durbar, and addressed him in Persian as follows :—

JANÁB-I-SHUMÁ,—Man az shumá khwáhish karda-am ki im-rúz bá man dar ín-já mulákí shavéd, tá ba shumá jawáb-í-t'alíka'e ki dar-án á'lá Hazrat-i-Sháh, ákú-i-zí-shaukat-i-shumá, az ráh-i-iltifát izhár farmúda-and, ki ba 'ulyá janáb Lady Dufferin kita-i-nishán-i-áftáb-i-daulatí-i-daulat-i-Irán 'atá farmúda-and, baráe tahvíl namúdan ba á'lá Hazrat-i-Sháh mufawazz numáyam.

Dar t'alíka-i-mazbúrah á'lá Hazrat-i-Sháh wajh-i-ín 'atíya-i-átifat-o-iltifát-i-khud rá mansúb ba dustí-o-ittihád-i-kalbí, ki az diryáz darmián-i-daulatain 'ání daulat-i-Iránwa daulat-i-

Inglis bar karár búda, izhár mí-farmáyand, wa ham ummíd mí-kunand ki ín-dustí-o-ittihád rúz ba rúz rú ba tazáyud-o-tarakkí numáyad. Wakte-ki janáb-i-shumá t'alíka-i-á'lá Hazrat-i-Sháh rá wa nishán-i-tabka-i-daulatí rá muhavval namúdéd, janáb-i-shumá hamín alfáz rá dar mahall-i-bayán áwurdéd, wa hamín ummíd rá izhár kardéd. Janáb-i-shumá az jánib-i-á'lá Hazrat-i-Sháh ba khátir-i-man awurdéd ki dustí-o-ittihád darmíán-i-har du daulat az pushthá káim-o-barkarár búda, wa janáb-i-shumá píshín-gúí-namúdéd ki, ba fazl-i-janáb-i-Bárí, ittihád-o-mawaddat áindah hamésha rú ba izdiád báshad tá wakte ki u'júba-i-zamána gardad.

Hích kalimát án kadar pur zúr-o-káfí níst ki ba-wásitah-i-án man kadar-dání-i-khiálát-o-maknúnát rá ki á'lá Hazrat-i-Pádsháh-i-shumá az ráh-i-iltifát tahríran, wa ham ba wásitah-i-mulázim-i-mu'tamad-'alaih-i-khud izhár namúda-and, ibráz numáyam ; wa na man mí-tawánam ki janáb-i-shumá rá, wa ba tawassut-i-janáb-i-shumá á'lá Hazrat-i-Sháh rá, mutayakkin sázam ki khiálát-i-man fakat 'aks-o-partaw-i-khiáslát-i-á'lá Hazrat-i-Sháh ast. Man dustí-o-khair-khwáhí-i-dáim rá ki daulat-i-'álíyya-i-Sháh ba daulat-i-bahíyya-i-Inglistán izhár namúda-ast ba ibtiháj-i-kalbí ba-yád-i-khátir mí-áram, wa man ba i'tikád wa niháyat khush-dilí dawám-o-izdiád-i-dustí-o-khair-khwáhí rá mutawakki'-am. Irán-o-Inglistán bisyár rawábit-i-ittihád dárand, wa hích amre níst ki darán masálih mutasádim shawand wa baham khurand. Man ummíd mí-kunam wa i'tikád dáram ki dar zamán-i-áindah har du millat o-kaum paiwasta chunánki alán and, dústán-i-hamím-o-rásikh khwáhand búd, wa chunánchi khud-i-janáb-i-shumá mí-guéd mawaddat-o-dustí-i-unhá pusht-ba-pusht mazbút-o-mustahkan khwáhad shud.

Man az janáb-i-shumá khwáhish mí-kunam ki á'lá Hazrat-i-Sháh rá bar-ánchi man gufta-am muttali'-o-hálí gardánied wa á'lá Hazrat-i-Sháh rá mutayakkin sázed ki chunánki man az jihat-i-'atá-i-nisbán-i-tabka-i-daulatí niháyat mukirr-o-káil bar ihtirám, e ki á'lá Hazrat-i-Pádsháh ba Lady Dufferin wa ba khud-i-man namúda-and hastam, man nishán-i-mazkúr rá az hama chizhá bísh-bahá khwáham dánist, wa Lady Dufferin ham án-rá az hama ashyá bíshbáha khwáhand dánist, chi, án 'alámat-o-nishán-i-dustí-i-á'lá Hazrat-i-Sháh nisbat ba kishwar-o-mulk-i-má hast.

Man bar án chi im-rúz ba wukú' rasída 'ulyá Hazrat-i-Malika-i-mu'azzama rá muttali'-o-hálí mí-gardánam, wa man ba yakín mí-dánam ki 'ulyá Hazrat-i-Malika-i-mu'az-zama rá az istimá'-i-ín amr *kh*aile bahjat o *kh*urramí rú *kh*wáhad namúd. Ba janáb-i-Lady Dufferin, wa ba *kh*ud-i-man bá-'is-i-inbisát-i-ziáda dar zamán-i-áindah *kh*wáhad búd, wakte ke ba yád mí-árem ki janáb-i-muhtasham ilaihá bá nishán-i-tabka-i-daulatí dar ín sál-i-kábil-i-yád-gár-i-hukúmat-i-'ulyá Hazrat-i-Malika-i-mu'azzama muhallá namúda shudand.

The following is a translation of the above speech:—

YOUR EXCELLENCY,—I have asked you to meet me to-day in order that I might hand over to you, for delivery to His Majesty the Shah, your august master, a reply to the letter in which His Majesty was good enough to announce that he had conferred upon Lady Dufferin the Imperial Order of the Sun of the Persian Empire.

In that letter his Majesty refers, as the reason for his gracious gift, to the cordial friendship which has so long existed between the Governments of Persia and England; and he expresses the hope that this friendship may grow closer day by day.

In presenting His Majesty's letter, and the Insignia of the Imperial Order, Your Excellency dwelt upon the same subject, and expressed the same hope. You reminded me, on His Majesty's behalf, that the friendship between the two Governments had endured for generations past, and you foretold that, by the grace of God, it would continue to increase in the future until it should be a wonder to the world.

No words would be too strong to convey my appreciation of the sentiments which your Sovereign has been pleased to express, both in writing and through the agency of his trusted servant. Nor could I too warmly assure your Excellency, and through you His Majesty the Shah, that my own feelings are but the echo of His Majesty's.

I look back with hearty pleasure upon the unfailing good-will which the Government of the Shah has shown towards England; and I look forward with confidence and deep satisfaction to the continuance and increase of that good-will. Persia and England have many bonds of union, and there is no point upon which their interests should conflict. I hope and believe that in time to come the two nations will ever remain, as they are now, warm and constant friends; and that, to use your own words, their friendship will grow closer from generation to generation.

I would ask Your Excellency to inform His Majesty of what I have said, and to assure him that, while I am deeply sensible of the honour which His Majesty has done to Lady Dufferin and myself by the conferment of the Imperial Order, I shall value it above all, and Lady Dufferin will value it above all, as a sign of His Majesty's friendship towards our country.

I shall inform Her Majesty the Queen-Empress of what has passed to-day, and I feel sure that Her Gracious Majesty will hear of it with sincere satisfaction. To Lady Dufferin and myself it will be an additional source of pleasure in the future to remember that Her Excellency was invested with the insignia of the Imperial Order in this memorable year of Her Majesty's reign.

PUNJAB TENANCY BILL.

At the meeting of the Legislative Council which was held at Simla on 22nd September, 1887, Lord Dufferin made the following remarks on the motion that the Punjab Tenancy Bill be passed into law:—

Before putting this motion to the Council, I desire to congratulate my colleagues in the Government, as well as the members of the Legislative Council, upon the successful termination which has been reached in this important matter. Undoubtedly we are under the very greatest obligation to those members of the committee who have undertaken the responsible and laborious task of shaping this Bill in so careful and conscientious a manner. Although it is perfectly true that the proposed Act may, in some sort, be called an amending Act, there can be no doubt that any piece of legislation which touches such important and extensive interests, unless very carefully drawn, is liable to inflict both injury and injustice. I am quite convinced that, thanks to the ability and care with which the clauses of the Bill have been framed, this danger has been reduced to a minimum. I think we are also very much indebted to the Government of the Punjab for the manner in which they have given their attention to the subject. I also wish to express, on behalf of all my colleagues, our thanks to Mr. Peile for the interesting and clear manner in which he—and no man is in a better position than himself to undertake such a task—has described the general scope and objects of the measure.

With these few observations, I now beg to put the motion made by Colonel Wace that this Bill, as amended, be passed.

The motion was put and agreed to.

ADDRESSES FROM THE KURRACHEE CHAMBER OF COMMERCE, THE INHABITANTS OF SIND, THE MAHOMEDAN CENTRAL ASSOCIATION, AND THE SIND SABHA.

At Kurrachee, on 12th November, 1887, four deputations waited on the Viceroy: the first, from the Chamber of Commerce, with an address which was read by Mr. McInch, the President; the second, from the inhabitants of Sind, with an address which was read by Colonel Cory; the third, with an address from the Mahomedan Central Association which was read by Mr. Hassan Ali; and the fourth, from the Sind Sabha.

The Hyderabad-Pachpadra Railway was the subject principally referred to. Colonel Cory made a long statement in support of the prayer of the memorialists for a reconsideration of the railway project, on account of the grave mistakes as to figures and facts which he alleged had been made by the Public Works Department. Besides referring to several local wants, the Sind Sabha asked that Kurrachee should be made the headquarters of the Government of India; whilst the Mahomedan Association referred especially to the backward condition of their co-religionists.

Lord Dufferin replied collectively to the addresses as follows:—

GENTLEMEN,—It is needless to say that I have listened with the greatest interest, gratification, and attention to the several addresses which have been presented to me. I am very sensible of the kind and friendly spirit in which you have met me here to-day, and of the warm and friendly welcome which the representatives of this important province have been pleased to accord to me. Any one in my position feels very deeply touched by finding, wherever he goes amongst the various communities of India, the same universal loyalty towards the throne and person of our Sovereign, and the same generous desire to place confidence in the Government representing Her Majesty in this country. Personally, I desire to express to you, both on my own behalf and on that of Lady Dufferin, to whom a very friendly allusion has been made, our best and most grateful thanks for your kindness.

I will now turn for a few moments to some of the points which have been brought to my notice in your respective addresses; and, in the first place, I desire to recognise in the most ample manner not only the force and lucidity, but the moderation and good feeling which have characterized all your references to what is undoubtedly a very burning question in this neighbourhood—I allude to the extension of your railway communications. Of course, when a Viceroy finds himself alone, and separated from his councillors and constitutional advisers and from those technical experts upon whose special acquaintance with these particular subjects he is forced so much to rely, his natural inclination is perhaps to sympathize overmuch with those who appear before him, and who are generally able to make out a very strong and cogent case for the particular line of policy they advocate. Undoubtedly, were I an inhabitant of Kurrachee and were my material interests bound up with the prosperity of this province, I should feel as deeply as any one here present the force of those representations which you have submitted to me. Indeed, it would be impossible to dispute the correctness of the view you take that the extension of your railway communications towards the north-east would materially improve the prosperity of this town and neighbourhood, and I may say of the greater part of the province. But, as I said before, in replying to the address with which I was favoured yesterday, the Government of India in relation to questions of this kind always finds itself in a very difficult and embarrassing position. We are strictly enjoined by the Secretary of State—and recently his instructions have been more imperative than ever—not to expend, either directly or through the medium of a guarantee, more than a certain sum annually in the construction of railways. On the other hand, the Government of India, long before I came to the country, was irretrievably committed to the construction of a great number of lines which are still incomplete, and which consume annually almost the whole of the capital which we are allowed to borrow for such purposes. By postponing indefinitely some of these lines we should not only cause an unjustifiable amount of loss to the Government, but we should also imperil the lives of thousands, nay of millions, of our fellow-subjects in the districts liable to famine. Then, as I have already said to the deputation which addressed me yesterday, we have also to consider our obligations to the new province of Upper Burma. The construction of railways from one end of that province to the other is not only required for preserving peace amongst our new subjects, but is also necessary to enable the province to assume that position of financial equilibrium which can only be brought about by the natural development of its resources. Here in Kurrachee, when listening to the eloquent and forcible language addressed to him, a Viceroy is apt somewhat to overlook the other obligations which must present themselves to the mind of the Government, and the claims of your town are only too likely to assume almost an undue importance; but when he goes to Calcutta and again finds himself surrounded by his advisers, when he hears this question discussed in connection with the claims of other communities, then, perhaps, even against his own amiable inclinations, he may be forced to attach greater importance to other considerations which tell against your wishes. Be that, however, as it may, I can assure you that I will do my very best fairly to study all those arguments which have been advanced in your several addresses; and although it would be both unwise and unfair of me to hold out any hopes that the present decision of the Government will be reversed, this at all events I can promise you, that, as far as my own judgment is concerned, I shall be prepared to go into the question in a very thorough and earnest manner. I am sure, under the circumstances, those gentlemen whose addresses were principally concerned with the railway question will consider that I have given them as fair and as conciliatory an answer as the case permits.

Passing from that topic, therefore, I will now thank the Sind Sabha for their loyal and hospitable sentiments. I am glad to find that they have fully appreciated as it deserves the great boon that was conferred on India at large when my illustrious predecessor granted municipal self-government to various communities, and I have observed with pleasure the singularly modest manner in which they have referred to the working of that institution in their own province. That modesty and moderation is in itself an assurance to me that those citizens who have been entrusted with the responsibility of conducting the municipal business of their fellow-townsmen, are likely to fulfil their duties to the satisfaction of those whose affairs they administer, as well as to that of the Government, which will always watch, with the greatest interest, the successful development of these institutions.

I have noted what has been brought to my attention in regard to the fact that those two important commissions, the Civil Service Commission and the Financial Commission, did not visit Sind. I certainly share the regret of the members of Sind Sabha that that visit should have been omitted, and I will take care that, should it be my duty hereafter to appoint any commission of an equally universal character, the population of Sind will not have any cause to complain of similar neglect.

With regard to the suggestion that the capital of India should be transferred from its present locality to this port, I am afraid it is a proposal that is likely very much to flutter the hearts of the inhabitants of Calcutta, who are peculiarly sensitive to any question of the kind. Personally, I am always glad myself to be in the neighbourhood of the sea, and, as far as my short experience goes, it appears to me that the air of Kurrachee is exceptionally pleasant and invigorating; but at the same time, as I am always careful never to raise hopes which I see no immediate prospects of fulfilling, I do not like to bind myself by any promise on the subject.

It only remains for me now to thank the Mahomedan gentlemen whom I see before me for the kind and sympathetic manner in which they have approached me. They are perfectly right in thinking that the fact of my having passed so many years of my life in close contact with Mahomedan communities, and in official relations with Mahomedan Governments, has naturally inspired me with the deepest and most genuine sympathy with the Mahomedan subjects of Her Majesty in India; but, on the other hand, it must always be remembered that one of the most important and righteous functions of the Indian Government is to administer the affairs of the State with the most absolute impartiality, and with an equal distribution of sympathy amongst all the classes, races, and religious communities of which India is the home. What we desire to bring about is a condition of absolute impartiality as between race and race, religion and religion, community and community. But, though firmly determined, as long as I shall have the honour to retain the great and responsible office which I now hold, to preserve inviolate this traditional impartiality, and to avoid, even in thought, any departure from those principles, I am certainly, neither in my individual capacity nor as head of the State, precluded from recognising the undoubted fact that, owing to various circumstances and to historic forces over which they themselves have had no control, the Mahomedan community in many parts of India hardly finds itself in that satisfactory position to which it has a right to aspire. I am, however, happy to think that wherever I have gone I have found the Mahomedans themselves most ready and willing to acknowledge what is the principal reason for this state of things, as well as to create and to apply the necessary remedy. In this province I am glad to find that the Mahomedans have an earnest zeal for the promotion of education among the youth, and are showing that they, too, are determined no longer to remain behind in the race of progress upon which all the communities of India are so happily embarked.

With regard to those other special points to which my attention has been called, I would only observe that they are questions which fall rather within the jurisdiction of the local government than that of the Viceroy, and inasmuch as Sind has recently had the advantage of a visit from Lord Reay, one of the most experienced, most intellectually gifted, and most scholarly Governors that have ever been sent to India, it is to be supposed that the circumstances referred to have been brought to his notice, and that he and his Government in due time and place will do their best to apply such remedies as are compatible with those principles of absolute impartiality to which I have already referred.

I have now, gentlemen, touched upon almost every point except one, to which reference has been made, but I should certainly fail in my duty if I did not take this opportunity—the first which has presented itself—of expressing publicly, in the most cordial terms which I can command, my sympathy with that just pride with which the Mahomedan community have signalized the fact that, amongst all the native chiefs of India, a Mahomedan Prince, the Nizam, has been the first to come forward with one of the most noble and generous offers ever made to the Government. The whole Mahomedan community may be proud of his wisdom, of his patriotism, and of his loyalty; and it has already been my duty to express to His Highness personally, both in my own name and in that of my Government and of Her Majesty the Queen-Empress, our very deep sense of the noble manner in which he has acted.

In conclusion, gentlemen, addressing you all collectively, allow me again to thank you for the manner in which you have allowed me to ascertain your views and sentiments. I only wish you to believe that I have no higher ambition, no stronger hope, than to promote, as far as lies in my power, the interests of this place, which I fully acknowledge to be already one of the most important harbours which exist in India, and one which undoubtedly, as time goes on, is destined to assume even greater prominence, both as a commercial port and as one of the bases of military operations in India.

DURBAR AT PESHAWAR.

On the 25th of November, 1887, the Viceroy held a Durbar at Peshawar for the reception of the Chiefs and Sirdars of the frontier. The ceremony took place in a spacious shamiana, in the presence of a large assembly of European and native gentlemen. On the left of His Excellency were seated the Lieutenant-Governor of the Punjab, the Commander-in-Chief, Sir Theodore Hope, and other high officers of Government. The representatives of the frontier tribes were accompanied by their followers. After the presentations had been made the Viceroy delivered the following speech:—

PERSIAN TRANSLITERATION.

Sardárán wa Khánán,—

Har chand ki man mí-khwástam tá ín waḳt mará hích mauḳa-i-dídan-i-Pesháwar dast na dáda; wa azin amr ki man imrúz bá shumá dar injá naubat-i-awwal mulákí shudam khailé mahzúz wa masrúr gardídam.

Chunánki shumá mí-dáned man du hafta-i-guzashta rá dar daura-o-safar-i-azlá'-i-sarhadd-i-Daulat-i-bahiyya-i-Británia ki az Karáchí ba samt-i-shimál mumtadd mí-shawad sarf karda-am; wa man az yak sar ta dígar sar sarhadd,e pur amn-o-amún muláhaza namúdam ki dar ḳabza-i-mustahkam wa khúb muntazam ast. Har jáo ki búdam az mulá-haza-i-ásár-i-sarsabzí-i-kámil ki har já ham-ḳadam-i-istih-kám-i-Hukúmat-i-Daulat-i-bahiyya-i-Británia ast, mará farhat wa inbisát rú dáda. Zirá'at wa daulat dar-mián-i-mardum rú ba taraḳḳí-st; khutút-i-buzurg-i-ráh-i-áhan muta'ilik ba tadábír-i-harb-o-tijárat bar sath-i-mamlukat rú ba imtidád dárad. Rawábit-i-dústána bá hukmránhá wa sákinín-i-diár-i-khud-mukhtár' e ki án rúe sarhadd-i-má-st ḳáim ast. Ín wa dígar 'alámát-i-ummíd wa himmat afzá-i-ḳuwwat wa taraḳḳí ba har taraf ba muláhaza-i-man rasíd.

Wa alán ki man darín shahr-i-Pesháwar, ki zikr-i-án dar tawáríkh bisyár ast, wárid shudam, humán haḳáiḳ wa wáḳiát-i-numáyán mu'áyana shud. Railway y'aní ráh-i-áhan az mián-i-mulk-i-pur amn-o-amán wa sarsabz-o-shádab marú ín já rasáníd,; wa ín laḥza man ra'áyá-i-wafá-kísh wa ḳáni'-i-'Ulyá Ḥazraṭ-i-Malika-i-Mu' azzama wa*kh*awánín-i-bá ittiḥád wa malikán-i-aḳwám-i-*kh*ud-mu*kh*-ṭár rá ḍaur-o-ḥauz-i-*kh*uḍ mí-bínam. Unhárá man ba farḥat-o-inbisáṭ az jánib-i-sani'-ul-jawánib-i-Malika-i-Mu' azzama marḥabá wa *kh*ush-ámaḍed mí-gúyam.

Ba hama wa ba har yak az shumá wa ba sáḥib-man-sabún-i-shujá' wa ḳábil-i-Daulaṭ-i-bahiyya-i-Briṭánia, chih az ahl-i-Inglistán wa chi az sákinín-i-ín mulk ki ín sarhaḍd rá ánche hast sá*kh*ta-and, man az samím-i-ḳalb tahniaṭ wa mubárakbád mí-diham, wa ummíḍ mí-kunam ki tá ba bisyár pushthá amn-o-faláḥ dar mián-i-shumá ḳáim mánad. Wa man yaḳín mí-kunam ki rawábiṭ-i-ḍil*kh*wáh ki alán, na sirf hamráh-i-aḳwám-i-sarhaḍd balki bá ḥukmrán wa sákinín-i-Af*gh*ánistán bar ḳarár ast, mújib-i-bisyár istiḥḳám-i-ín amn-o-amán *kh*wáhad shud, ki ín amn-o-amán alán dar ín ḥissa-i-muhimma-i-Salṭanaṭ-i-Hind-i-'Ulyá Ḥazraṭ-i-Malika i Mau'azzama shái' ast.

The following is a translation of the above speech:—

GENTLEMEN, CHIEFS, AND SIRDARS,—Until now I have had no opportunity of visiting Peshawar, and as I have always wished to do so, it is with deep interest and pleasure I meet you here for the first time to-day. As you know, I have spent the last fortnight touring along the British border districts from Kurrachee northwards. I have found throughout a peaceful frontier, firmly held and firmly administered; and I have been gratified to observe, as I passed, the evidences of material prosperity which everywhere follow the establishment of British rule:—cultivation and wealth increasing among the people, great lines of strategical and commercial railways spreading themselves over the face of the land, and friendly relations existing with the rulers of the people in the independent tracts on the frontier. These and other hopeful and inspiring signs of progress have met me on every side, and now that I have arrived in this historical city I am impressed by the same significant facts. The railway has brought me here through a peaceful and prosperous country, and I stand at this moment surrounded by loyal and contented subjects of the Queen and by the friendly chiefs and representatives of the independent tribes whom I am rejoiced to welcome in Her Majesty's name. To one and all of you, and to the brave and able officers of the British Government in India who have made the border what it is, I offer my heartiest congratulations; and I hope that for many generations to come peace and prosperity may continue among you. I am confident that the friendly relations now established, not only with the border tribes but with the ruler of Afghanistan, will do much to strengthen the feeling of rest and security which prevails in this important portion of Her Majesty's empire.

ADDRESS FROM THE PESHAWAR MUNICIPALITY.

After the conclusion of the Durbar at Peshawar on the 25th of November, the Viceroy and party, including the Commander-in-Chief and the Lieutenant-Governor of the Punjab, drove through the city in the afternoon. Outside the Edwardes Gate the Yusufzai armour men were drawn up, and guards of honour of 100 men with band were placed inside the Kotwali and Gor Khatri.

At the Tahsil, Lord Dufferin received a loyal address from the Municipal Committee, to which His Excellency replied as follows:—

GENTLEMEN,—I desire to express to you my warmest thanks for the kind reception you have prepared for me on entering your city. It so happens that during the first year of my residence in India I had formed all my plans with the intention of coming amongst you, for though you allude to Peshawar in very modest terms, I can assure you that in the estimation of the rest of your fellow-subjects, whether native or English, it is regarded as one of the most important cities in Hindustan. Now at last I have been able to accomplish my desire, and I need not say with what pleasure I have driven through your orderly streets, or how deeply I feel those marks of respect which I have encountered on every side at the hands of its inhabitants. As you are aware, during the past two or three weeks I have been engaged in visiting the whole of the frontier of British India from Kurrachee to this place, and I have been glad to find wherever I have gone, the marks of prosperity, of contentment, of good government, of loyalty, and of peace, which characterise what at one time was a distracted and disorderly region. One of the great benefits of British rule, which every one in India, I think, is ready to acknowledge, is that, wherever the sway of Her Majesty extends, there at all events, peace is insisted on, and justice is administered with impartiality to all persons, no matter to what community or to what religion they may belong. I have also to congratulate you upon what is always a matter of importance to those inhabiting a frontier region; namely, upon the amicable relations between us and our immediate neighbours. A most excellent understanding exists between the Government of Her Majesty and the Government and people of Afghanistan; and there is no doubt that the recent conclusion of the frontier convention with Russia—which was inaugurated, to his credit be it said, by my illustrious predecessor—will still further add to that feeling of satisfaction to which I have already referred.

I am glad to learn from the authorities of your town whom I have met that its condition is prosperous and its trade flourishing, and that every year the industries of its inhabitants attain greater dimensions. I have no doubt that under your auspicious direction that satisfactory state of things will continue, and that Peshawar will become year by year a still greater and more prosperous city among the great and prosperous cities of Hindustan.

OPENING OF THE DUFFERIN BRIDGE, BENARES.

On Friday, the 16th December, 1887, the Viceroy arrived at the bridge soon after noon. There was a large gathering of ladies and gentlemen, and His Excellency at once proceeded to the dais, accompanied by the Duchess of Montrose; Sir Auckland Colvin, Lieutenant-Governor, North-Western Provinces; the Maharaja of Benares; the Kumar Sahib; and the members of His Excellency's personal staff. Colonel Jenkins, agent of the Oudh and Rohilkhund Railway, read a history of the bridge, after which His Excellency addressed the assembly as follows:—

Your Honour, Ladies and Gentlemen,—We have all listened with the greatest interest to the clear and lucid account which has been read by Colonel Jenkins of the manner in which this bridge was originally initiated, its design conceived, and its subsequent construction accomplished. I confess that, in hearing that description, the feeling impressed upon my mind was one of wonder that the structure should ever have come into existence at all; but I believe that, if only we give them enough money—and in that direction engineers seem to imagine that our supplies are inexhaustible (laughter)—there is nothing which the mechanical skill of the present day is unable to accomplish. (Cheers.) Be that, however, as it may, I cannot sufficiently express to Colonel Jenkins, the representative of the company, Sir John Pender, its chairman, and to all its directors, how deeply I feel the compliment paid to me in calling this bridge after me, and at their request I give it the name of the Dufferin Bridge.

The assembly then adjourned to lunch in an adjoining shamiana. After the tables were cleared, Colonel Jenkins proposed the health of the Viceroy, and Lord Dufferin in reply spoke as follows:—

Ladies and Gentlemen,—I need not say that I am very sensible of the kind reception you have given to the toast which has been proposed in such flattering terms by Colonel Jenkins. It is, however, even a greater satisfaction to me that the interesting ceremony upon which we have been this day engaged should have attracted to Benares so large a gathering of distinguished and influential persons, both European and native, for it indicates how fully the significance of these great triumphs of engineering skill are appreciated by all the intelligent classes in this country. (Cheers.) To me personally the completion of the Dufferin Bridge has been an especial source of pleasure, not merely on account of the kind thought which inspired the directors of the company when they gave the bridge my name—though no one could desire his service in India to be associated with a more noble monument—nor on account of its having brought me into contact more closely than otherwise might have been the case with

His Highness the Maharaja (cheers) as well as with many of the other distinguished inhabitants of the famous city of Benares; but chiefly because the great and arduous engineering task of bridging the Ganges, at what is perhaps the most interesting as well as the most difficult part in all its course, has been executed under the immediate superintendence of Mr. Walton, whose father is one of the dearest and kindest friends I ever had, having been the instructor of my earliest youth—an instructor, I may mention in passing, who knew the principles recommended by King Solomon—(laughter), and who, I am happy to think, is still alive to witness and rejoice in the success and triumph of his accomplished son. (Cheers.) This is now the fifth or sixth great bridge that I have passed over during my recent travels, and I do not know to what more striking proof we could point of the benefits which the British Government is conferring, not merely upon the trade, commerce, and industry, but upon the social life of the people of India, than to these stupendous instruments of communication which are so rapidly unifying the interests, harmonizing the modes of life, thought, and feeling, and consolidating the sympathies of the various races, states, and communities which, under the mysterious guidance of Providence, have been united into one great imperial whole beneath the benign sway of Her Most Gracious Majesty. (Loud cheers.) But however much we may have occasion to admire the technical skill by which all these great works are characterised, I imagine I am right in saying that nowhere in India has a more difficult engineering task been performed than that whose triumphant accomplishment we celebrate to-day. Nor, in connection with it, can I resist the temptation of offering my humble meed of admiration and my best congratulations to those eminent gentlemen whose knowledge of their profession, whose practical skill, and whose fertility of resource, have enabled them to triumph over every impediment, and to master and enthral the gigantic forces of nature with which they were contending. (Applause.) To Mr. Hederstedt, the present chief engineer of the Oudh and Rohilkhund Railway, belongs the praise of having designed the structure, and of having organized the method of its erection. On the shoulders of Mr. Walton, as I have already mentioned, has fallen the unceasing and anxious responsibility of its construction ; while the late Mr. Batho, Sir Bradford Leslie, Colonel Jenkins, and Mr. Sydney Hartwell, have each and all in their various spheres contributed their experience and their valuable counsels to the successful termination of the work. (Cheers.) Nor, in mentioning the names of these distinguished persons must I omit those of their subordinate coadjutors—I mean the superintendents and skilled artizans who, with indomitable pluck, and in spite of the discouragement of sickness and a trying climate, have seconded Mr. Walton's efforts with so much loyal gallantry. (Applause.) Ladies and gentlemen, so many and so numerous are the reflections which such an occasion as this naturally suggests to us all, that one might continue for a long time to enlarge upon so interesting a topic ; but I am always unwilling to trespass too long upon the indulgence of audiences who never fail to accord to the representative of the Queen an indulgent and sympathetic attention. Still, before concluding, I must in a few words express my thanks for the friendly terms in which Colonel Jenkins has referred to the Government of India, as well as for the manner in which you were pleased to receive his observations. All I can say is that my colleagues and myself will do our best to merit a continuance of the confidence you have accorded to us. It is true that at the commencement of my term of office unexpected circumstances forced upon us a policy, both with regard to Burma and our military preparations, which, had it been possible, we should willingly have avoided ; but I am happy to think that at present I do not see any reason to anticipate any disturbing causes to divert the attention of our administration from internal progress and improvement and those works of peace upon which the happiness of the people so largely depends. (Cheers.) Ladies and gentlemen, I again thank you from the bottom of my heart for the kind way in which you have received the mention of my name. (Loud applause.)

CUSTOMS DUTY ON PETROLEUM.

In the Legislative Council which met at Calcutta on Friday, 27th January, 1888, Mr. Westland, the Finance Member of the Viceroy's Council, moved for leave to introduce a bill for levying a customs duty on petroleum, and made an exhaustive statement explanatory of the financial position of the Indian Government.

His Excellency the Viceroy spoke as follows:—

GENTLEMEN,—I do not think it necessary at this stage of the proceedings to trouble the Council with any special observations in regard to the motion before it. But I cannot help expressing my satisfaction at hearing from our honourable colleague Rájá Peári Mohun Mukerji that the recent increase which we have made in the salt duty has met with his approval. Representing so fully as he does the views of the intelligent and educated native community of India, that expression of opinion on his part is very valuable. Of course it is with extreme reluctance that any one in my position can give his consent to any increase to the burdens of the people of India. Unfortunately it has become my lot on two several occasions to add to the taxation of the country. But, in justification of this hard necessity, it is sufficient for me to remark that since my arrival in India, owing to the depreciation in the price of silver, the annual accumulative loss to the Government has progressively increased year by year by a million pounds sterling. The loss in 1884-85, when I first took up the reins of Government, stood at £3,400,000; in 1885-86 it amounted to £4,400,000; in 1886-87 to £5,400,000; and now in 1887-88 to £6,200,000. But, even in the presence of these growing embarrassments, I would certainly have been unwilling to agree to an increase of the salt tax, had it not been, as the Honourable Mr. Westland has most clearly explained to the Council, that a somewhat unexpected loss of revenue had declared itself during the last year under two other heads—through a fall in the price of opium and in our railway receipts. As the Government would not have been in a position to suggest to the Council on other grounds than those of mere conjecture that any improvement would take place in future years under the head of exchange, or even under either of the other two heads of income I have referred to, it became obviously our duty at once to strengthen our financial position and to provide ourselves with a working surplus. By the executive measure which we adopted a few days ago, and by the bill which is now about to be introduced into the Council, I trust that this satisfactory result will be obtained. I am very glad that my honourable friend Mr. Westland has noticed the circumstances under which the Government was induced to issue a *Gazette* notification raising the salt duty. In acting as we have done, we have merely acted in accordance with the intentions of an Act of the Legislature which placed us in possession of those powers which we have put in motion. To have adopted any other course would have been undesirable. To have given the kind of notice which some persons seem to have wished would have only benefited a certain number of individuals at the expense of the community at large. I can quite understand that my honourable colleague Rájá Peári Mohun Mukerji should have felt himself—and in that respect he has merely expressed what, I am sure, is the feeling of his colleagues—unable at this stage of the proceedings to enter into any of those larger questions of finance which my honourable friend Mr. Westland has brought to the notice of the Council. But I hope that he will appreciate the desire of the Government of India, in submitting to the Council so full a financial statement as that made by Mr. Westland, to profit by the experience and advice of those eminent gentlemen I see around me.

The motion was put and agreed to.

CUSTOMS DUTY ON PETROLEUM.

At the meeting of the Legislative Council held at Calcutta on Friday, the 3rd February, 1888, the Hon. Mr. Westland, the Finance Member of the Viceroy's Council, moved that the bill for levying a customs duty on petroleum be referred to a select committee consisting of the Hon. Messrs. Scoble, Whiteside, Steel, and the mover.

At the conclusion of the debate which ensued His Excellency the Viceroy spoke as follows:—

Gentlemen,—Our honourable colleague the Finance Member may certainly be congratulated on the candid and generous manner in which his financial statement has been received by all the members of this Council; and it is gratifying to the Government to feel that not only do we possess the unanimous approval and support of the Council, but that we may fairly conclude that the views which have been expressed by Mr. Steel in his very weighty speech, by Mr. Evans, and by all the native members, are the reflex of that intelligent public opinion which they are so well entitled to represent. The question has been so ably dealt with by every member who has spoken, and the consensus of opinion is so general, that it is unnecessary for me to trouble the Council further. Of course the real difficulty attending our financial policy is the instability of silver. With an uncertainty of that kind introduced into all his calculations, no Finance Minister can ever enjoy any real repose. He must be always conscious that in the unknown future there may exist contingencies which will upset all his calculations and destroy the anticipated equilibrium in his budget; but from the very nature of the case all that the Government can do is to exercise its best intelligence in calculating the probabilities of the actual situation, and leave the ultimate issue in the hands of Providence. As I have already had occasion to say, had it not been for the fall in silver which has made me three millions a year a poorer Viceroy than I was when I first came to the country, I think we might, notwithstanding even the fall in opium and the expenditure in Burma, have tided over our present difficulties without any resort to increased taxation. From what I have recently heard from our minister in China it does not seem likely that any very considerable change in the mercantile relations between China and India as regards opium is likely to ensue. Again, though we have no right to allow such an anticipation to influence our practical policy, we may fairly hope that our railway receipts will gradually recover. With regard to Burma, there is no doubt that, although during the last year the expenditure has been very heavy, heavier even than was anticipated, it will be a diminishing charge, and even in the budget we are now preparing a change for the better will be shown. Moreover, it must be remembered that Lower Burma may soon be expected, if not altogether, at all events to a considerable extent, to be able to carry Upper Burma on its back. It is true the surplus revenue of Lower Burma which annually accrues over and above the expenses of its own administration and now amounts to nearly a million, only represents the fair share which that province might be called upon to pay towards the general imperial expenses of administration; but, on the other hand, it is clear that if Lower Burma did not exist, the large sums which for some years past we have received from thence would have had to be supplied by India herself from extra taxation from which she has now been relieved. Consequently, were the accounts of the two provinces to be united, the deficit in regard to Upper Burma, even for the present, will be found to be inconsiderable. It will be interesting to the Council to know that not only are we daily receiving satisfactory proofs of the rapidity with which Upper Burma is settling down and order is being established, but that we have made most satisfactory progress in dealing with all those subordinate questions which affect the Shan States and our relations both with Siam and China. It has been stated that this Government has determined upon the subjugation of the Shan States, and that we are about to send a *corps d'armée* in order to carry this purpose into effect. Such an observation only shows how very great is the misconception which prevails in regard to the political and geographical condition of what are known as the Shan States. As you are aware, Burma may be described as a broad valley traversed by the Irrawaddy and the Chindwin, with the Arracan mountains on the western side, and a corresponding high plateau on the eastern side. It is upon this plateau, which extends as far as the Salween, that the Burmese Shan States are situated. These states have always been subject to Upper Burma, and when we took possession of that country we sent messages to their various chiefs that from henceforth they were to regard Her Majesty the Queen as their Sovereign. This information was received upon their part in a satisfactory manner, and they suggested that we should send up some officers to settle the exact nature of their future relations with us. We have taken advantage of the cold weather to despatch two political officers into the Shan States, accompanied each by a small column. These gentlemen have traversed the whole district from one end to the other in perfect security, and have been everywhere received in a cordial manner both by the population and by the various chiefs. Not only so, but our agents have met on the extreme eastern frontier of Shan Burma the authorities of Siam, and have come to a preliminary understanding with them as to the frontier which is hereafter to divide the Shan States under British rule from those under Siamese jurisdiction. But what perhaps is even a more gratifying feature in the situation is the fact that the government of His Majesty the Emperor of China is exhibiting towards us a most friendly spirit, and is doing everything we could desire to render the settlement of that part of Burma which borders on China easy and successful. The Viceroy of Yunnan has received instructions to order the officials on the Chinese frontiers to cultivate friendly relations with us, and the effect of this action upon the part of China is now becoming very marked. I may mention, as an additional proof of the desire of China to exhibit a conciliatory spirit towards the Government of India, that she is using her best efforts to induce the garrison of Thibetans, who have passed beyond their own frontier and built a fort on a road which was made by the Indian Government in Sikkim—a road over which we have definite and strict legal rights—to retire within their own territories. Consequently, although, as must always be the case in a new province recently added to the empire, a very considerable outlay will be necessary in Burma with the view to furnishing it with roads, jails, barracks, and public buildings, and for the purpose of opening up what are undoubtedly its large material resources, I do not think that any one need apprehend that our expenditure in Burma will eventually prove a source of financial embarrassment to the Indian Government. Thanking the members of the Council for the patience with which they have listened to my few observations, for the generous spirit in which they have received the financial statement which has been placed before them, as well as for the valuable suggestions which have fallen from various members, I proceed to put the motion, namely, that the bill to provide for the levying of a customs duty on petroleum be referred to a select committee consisting of the Honourable Messrs. Scoble, Whiteside, Steel, and Westland.

The Motion was adopted.

COUNTESS OF DUFFERIN'S FUND.

The Viceroy presided at the annual meeting of the supporters of the "Countess of Dufferin's Fund for providing medical aid to the women of India," held in the Town Hall, Calcutta, on Wednesday, the 8th February, 1888. In reply to a resolution thanking him for presiding on the occasion, His Excellency said:—

LADIES AND GENTLEMEN,—I feel that it is not from you to me, but from me to you, that thanks are due for the privilege afforded to me of presiding on this occasion, for who is there that would not feel gratified to find himself associated with those patriotic gentlemen who, by their generosity and energy, whether as members of the committee, as subscribers to the fund, or as general supporters of our institution, have so ably seconded the efforts of our Lady President? (Applause.) When we first met here three years ago, we must have felt that, after all, we were embarking upon a tentative experiment; but no one, I am sure, can leave this room to-night without feeling that the institution has been placed upon a basis which can never fail, and that henceforth and for ever its benevolent operations will extend wider and wider, and penetrate further and further into the homes of India. (Cheers.) Not only so, ladies and gentlemen, but there is another reason on account of which I feel proud to be present upon this platform. To-night we have received the assistance of the brother of one of the noblest Viceroys that ever presided over the destinies of this country (cheers), who sacrificed his life in the discharge of his duty, and to whose memory the affectionate reminiscences of the grateful people of India still cling with undying fidelity. (Applause.) Then again, on the other side of me there sits the daughter of one of the most illustrious statesmen that ever left the shores of England in order to devote their great talents and undaunted energies to the service of their country, the memory of whose achievements will last as long as history itself. He, too, ladies and gentlemen, it will be remembered, laid down his life for India, for though he left these shores alive, he soon afterwards succumbed to those unparalleled labours which signalized his Viceroyalty. Ladies and gentlemen, I also desire to thank those who have addressed you, and you who have so generously accepted their observations, for the kind way in which Lady Dufferin has been remembered by you on this occasion. (Applause.) There is no one perhaps more capable than myself of bearing testimony to the constant and earnest attention which Her Excellency is continually paying to your interests; for only too frequently when the hard labours of my office are concluded, and I repair to the retirement of my zenana for the purpose of seeking that repose which my conscience tells me I have earned, I am grievously disappointed by finding Her Excellency so closely engaged upon the various matters connected with her "fund," that she is unable to pay me any attention whatsoever. (Cheers and laughter.) Nor, ladies and gentlemen, must I forget on this occasion to pay, on behalf of the committee and on your behalf, a well-merited tribute of gratitude to a gentleman of whose exertions and of whose devotion and industry I cannot speak in too high terms, but who, very much to his own regret, has now been compelled to dissociate himself from those labours which he has so efficiently discharged, and to which he is so much attached—I allude to your late honorary secretary, Major Cooper. (Cheers.) Though we have been sufficiently fortunate in finding a successor who, I am sure, will be prepared to tread conscientiously in his footsteps, of this I am certain, that you will never have a more devoted or a more single-minded friend and servant than Major Cooper. (Cheers.)

Ladies and gentlemen, it now only remains for me to thank you for the kind reception you have given me, and to congratulate you, as I do with all my heart, upon the proud position which you have already attained, and which I hope you will seek still further to improve, for I trust that you will never rest until the capital sum in your possession shall at all events reach the very moderate figure of a hundred thousand pounds. (Applause.)

ANNOUNCEMENT OF HIS EXCELLENCY'S RESIGNATION OF THE OFFICE OF VICEROY.

At the close of the business of the Legislative Council held at Calcutta on Friday, the 10th February, 1888, His Excellency addressed the members as follows in reference to the announcement of his resignation of the office of Viceroy at the end of the year 1888, which had appeared in the newspapers on the preceding day:—

GENTLEMEN,—It would be scarcely respectful that I should allow the members of this Council, with whom I have been so frequently associated in devising legislative measures for the good of this country, to separate without referring to the announcement which was made public yesterday, that I had obtained the permission of Her Majesty's Government to resign the Viceroyalty of India at the end of the present year. It may be well imagined that no one in my situation would take such a step without feeling both pain and regret; for the post I am now filling is at once the most honourable and the most important that can be held by a subject of the Crown. It was with no light heart that I accepted it, and it is with a deep sense of the responsibility I owe to my Sovereign, to my fellow-countrymen at home, and, above all, to the inhabitants of India, that I have endeavoured, however imperfectly, to discharge the laborious duties attaching to it. I desire it, therefore, to be understood that I have been actuated by imperative private considerations alone in pursuing the course I have adopted. From the time I set foot in India till the present moment not a shadow of difference has arisen between myself and the Government at home, nor, as I trust, have I in any way forfeited the confidence of the Secretary of State. Indeed, I cannot sufficiently express my deep gratitude for the generous support I have received at the hands of the successive ministers who have presided over the India Office since 1884. Neither has anything occurred in India itself to render my position as Viceroy less agreeable or less attractive than it was when I first came to the country. On the contrary, from the entire European community, from all classes of my native fellow-subjects, whether Hindu or Mahomedan, whether princes or private persons, whether in Calcutta or in other localities, I have received constant and innumerable tokens of sympathy and good-will. I only wish I had been better able by my public exertions to show my appreciation of so much loyalty and kindness. Domestic reasons alone have induced me to return home a year before the regular effluxion of my term; but, after all, it must be remembered that in limiting my service in India to four years, I shall have stayed in this country as long, or almost as long, as any of my immediate predecessors, and four years of such constant labour and anxiety as a Viceroy is called upon to bear are almost as much as is good for any one, so that I cannot but feel it may be for the public interest that I should resign my charge into the hands of a younger man, especially as the general political condition of the country, whether we regard its domestic affairs or its external relations, is prosperous and peaceful. Had it been otherwise, I would have gladly sacrificed every personal consideration in the cause of duty. With regard to my successor, all I can say is that had the choice lain with me, he is the very person whom I would have suggested, possessing, as he does, every quality to recommend him to the confidence of the Crown and of the nation. A grandson of one of our most venerable statesmen, and initiated from his earliest youth in the conduct of serious political affairs, he is now discharging the duties of Governor-General of Canada in a manner equally satisfactory to the people of that great Dominion and to the Government at home. He is in the prime of life, and married to one of the most charming ladies that ever graced London society, and whether as presiding over the social or the political world of India, I prophesy for him universal popularity and acceptance. Gentlemen, I feel that I have already occupied you too long with my own personal affairs, but my great gratitude for your constant kindness and assistance, and the friendly regard in which I hold every member of this Council, have induced me to trouble you with these observations.

THE VICEROY'S ADDRESS TO THE MEMBERS OF THE LEGISLATIVE COUNCIL, IN CALCUTTA.

At the conclusion of the business of the Legislative Council held in Calcutta on Friday, 23rd March, 1888, His Excellency the Viceroy addressed the members present as follows:—

GENTLEMEN,—This Council will now adjourn *sine die*, and as it will probably not be my good fortune to preside again over so full a meeting, or in the presence of His Honour the Lieutenant-Governor of Bengal, I trust I may be permitted to express my deep sense of obligation to all its members for the great assistance which they have given to the Government in the discharge of its legislative duties. I especially desire to tender my thanks to the non-official members who have been good enough to sacrifice their time and pretermit their private and professional pursuits in order to devote their energies to the business of the country, and to give us the advantage of their experience. I can assure them that, as representatives of an independent public opinion and of those various important interests which form so large an element in the Indian commonwealth, my colleagues and myself have welcomed their presence and assistance with the greatest satisfaction. I also wish to convey to our native colleagues my deep sense of the ability with which, from time to time, they have handled the various matters which have come up for consideration. The manner in which they debate the several questions under discussion in a language which is not their own, has always been to me a matter of surprise and admiration. I have been equally struck by the good temper, the courtesy, and gentlemanlike bearing with which they engage even in the warmest controversies. I think I may congratulate the Council on the very considerable amount of work which has been done during the four sessions over which I have presided. The number of bills which have been passed has been no less than 73. Amongst these may be mentioned the Bengal Tenancy Bill, the Oudh Rent Act, the Provincial Small Cause Courts Act, the Indian Marine Act, the Punjab Tenancy Act, the Punjab Land Revenue Act, the Invention and Designs Act, and last, though by no means least, the Debtors Act. It must always be remembered that the debates which take place round this table and to which the public are admitted, form but a very small part of the labours of the Legislative Council, inasmuch as the time, thought, and attention devoted to bills in committee are infinitely greater than that which the Council when assembled in its full numbers is required to give them. It is true the bills I have enumerated do not belong to that category which excite abnormal and universal attention throughout the country, but they have not for that reason been the less beneficent in their operation. In fact, if we regard our land legislation alone as it affects Bengal, Oudh, and the Punjab, it will be found that the labours of this Council have contributed vastly to the security, happiness, and content of many millions of our fellow-subjects. I have also especially to express my thanks to the Legislative Department, and I shall always remember with gratitude the industry and devotion which Mr. Ilbert and Mr. Scoble, assisted by Mr. James, have given to the preparation of these various Acts which have eventually secured the assent of the Legislature. Neither their colleagues nor the general public have any adequate idea of the amount of thought, correspondence, labour, and research which are necessary before a bill can even be brought up for the consideration of the Council. I am glad to be able to add that experience has proved—and a sufficient time has now elapsed to justify the statement—that the legislation upon which we have been engaged during the last four years, what-

ever opinions or doubts existed at the time, is now admitted
to have been necessary and desirable, and to have worked
advantageously.

PRESENTATION OF FAREWELL ADDRESSES TO THE EARL AND COUNTESS OF DUFFERIN IN THE TOWN HALL, CALCUTTA, IN VIEW OF THEIR DEPARTURE FROM INDIA.

On the evening of Friday, the 23rd March, 1888, a very large and enthusiastic gathering of the general public of Calcutta and of the neighbouring stations assembled in the Calcutta Town Hall to witness the formal presentation of the farewell addresses from the inhabitants of Bengal which had been voted at a recent meeting of the public to Their Excellencies the Earl and Countess of Dufferin.

On the arrival of Their Excellencies they were received by His Honour the Lieutenant-Governor of Bengal, Sir Comer Petheram, and other members of the committee, and were greeted by the assembled public with repeated cheers and acclamations.

The proceedings opened with the reading of the address to the Viceroy by Sir Steuart Bayley, Lieutenant-Governor of Bengal, to which His Excellency replied as follows:—

GENTLEMEN,—I am sure you will readily understand that it is almost impossible for me to express in words my deep sense of the honour conferred upon me by the presentation of such an address as that which you have just read. To be assured of the good-will, the confidence, and the approval of his fellow-countrymen and fellow-subjects, whether English or native, is the highest and the most legitimate reward to which a person in my situation can aspire. (Cheers.) Indeed, the marks of approbation which I have received from so many different quarters have taken me almost by surprise. A Viceroy is so continually engaged every hour of the day in labours requiring all his energy and attention, problem after problem presses so uninterruptedly upon his consideration, that he has not even breathing-time to ask himself whether he is satisfying the expectations of his friends or the reverse. (Cheers.) Nay, more, the issues with which he is confronted are so vast and far-reaching, affecting as they do the destinies of millions and millions of men, that his own individuality and personal interests sink into insignificance in the presence of these mighty multitudes for whose welfare he is responsible. (Applause.) And it is very fortunate that this should be the case, for I cannot conceive a greater danger to India than that a man, in assuming this great office, should be preoccupied with such trivial considerations as his fame or popularity. (Cheers.) His duty is to efface himself as much as possible, and to forget his own identity in his devotion to those absorbing duties with which he is intrusted. It is in accordance with this golden rule that my illustrious predecessors have invariably lived and laboured, and it is the same spirit of self-abnegation and unostentatious devotion to duty, irrespective of recognition or reward, that has characterised the successive generations of those public servants of all ranks who, at the sacrifice of ease, health, and even life itself, have built up the India of to-day—the loyal, contented, and prosperous India of Queen Victoria. (Loud cheers.) Nor, in thanking you for the kind expressions you use towards me, must I forget to remind you that it is to the Government of India and to my colleagues that the largest measure of the approval you are pleased to bestow upon me is justly due. If I have succeeded in steering the ship of State with success through the troublous period we have recently traversed, it is owing to their wise assistance in council, and to the energy and skill with which they have administered their several departments. (Applause.) Not only so, but it must also be remembered that a great deal of the harvest reaped in one Viceroyalty is the fruit of the seed sown and the labours inaugurated in the preceding reign, and I gladly acknowledge that much of the policy of the existing Indian Government which has met with cordial acceptance, both here and at home, received its original impulse from my predecessor, with whom, as is well known, originated the demarcation of the northern frontier of Afghanistan, the retention of Quetta and the Harnai line, and similar measures. The settlement finally arrived at between ourselves and Russia, though some people make light of it, is in my eyes a most valuable diplomatic achievement, and I venture to think that our policy as a whole in that region has been eminently successful. (Cheers.) The fixing of the confines of India proper at the Amran range has placed us in possession of an advanced military position of almost impregnable strength, and my interview with the Amir not only prevented a war which would certainly have broken out between England and Russia in connection with the Panjdeh affair had he not been in my camp when that sinister event occurred, but by the knowledge it gave me of his character, wishes, and modes of thought, and by the mutual good feeling which was then established, it has enabled me to secure his assent to the Russo-Afghan agreement, and to deal with many other delicate questions which have since arisen between us, in a manner to increase and corroborate his confidence in the friendship and good faith of the English Government. (Applause.) Nor is it merely with the Amir himself that better relations have been established; the Afghan people generally have assumed a totally different attitude towards us during the last three years from that which previously prevailed, as was exemplified not only when Sir West Ridgeway and his companions returned through Cabul to India, but in a still more remarkable degree by the cordial reception given to our boundary escorts at those very places near which a little while ago they dared not even pass by reason of the hostility of the inhabitants. (Cheers.)

Turning to the next topic upon which you have touched, the conquest of Burma, I need not assure you that it is a great satisfaction to me that our policy in this respect should meet with your approval. War is always a hateful and an evil thing; no one detests the very thought of war more heartily than myself. Again, annexation, the increase of our territories, and consequently of our responsibilities, is confessedly undesirable; yet I never had a clearer conviction of anything in my life than as to the necessity, under the then existing circumstances, of extending our control over the whole of the Irrawaddy valley. (Applause.) What was Burma? It was neither a government nor a kingdom. There was no central authority. Even after massacring most of his relatives and kindred, the king did not dare to leave the precincts of his palace. His whole territory was the theatre of anarchy and lawlessness. One half of the population lived by plundering the other half. The local chiefs were cruel and rapacious brigands, extorting money from the helpless villagers at the point of the sword. A Chinese horde had a short time previously taken possession of one of Burma's most important northern towns, and the government of Mandalay had embarked upon a line of diplomacy which would have infallibly brought us into hostile collision with a great European power. (Cheers.) English merchants who had sunk large sums at the express invitation of the Burmese Government in developing the resources of the country were treated with the greatest injustice, and the friendly remonstrances of the Government of India on their behalf were replied to with insolence and contempt; while the total disintegration of all civil society in Upper Burma was exercising a most pernicious and baneful influence on the peace and prosperity of our own province. In these circumstances something had to be done; and if only the moderate and benevolent terms of the Indian Government had been accepted, the tottering Court of Ava might have been kept upon its legs a little longer, though under no conceivable circumstances could the catastrophe have been very long delayed. As it was, our proposals were met with a cry of insolent defiance, and, as a consequence, Upper Burma became a province of the British Empire. (Cheers.) I am well aware that this result has not been regarded with great satisfaction by some of our fellow-subjects. On the one hand, they could hardly be expected to look at the question from the imperial standpoint, while, on the other, they naturally dreaded the expense inevitably attending conquest; but it is evident, even taking the most restricted view of the matter, that India was bound, after drawing for several years a surplus revenue of a million a year from Lower Burma, to come to the assistance of the province when it had become so obviously necessary to provide for its protection. Nor do I think that any apprehension need be entertained as to the ultimate financial effect of what we have done. (Cheers.) At first, of course, there must be a great deal of expenditure on courts of justice, barracks, jails, and the other appliances of civilization, but the more we know about the country the more extensive and the richer seems to be its resources, and the more certain it is that in the course of some years it will become an even more prolific contributer to the Indian Exchequer than Lower Burma. (Loud applause.) In any event, the verdict of history I am sure will pronounce that by establishing in that unfortunate country order, security, peace, and justice, in the place of anarchy, rapine, torture, and murder, and by replacing the late king's helpless and hopeless administration by the temperate and benign rule of Queen Victoria, we have reached a consummation as beneficent as it was unavoidable. (Cheers.)

I approach the next topic to which you have alluded with great reluctance, notwithstanding the gracious language in which you have been pleased to clothe your reference. How can the head of any Government reflect otherwise than with pain and regret on the hard fate which has compelled him on two repeated occasions to add to the burdens of the people? That after this he should be regarded with tolerance and equanimity would itself argue great generosity of nature in those to whom he has dealt such hard measure; but the fact of their so candidly recognising the necessity of these unpopular expedients, which, in the case of the income-tax, so immediately affects our industrious classes and the Civil Service, is indeed to pour coals of fire on his head. (Applause.)

To the Finance Committee and to the Public Service Committee I can turn, however, with a far happier feeling; for if ever two committees did their work honestly, thoroughly, and effectually, it is those two bodies; and glad am I to have this opportunity of expressing my deep thanks to Sir Charles Elliott and Sir Charles Aitchison, and their respective colleagues, for the great services they have rendered to the Government by their arduous labours. (Applause.) The report of the Finance Committee will, I hope, soon be in possession of the public. That of the Civil Service Committee has already, I believe, been laid on the table of the House of Commons, and it is now in the hands of the local governments, on receipt of whose opinion it will be at once dealt with by the Government of India. (Applause.)

Leaving, however, these two important topics, I turn even with greater pleasure to your allusions to the noble spirit which has been recently displayed by the feudatory princes and chieftains of India. Most heartily do I agree with you in all that you have said in their regard, for certainly a finer example of patriotism and loyalty has seldom been witnessed than that displayed by these august personages. (Cheers.) The Nizam, the Gaekwar, Holkar, the Maharaja of Cashmere, the martial chiefs of Rajputana and of the Punjab—one and all, with an enthusiasm and a spontaneity without parallel, have not merely made offers of large sums of money, but have placed their persons, their swords, and all the resources of their states at the disposal of Her Most Gracious Majesty. (Cheers.) What more signal justification could we have of that sound and generous policy which has made their power, their independence, and their dignity an integral part of the imperial system! Most of them are my personal friends; and though here and there may be a ruler less appreciative than his fellows of the responsibilities imposed upon him by his great position, without flattery I can say that, both as regards their private characters, their sense of duty, their desire to benefit their subjects, and their friendly feelings towards the British Government, there is every cause for satisfaction. (Applause.) And I can assure them that the British Government desires no better than that they should administer their several states in accordance with their own lights, untrammelled by undue interference, and along whatever lines are most natural to the habits and customs of their people. (Applause.) Above all things I hope it will be remembered both by them and by the Indian people at large that, if here and there the Government has had to make its influence felt in a native court, so exceptional a procedure has only been adopted in the last resort, most unwillingly, and in the interests of the chief himself, and of the people for whose welfare he is responsible. (Cheers.)

And now, gentlemen, what more am I to say? You all

know how deeply I have had at heart the interest and the welfare of all classes of the community, how impartially I have endeavoured to promote the welfare of each in turn, how faithful I have been to that obligation which has been always felt by the Government of India to see in every subject of the Queen, not the member of a sect, of a caste, of a religion, but a citizen of the empire possessed of rights and privileges which are equally the property of all. (Loud applause.) What can I say to you, Europeans and natives alike, but this?—Whatever you do, live in unity and concord and good-fellowship with each other. Fate has united both races in a community of interests, and neither can do without the other. (Cheers.) The rule of England maintains peace and justice within the borders of India, and secures its safety from outside dangers, but that rule cannot be exercised either effectually or acceptably without the loyalty and assistance of the native races. (Applause.) Therefore again I say co-operate with each other in a generous and genial spirit. I confess I would rather see the Europeans, the Hindus, and Mahomedans united in criticising the Government than that the Hindus and the Mahomedans, the Europeans and the natives, should become estranged from each other by unworthy prejudices or animosities of race and religion. God forbid that the British Government should ever seek to maintain its rule in India by fomenting race hatreds amongst its subjects. Its antecedents, its strength, its self-confidence, and its dignity will for ever render a recourse to such expedients unnecessary and impossible. (Cheers.) To those amongst my native friends who, imbued with the political literature of the West, are seeking to apply to India the lessons they have learnt from the history of constitutional countries, I would say, pursue your objects, which no one can pronounce to be unworthy, with temper, with moderation, and with a due perception of the peculiar circumstances of your native land. (Applause.) Found your claims, whatever they may be, upon what is real and true, and not upon what is baseless and fantastic. It is by this method, and by this method alone, that you have a prospect of realizing anything practical. (Cheers.) My general feelings on these subjects I have already expressed in the speech I delivered on the occasion of the Queen's Jubilee, and to what I then said it is needless to say I still adhere. (Cheers.) To the writers in the public press I would say, follow your most honourable vocation in a manly, courageous, and faithful spirit. When England gave you a free press she intended that it should become an instrument for the guidance, the assistance, and the enlightenment of the Government and the protection of the people; nor will any Viceroy or any Government ever complain, no matter how severely you criticise what they have said, written, or done, provided there is that ring of sincerity and conviction in your utterances which none can mistake. (Applause.) But do not seek to excite the hatred of the people against the Government by wilfully and maliciously attributing to it intentions and designs which are the fruit of your imagination. (Cheers.) It was misrepresentations of this kind that thirty years ago helped powerfully to deluge the land with blood, and those who indulge in them are abusing the protection and freedom of speech extended to them by the laws of England—a freedom which a considerable portion of the Indian press, I gladly acknowledge, exercises with sagacity, discretion, and moderation, and which I trust it will every day be found more worthy to enjoy. (Applause.)

These I think are the only valedictory words with which I need trouble you. It only remains for me again to assure you, from the very bottom of my heart, that I have been deeply touched by this proof of your good-will and generous appreciation. (Cheers.) I shall never forget my friends in this country. It will always be my earnest endeavour, if I ever again take part in public life in England, to further the interests of my Indian fellow-subjects, and to consider in a sympathetic and liberal spirit whatever demands they may prefer. (Cheers.) The English empire in India is, indeed, the marvel of the world; and, encouraged by your approbation, I can carry home with me the conviction that, in the opinion of my Anglo-Indian countrymen, and of my Indian fellow-subjects, I have done nothing during the four years of my anxious rule to shake its stability, to dim the glory of its majesty, or to tarnish that reputation for humanity, justice, and truth, which is its crowning and most precious attribute. (Loud and long-continued cheers and applause.)

<small>The Hon. Mr. Steel, chairman of the committee for organising the meeting then read an address to the Countess of Dufferin, to which Her Excellency made the following reply:—</small>

It is indeed difficult for me to express my very deep sense of the kindness I am receiving at your hands. Your overappreciation of the little I have been able to do here makes me feel painfully how much more I might have done, and this regretful thought is the only one which, when I leave this country, can in any way mar the pleasant recollections of the years I have spent here, and of the exceeding kindness and consideration I have experienced on all sides.

I am grateful too for the expressions you use with regard to the project for supplying female medical aid to the women of India. The success of that movement I have most deeply at heart, and I should resign the conduct of its affairs with very great regret, had I any misgivings as to the permanent character of the work. I have none. From the first moment that I undertook to organize this association, I have received the most valuable and the most cordial help from persons of all classes and conditions, and from every part of the country. I have found that when from time to time presidents, or secretaries, or members of committees have been forced to abandon the work, others have been found ready to take it up, and in no single instance has the association had the smallest difficulty in finding earnest and capable workers to carry out its objects.

Moreover, these committees have been constituted in a great variety of ways, but whether their members have been drawn from different nationalities, whether they have been European or native, whether the secretaries have been men or women, English or Indian—in whatever form, in fact, the experiment of forming such committees has been tried, the result has in every case been equally and perfectly successful.

With its organization established; with committees such as these at work all over the country; with local bodies daily waking up to their responsibilities in this matter; with a respectable, if not an adequate endowment-fund in its possession; favoured by the friendly countenance and approval of the Government; with all these advantages and securities on its side, the association surely cannot fail to prosper. And I appeal with confidence to the people of India, and especially to the municipal councils of this great country, to take up earnestly, and to support liberally, a movement which, with God's blessing upon it, will, I trust, bring an increase of health and happiness to countless Indian households.

I thank you with all my heart for your friendly words and for your good wishes. I shall never forget this day, and shall ever retain feelings of the warmest interest and affection for the people of Calcutta, whose kindness to me during the three past years has culminated to-night. (Loud and continued applause.)

FAREWELL ADDRESS FROM THE OOTERPARA MUNICIPALITY.

On the afternoon of Saturday, the 24th March, 1888, the Viceroy and the Countess of Dufferin, on their way to Barrackpore, visited Ooterpara, and were present at a garden party given by the Hon. Rájá Peáry Mohun Mukerji. The local municipality took advantage of the opportunity to present a farewell address to the Viceroy, who replied as follows:—

GENTLEMEN,—I beg to return you my best thanks for your friendly welcome, as well as for the address you have presented to me. I recognise with pleasure that you take a proper pride in the town with which you are connected. Local patriotism is as desirable and useful a sentiment as the same feeling when applied to a country at large, for it frequently leads the members of the community not merely to take a pride in everything that concerns the prosperity of their native place, but also induces them to endow it with institutions similar to those which you have enumerated.

It is quite true that during the last four years the Government of India has had many difficulties to contend with, both as regards its external relations, its internal development, and its financial condition; but I am glad to learn that the various circumstances which have arisen out of this state of affairs have, in your opinion, been satisfactorily dealt with by my administration.

I am indeed sorry to bid you good-bye, for I have always regarded you as my neighbours, and have frequently had occasion to admire those marks of prosperity and improvement which characterise this locality, as I passed up and down the beautiful banks of the Hooghly on my way to and from Barrackpore.

The ladies of Ooterpara presented an address to the Countess of Dufferin, expressive of their gratitude for her efforts on behalf of the ladies of India, to which Her Excellency replied as follows:—

MY FRIENDS,—I thank you sincerely for the warm welcome you have given me, and for the kind words you have addressed to me. I am especially grateful for the expressions of your sympathy and interest in the aims of the National Association. Your countrymen have come forward generously and effectively to establish this work, and the hearty though unseen co-operation of the women of India can do much to ensure its universal success.

It is doubtless difficult for you who have not yet profited by those remedies and alleviations to which women of other countries are accustomed, to understand that you often have to suffer unnecessary pain; that many lives are lost through ignorant treatment, and that much ill-health is entailed upon yourselves and upon your children by the employment of unskilled practitioners, or by the absence of all medical aid. But if once you realize these facts, I feel sure you will use the influence you possess in your own homes to advance the work of an association which is endeavouring to bring these remedies and this relief into your households.

I would appeal to you also on behalf of those Indian women who undertake the study of medicine as a profession. I ask you to give them your sympathy and your support, and, wherever it may be needed, your protection. They have no light task before them; they have much to learn, much to bear, many prejudices to overcome, many cherished customs to give up, and they will need all the encouragement and all the respect their countrywomen can give them to carry them through their arduous duties.

I thank you again for your kind reception and for giving me this opportunity of meeting you. I trust that health and happiness and every blessing may attend you, and I can assure you that wherever I may go no subject will ever interest me more deeply than that of the welfare of the women of India.

FAREWELL ADDRESS FROM THE CENTRAL MAHOMEDAN ASSOCIATION.

On Saturday, the 24th March, 1888, a deputation from the Mahomedan Central National Association waited on the Viceroy at Government House, Calcutta, and presented a farewell address on behalf of the Mahomedan community. Delegates from several parts of Bengal, Behar, and the north were present. Mr. Amir Ali, the secretary of the association, read the address, and His Excellency replied as follows:—

GENTLEMEN,—It is indeed extremely flattering to me that the large deputation which fills this hall should have come from so many important and distant cities of India to present me with an address expressive of your good-will and confidence. As the representative of Her Most Gracious Majesty and of the people of England, it is one of the first duties of the Viceroy so to conduct his administration as to render it, as far as possible, acceptable to the people over whom he rules, and especially is he bound to make those races who are in any way disadvantageously situated feel that they are the objects of his sympathy and solicitude. The guiding principle of English rule has always been to administer the affairs of the empire with absolute impartiality in the presence of the diverse religions and nationalities of which it is composed, and, in order that this may be effectually accomplished, it is its duty to see that each denomination obtains a fair start, and that the conditions upon which they enter on the contests of life are equalized and fairly adjusted. The Mahomedans of India may, consequently, rest assured that the Government will always view with the utmost sympathy and approval their endeavours to remove the peculiar impediments which hamper their efforts, especially when those impediments result from a conscientious adherence to the behests of their religion. Fortunately the whole Mahomedan community, under the intelligent leaders I see before me, and with the assistance of many other wise and thoughtful Mahomedans whom I have met in the provinces, are energetically working for this end, and we already see the fruits of their labour both in the increase in the number of Mahomedan students at our various educational centres and in the high places which they have begun to take in the university and school competitions. I trust, therefore, that ere long the whole Mahomedan youth of the country will be marching abreast with their Hindu brethren, and that all the present causes of complaint and dissatisfaction which you have so keenly felt will eventually disappear. In any event, be assured, gentlemen, that I highly value those marks of sympathy and approbation which you have been pleased to express in regard to my general administration of the country. Descended as you are from those who formerly occupied such a commanding position in India, you are exceptionally well able to understand the responsibilities attaching to those who rule; nor does it surprise me to learn, considering the circumstances under which your forefathers entered India, that you should be fully alive to the necessity of closing its gates, for it is only by such precautions that content can reign, that commerce can flourish, or wealth increase.

In conclusion, allow me to thank you on behalf of Lady Dufferin for the kind expressions you have made use of in her regard. She will be the first Viceroy's consort—and I say it with pride—whose popularity will be more extensive and her fame more enduring than that of her husband.

FAREWELL ADDRESS FROM THE CALCUTTA MAHOMEDAN LITERARY SOCIETY.

On Monday, the 26th March 1888, a deputation of the Mahomedan Literary Society waited upon His Excellency the Viceroy at 3 P.M. His Excellency received the members of the deputation in the Throne-room of Government House. Nawab Abdool Latif Bahadur, the secretary of the association, read the address, to which His Excellency made the following reply :—

GENTLEMEN,—It is needless for me to assure you that I am very sensible of your kindness in presenting me with an address which at once assures me of your personal regard towards Lady Dufferin and myself, and of your general approval of the way in which the administration of India has been conducted during the period that I have presided over its Government. I can well understand the satisfaction with which as Mahomedans you have watched the growth of the better understanding which has come to exist between ourselves and the Amir of Afghanistan. From the moment I came into personal relations with His Highness at Rawalpindi until now, I have done everything in my power to make him and his people understand that there is nothing we more desire than the maintenance of Afghan independence and the prosperity of Afghanistan and its inhabitants. The delimitation of the Russo-Afghan boundary has undoubtedly removed a fertile occasion of friction, dispute, and uncertainty, and the very fact of Russia having herself drawn a line beyond which her progress southwards is not to extend is an additional element of security. This fortunate circumstance, however, should not tempt us to neglect those ordinary precautions which all nations take, and are bound to take, when they are conterminous or nearly conterminous with great military monarchies. The most peaceful and well-disposed governments are sometimes powerless in the presence of a wave of popular feeling, or the ambition of a strong military party, and if a nation wishes to maintain its territory inviolate, the only certain way of doing so is to render its frontier impregnable to attack. Fortunately the natural features which characterise the boundaries of India are such as to render this task both of easy and comparatively cheap accomplishment. The system of railways which we have recently constructed would enable us in a very short period to concentrate the whole forces of India at whatever point might be threatened; and the passes that lead from the outside world are easily defensible. Inasmuch as the one desire both of the Government and of the people of India is to be left alone in order that they may tread the paths of peace and progress, the conditions I have referred to are sufficiently reassuring, but, if anything were wanting to enhance our satisfaction, it would be the spontaneity and patriotism evinced by our Indian princes in placing large sums of money at the disposal of the Government, with a view to rendering still more effectual those precautionary measures upon which the executive has so prudently embarked; nor is it unnatural that a Mahomedan community like yourselves should take a just pride in the fact that His Highness the Nizam, the chief Mahomedan ruler in India, should have put himself at the head of this movement and afforded so splendid an example.

I see with pleasure that you have been good enough to allude to the arrangements made with the firm of Messrs. Cook and Son for the promotion of the comfort of the Mahomedan pilgrims to Mecca. This was a matter in which I took the deepest personal interest, as during my stay at Constantinople I had been made aware of the extortions and hardships to which they were exposed; and it is already evident that the system is working well, and that the benefits attained under it are considerable.

I must also thank you for the specially friendly terms which you use towards Lady Dufferin and her efforts to be of service to the suffering women of this country. However fully her endeavours may be appreciated, there is no one but myself who knows the unremitting labour, attention, thought, and anxiety which she has given to this subject; but I assure you she feels herself more than rewarded by the generous support which she has received on all sides, and by the fact that the institution she has established should have become so thoroughly incorporated with the social system of the country.

And now, gentlemen, in conclusion, allow me to assure you that I shall never forget your kindness; that I shall watch with extreme interest the efforts of the Mahomedan community to place themselves in line with their Hindu fellow-subjects in the matter of education and the other requirements of modern civilization; and that the success which I do not hesitate to predict for you will always command my warmest sympathies.

FAREWELL ADDRESS FROM THE TALUKDARS OF OUDH.

On the night of Saturday, the 7th April, 1888, His Excellency the Viceroy and Lady Dufferin were entertained at a grand fête by the Talukdars of Oudh at the Baradari in Lucknow. Raja Ameer Hossein read an address to the Viceroy on behalf of the Talukdars, and His Excellency replied as follows:—

TALUKDARS OF OUDH,—Being well acquainted with the history of your country, I am fully able to appreciate the significance of the gathering I see before me. Representing as you do its great territorial families and both its agricultural and its political interests, it is a matter of deep satisfaction to me to be assured of your confidence, as the head of the Government of India, and also of your good-will as the representative of the Queen. There is nothing Her Majesty more desires than that it should be brought home to the convictions and consciences of her subjects in India, great and small, not only that she has their general welfare at heart, but also that she takes a deep personal interest in everything that concerns them. By no means the least of my important functions is so to carry myself towards Her Majesty's Indian subjects as to make this thoroughly known and understood, and I am pleased to see from the language you use that my efforts to produce this result have proved effectual. Unhappily, with every desire to keep himself in touch with all classes and communities, a Viceroy's occupations confine him necessarily so much to his office, that it is only with an infinitesimal portion of his Indian fellow-subjects that he ever succeeds in coming into contact; consequently, I must ask you to be my interpreter to those large populations with which you are connected, and to convey to them in my name my warm appreciation of the loyalty which animates the whole of Oudh from one end to the other, at the same time that you assure them of the deep solicitude felt both by the Queen and by the English people for the prosperity of this great province. Fortunately, for the last five years it has been in the charge of one of the ablest and most eminent statesmen that this generation has seen, of a writer who has done more than almost any one else to disseminate in Europe an adequate idea of the history, the philosophy, the poetry, and the characteristics of the Indian peoples. Moreover, combining as he does eminent practical ability with the highest literary attainments, he has left behind him in the University of Allahabad, in the Legislative Council of the North-west, and in various other measures adopted by the Government of India at his instance, innumerable monuments of his zeal, wisdom, and forethought. And now he has been succeeded by a ruler whose father sacrificed his life in the public service, who has been long connected with you by the closest ties, who has occupied positions of the highest responsibility both under the Home Government and under the Government of India, and who has already given abundant proofs of his deep and earnest desire to guide you in a wise, sympathetic, and benevolent spirit along that path of reasonable progress and material and political improvement which you have so wisely chosen.

I will not attempt to follow you through your review of the policy of the Government of India during the last four years, which you have embodied in terms so kind and so flattering to myself, though I cannot help expressing my satisfaction at finding that you appreciate in an adequate manner the efforts we are making to secure the peace of India by rendering our frontiers impervious to attack on the north-west, and by the extension of our jurisdiction over the entire valley of the Irrawaddy on the east. Our action in both directions has been forced upon us by external conditions over which we had no control. They must be regarded as simple measures of home defence, which cannot fail to contribute powerfully to the quiet and security of our own house for many a year to come.

But, though unwilling to detain you long, I must return you my special thanks for your expressions of gratitude to the Government of India for the establishment of the Allahabad University and the creation of the Provincial Legislative Council of the North-west. As I have already mentioned, both these measures were originally suggested by Sir Alfred Lyall, and what better proof could you have than these of the desire of the Government of India to sympathize with your aspirations, and to do everything in its power to enable this province to hold its head high amongst its neighbours? Most heartily do I congratulate you on their acquisition, for I am fully persuaded that you will make a good and effectual use of both.

There is one other most important legislative measure upon which the Government of India also embarked at the instance of Sir Alfred Lyall, to which I must also refer, namely, the Oudh Rent Act. That Act was introduced with the view of terminating in a fair and impartial manner those disputes, uncertainties, and complications which had arisen regarding the status of the Oudh ryot, and I am glad to have this opportunity of expressing my high appreciation of the liberal and hearty manner in which the talukdars of Oudh met the Government on this question. Had it not been for the fair and generous way in which they consented to assist us, the matter which has now been happily settled in a way greatly to benefit the cultivator, without, I trust, in any degree injuring the talukdar, might have grown up into a controversy only too well calculated to sow ill-feeling and dissension between two classes whose interests, if only properly regarded, will be found to be interdependent and closely connected with each other. Again I say, gentlemen, I thank you heartily, and especially my honourable colleague Rana Shankar Baksh, for the manner in which you have dealt with the land question in Oudh.

Turning now to two matters upon which you justly pride yourselves—the success with which you are working your local self-government, and the auspicious fact of Her Majesty's jubilee having resulted in the foundation of a School of Arts and Industries—I would observe that, as I have frequently stated, local self-government has never had a better friend in India than myself. I have watched its operations throughout the country with great interest, and though, as was to be expected, there is a considerable difference in the results which it has produced in different localities, there seems to be a very general consensus of opinion that the system is as a whole working in a promising and successful manner, especially in the larger centres of population. Some municipal bodies may be inert, local and district boards may fall short of the expectations formed of them by their friends, but the great fact remains that from one end of the country to the other, whether in the urban or the rural districts, there are numerous bodies of men who are busily occupied in looking after the affairs of the important communities they represent, who are being made to feel the responsibilities attaching to a public post, and who are gradually learning to look beyond the range of their own private interests and businesses, and to entertain an intelligent and lively concern for the common good. It is in this way, and under this discipline, that true patriotism and a wise public spirit can alone be generated, and glad am I to learn from several independent sources of the successful way in which both have been developed in your own midst.

I need hardly observe that I am much pleased to learn that you are in a fair way of establishing a School of Arts and Industries. Both as the head of the Government and personally I have always taken the deepest interest in technical education. I have called the attention of all the subordinate Governments to the desirability of promoting this branch of instruction by every means in their power, and I never lost an opportunity of reminding the general public of the many benefits to be derived from a large measure of technical skill being diffused amongst the people. But I must ask you always to remember that it is not within either the competence or the functions of the Supreme Government to give practical effect to its views. This latter responsibility devolves upon the local governments in a certain degree, but still more largely upon the various Indian communities. Even the local governments, unassisted by the liberality and by the counsels of those who are in a position to support and direct their efforts, can do but little. Indeed, I know no road along which it is so desirable to march with caution and discretion, and with a view to the local needs, opportunities, and requirements of each district; but you at all events in contributing no less a sum than five lakhs to this most noble and practical mode of meeting the needs, embarrassments, and wants of modern Indian civilization, deserve the highest praise, and most warmly do I congratulate you on the extraordinary success which has attended your efforts.

And now, gentlemen, allow me to thank you from the bottom of my heart for the kind expressions which you have used towards Lady Dufferin and her efforts to mitigate the trials to which for so many generations Indian ladies have been exposed, without any of those alleviations with which Western science has so amply provided their sisters in other lands. I am indeed happy to think that the institution which my wife has founded has taken such deep root in the confidence of the people, has been so nourished and supported throughout the length and breadth of the land by all the intelligent classes, has been so endowed with princely gifts, that its permanent vitality and continued existence are amply secured. With these auspicious results already obtained, Lady Dufferin will leave your shores with the happy assurance that she has really accomplished a useful and successful work amongst you, and that her name will be remembered with gratitude not merely in the mansions of the rich and of the great, but in the humble dwellings of the poor, for many a generation.

In conclusion, gentlemen, I must again bid you good-bye. I shall lay down my great office at the end of this year with many a regretful feeling, but at the same time with a most grateful recollection of the universal indulgence with which my humble endeavours to do my duty amongst you have been met. I am already the oldest Viceroy that has ever ruled in India, and I feel the time has come when in the public interests the heavy responsibilities of my office should be confided to the hands of a younger man; but at least I can carry away with me the consolation of knowing that at no time during the past hundred years has there prevailed a deeper feeling of security in reference to all those great interests upon which the happiness of every nation so much depends as at the present moment, and that, while the prince in his palace is conscious that his throne is as firmly and irrevocably secured to him and his dynasty as is that of the Queen-Empress herself, the zemindar in his country-house, the trader in his shop, the humble ryot in his cabin, are all equally convinced that where they have sown there also they shall reap, and that English might and English justice are ever ready at hand to protect the land from outward aggression, and to ensure to every citizen the untroubled enjoyment of his rights and privileges within its borders.

FAREWELL ADDRESS FROM MAHOMEDAN ASSOCIATIONS AT LUCKNOW.

On Tuesday, the 10th April, 1888, at 3 P.M., the Anjuman-Jhalsa-i-Islamia, and other Mahomedan societies in Lucknow, waited on His Excellency the Viceroy at Government House in Lucknow, and presented him with an address, which was read by Munshi Imtiaz Ali.

His Excellency, in reply, spoke as follows :—

GENTLEMEN,—I return you my best thanks for the friendly and flattering address with which you have presented me. I need not now repeat what I have often said, that having for so many years of my previous public career found myself closely connected with Mahomedan Governments and Mahomedan populations, it was an additional pleasure to me in coming to India to remember that it would be one of my duties to watch over the interests of fifty millions of Her Majesty's Mahomedan subjects. Fifty millions of men are themselves a nation, and a very powerful nation; and when we remember the circumstances under which the Mahomedan community has come to form an integral part of the Indian people, and all the splendid antecedents attaching to their history, a ruler would indeed be devoid of all political instinct if he were not careful to consider their wants and wishes, and to bring their status and condition into harmony with the general system over which he presides. But you have another especial claim upon my sympathy and good-will. Owing to circumstances beyond your own control and to the necessity of conforming to certain accepted traditions attaching to your religious convictions, you long occupied a disadvantageous position in relation to your Hindu fellow-subjects, for, whereas their youth were free to master at an early age those acquirements which are the essential preliminaries to most employments in the public service, the Mahomedan children were required to devote themselves to the studies enjoined by their spiritual guides. Consequently you were beginning to lag behind in that arduous race in which it is so desirable that all sections of our body politic should be able to engage upon equal terms. But, however great might be the sympathy of Government with your unfortunate position, it was precluded by those strict principles of impartiality which, I trust, no Indian administration will ever be tempted for a moment to violate or neglect, from extending to you advantages which could only be enjoyed at the expense of the interests of Her Majesty's other Indian subjects. But what it could do it did. It issued the resolution of the 15th of July, 1885. For the reasons I have stated, that resolution undoubtedly fell short of the expectations you had conceived, but, as I trust will be the case with many other acts of the Government, as time went on it was found to be of a more beneficial and effective character than was at first supposed, and I am proud to think that by this bare act of justice I have been able to give you a satisfactory proof of my deep and warm solicitude.

Acknowledging, as I do with thanks, the favourable opinion which you have expressed in regard to the general policy pursued by my colleagues and myself, I desire in a special manner to recognise the generous terms in which you have referred to the Civil Service Commission. When that commission was appointed, the commission itself and the motives of the Government in nominating it were denounced by a certain portion of the native press in a very unworthy manner; but there is no honest person in India, I imagine, who is not now satisfied that the commission was actuated by a single-minded desire to open still wider the doors of our public offices to the natives of India, and that its members have discharged the task intrusted to them in an earnest and liberal spirit. Their recommendations are now being considered by the local governments, and I do not think Sir Charles Aitchison and his able associates need be anything but gratified by the way in which their proposals have been generally received by the public at large.

I also note with pleasure that you are good enough to refer in terms of approbation to that portion of a recent speech I made at Calcutta, in which, with all possible earnestness, I endeavoured to impress upon the various communities which are united into a whole under the Imperial Crown of India to live in peace and good-fellowship with one another. Divergences of race and differences of religion, and the historical circumstances in which those divergences and differences have originated, must inevitably give rise from time to time to occasional discrepancies of opinion, as well as to political and social friction; but the causes which generate these evanescent fires will be found, on examination, to be absolutely insignificant in the presence of those far mightier forces which work for peace and amity amongst you. The former are too frequently born only of prejudice, fanaticism, misapprehension, and perversity; the latter are closely incorporated with your most precious material interests, and are essential to the well-being of yourselves and of your children's children. Those amongst you who are acquainted with history, whether in the East or the West, will have observed that there is no circumstance which better exemplifies the occasional folly of mankind than the absolute indifference of subsequent generations to those very disputes and controversies for the sake of which their forefathers only too frequently persecuted and destroyed each other.

And now, in conclusion, to you also I must return, as I have already done to so many others, both in my wife's and my own name, our united and heartfelt thanks for the kind manner in which you have recognised her efforts for the amelioration of the condition of the ladies of India. In bidding you good-bye, I wish you all prosperity and happiness, and I would ask you to remember that, when all is said and done, your future is very much in your own hands. Government can do far less than is imagined either for the happiness or the advancement of the people; but the intelligence and energy with which your leaders in all parts of the country are promoting the cause of education, and are affording facilities to the rising generation to make up for the time that has been lost, is itself a certain pledge of eventual success.

SPEECH AT FAREWELL BALL AT SIMLA.

On the evening of the 24th September, 1888, the Viceroy and the Countess of Dufferin were entertained at a farewell ball, given in the Town Hall of Simla, by the members of the Simla United Service Club. All the society of Simla was present on the occasion. At supper the Hon. Lieutenant-General Chesney, military member of the Viceroy's Council, proposed the health of Lord and Lady Dufferin, in reply to which His Excellency spoke as follows:—

GENERAL CHESNEY, LADIES, AND GENTLEMEN,—To say that Lady Dufferin and I are both deeply touched by the kind way in which the society of Simla has joined together in giving us this farewell entertainment, is to say very little in comparison with what we both feel. If anything could enhance our gratitude, it is the eloquent and graceful manner in which General Chesney, as your representative, has conveyed to us your good wishes and adieus. (Applause.) The viceroys of India, as other representatives of Her Majesty elsewhere, are called upon to lead a kind of double life and to discharge twofold functions. On the one hand, as governors and administrators, burdened with heavy and anxious executive responsibilities, they are bound to give their time and their best energies to those important duties upon the proper discharge of which the welfare of their fellow-subjects depends. On the other hand, as heads of the communities amongst whom it is their happiness to live, they are called upon to dispense those hospitalities and to exercise those representative functions which tradition has recognised as appertaining to their state. Unfortunately, however, the conditions of this great empire are such, the cares and anxieties of Indian administration are so constant and absorbing, as greatly to impede and fetter the Viceroy in the execution of these his lighter and more genial labours. Secluded all day within the four walls of his office, he is compelled to lead a monastic—indeed, so little does he see even of his own wife, I might almost say a celibate—existence. (Laughter.) Consequently he has neither the time nor the opportunities to give so much thought as he might otherwise desire to ministering to the well-being and content of that fairer portion of the society upon whose verdict his popularity and estimation so largely and so properly depend. Conscious, therefore, of my shortcomings in this respect, I am all the more glad to find that my own enforced austerity—which, I hasten to assure every lady present, is merely official and assumed, and altogether foreign to my real inclinations—has been forgiven and condoned, in consideration of the way in which Lady Dufferin—whom I am almost disposed to refer to rather as my colleague on the Viceregal throne than as my wife—has endeavoured to supplement my *laches* and deficiencies. (Applause.) In one respect, at all events, I know I shall have merited some recognition from a very influential and powerful class—I mean the young ladies—for now that a decent Viceregal residence has been erected, all future generations of Simla maidens will have far better opportunities of displaying both their graces and their pretty frocks, when they honour Government House with their presence, than had any of their predecessors. (Cheers.) Be that, however, as it may, I am sure it will be gratifying to all my friends to know that, no matter how little he may be able to show it, it is always a great comfort and consolation to any one in my situation to feel that, while he is pursuing his solitary labours, uncheered by those social relaxations which are open to others, he is, nevertheless, surrounded by an atmosphere of sympathy and good-will on the part of his countrymen and countrywomen. Such genial and subtle influences have an effect little comprehended perhaps by those from whom they unconsciously emanate, in sustaining his energies, encouraging his efforts, and soothing his ruffled spirits. For four successive years Lady Dufferin and myself have had the honour of presiding over the society of this place, and during the whole of that period we have experienced nothing but the greatest kindness from all its members. That unvaried good-will has now found its final consummation and expression in this beautiful ball and banquet. It therefore only remains for me, ladies and gentlemen, to express to you our heartfelt gratitude, and to assure you, both in Lady Dufferin's name and my own, that those kind, and I hope I shall not be thought impertinent if I add beautiful faces, whose friendly and sympathetic smiles have so often gladdened our sojourn amongst you, will always be a welcome sight to us wherever we may be, whether in our home in Ireland or in the ambassadorial palace at Rome. (Loud and continued applause.)

REPLY TO ADDRESS FROM THE MUNICIPAL COMMITTEE OF LAHORE.

The Viceroy left Simla on his final autumn tour on the 13th of November, 1888. On the 14th of November he arrived at Lahore, and at the railway station was presented with a farewell address by the Municipal Committee of the city. In reply, His Excellency spoke as follows :—

GENTLEMEN,—I beg to return you my most cordial thanks for your address, and for the loyal expressions contained in it towards Her Majesty the Queen-Empress, as well as for the kindly terms in which you have referred to my approaching departure from India. Having had many occasions of becoming acquainted with the public-spirited citizens of Lahore, I should indeed have been sorry had I not had an opportunity of bidding them good-bye before leaving India.

I have to thank you for the flattering manner in which you refer to the results of my administration. Prosperity and contentment can only be secured in times of peace. Peace is the greatest blessing which a country can enjoy, and, living as you do in a frontier province, it does not surprise me that you should appreciate to the full the value of the precautions which the Government of India has taken against all possible risks of aggression. The best security against so great a calamity is timely preparation. Any want of preparation is itself an invitation to attack. Not only so, but by encouraging the hopes of those sections of a neighbouring people who may be anxious for war, it weakens the hands of their governments when endeavouring to maintain a friendly attitude towards you. Happily, at a cost which is infinitesimal as compared with the expenditure of European nations for a similar purpose, we are in the course of putting the whole of our north-west frontier into such a state of reasonable defence as will enable you to continue to cultivate your fields in peace and contentment.

And now I must thank you for the kind manner in which you have alluded to the efforts made by Lady Dufferin to improve the condition of the women of India. The association over which my wife now presides, and the presidentship of which has, I am glad to say, been accepted by the Marchioness of Lansdowne, stands now on an assured basis of success. It has a sound system of organization, and, thanks to the readiness with which people in India, both European and native, have contributed towards it, it is in a favourable position financially. With these conditions we may anticipate its future success, and look forward with confidence to the day when India will be adequately provided with hospitals for the reception and treatment of women, and with women practitioners capable of affording proper medical attendance to their own sex. Each institution, such as that which will be opened by Lady Dufferin to-morrow, may be regarded as one more step towards this consummation, and it affords the greatest pleasure both to Lady Dufferin and myself that the most important institution of this kind in the Punjab will bear the name of Lady Aitchison, which I feel sure you all prize and venerate equally with that of her husband.

And now, gentlemen, I will bid you farewell. You have always received me with kindness. You have judged my conduct with indulgence, and have never withheld your generous appreciation of the endeavours of my Government to do its duty. As long as I live I shall always retain a most affectionate recollection of the brave and high-minded races of the Punjab, with so many of whose chiefs and leading men I have formed ties of personal friendship. May every blessing that Providence has in its gifts rest upon you and yours for many a generation!

REPLY TO AN ADDRESS FROM THE ANJUMAN-I-ITIHAD, LAHORE.

On the 15th of November, 1888, a deputation from the Anjuman-i-Itihad waited on the Viceroy at Government House, Lahore, and presented him with a farewell address on behalf of their Association, to which His Excellency replied as follows :—

GENTLEMEN,—I have much pleasure in accepting the address which you have been kind enough to present to me, and in listening to your expressions of approval of the work which I have been able to do as Viceroy. The cares and responsibilities of a Viceroy are, as you yourselves realize, very great, and with the development of our system of government in India they show a tendency to increase rather than diminish. Nor can the public at large have any conception either of what is being accomplished by the Government for the good of the people over so vast an area as that comprised within the peninsula of Hindustan, or the enormous amount of anxiety and labour which it entails. In the Punjab alone, to mention a single subject, the Swat River, Sidnai and Chenab Canals have been opened, fertilizing nearly a million acres, while projects for the extension of the Western Jumna Canal and for the construction of the Jhelum Canal, which, it is estimated, will irrigate between them another half million acres, have received the approval of the Government of India and been recommended to the Secretary of State. The wealth of the country, and the outlet which will thus be afforded to the inhabitants of congested districts for improving their material conditions, cannot fail to be very considerable.

To the extension of railways, again, great attention has been paid by my Government, and not only have 670 miles of military railways been opened during the past four years, but 2235 miles of commercial and protective railways have also been completed within the same period; and 2634 more are now under construction.

Nor have the more domestic concerns of the people of the country escaped our attention. The Government has long realized the extent to which disease which is the direct product of insanitary conditions affects the energy and retards the advancement of the population of India. The efforts made in the past towards improved sanitation have been less fruitful of good results than they might have been had funds been more easily procurable, and had there been proper agencies for directing reform. The recent legislative enactments relating to municipal committees and local boards have provided the agency required, and the rules which restricted the advancement of money on loan to local bodies for sanitary and other similar purposes have been considerably relaxed. To assist the local agencies in directing sanitary improvements, we intend to appoint a central sanitary board in each province, and I sincerely trust that these measures will gradually result in the improvement of drainage throughout the country, in the provision of a supply of pure water in towns and villages, and in the general adoption of simple rules to regulate village sanitation.

LADY DUFFERIN'S REPLY TO THE REPRESENTATIVES OF THE WOMEN OF THE PUNJAB.

On the 16th of November, 1888, a deputation of Native gentlemen waited on the Marchioness of Dufferin and Ava at Government House, Lahore, and presented her with an Address on behalf of the women of the Punjab. The Address bore 25,000 signatures. In reply, Her Excellency spoke as follows :—

GENTLEMEN,—The very kind words you have addressed to me, and the warm approval you express of the scheme with which I have been specially connected here, touch me deeply. It is true that I have taken the greatest possible interest in the inauguration of the National Association for Supplying

Medical Aid to Women, and that, thanks to the position I have held in this country, I have had exceptional opportunities and facilities for pressing the needs of our Indian sisters, and their claims to all the benefits which medical science can procure for them, upon the Indian public. But my interest in the matter, or my efforts, or my words, would have been of no avail, had they not met with a ready response in the hearts of their countrymen; had I not found fellow-labourers in every province, and sympathy and practical support in every place where I have sought it.

I am glad to think that I am only one of the many hundreds to whom this movement owes its vitality and its great success, and to whom the kind words addressed to me might equally well be directed. I rejoice too in the belief that the people of India have accepted and acknowledged this work as one that has to be done and as one that they must do themselves; and I feel sure that, having recognised their duty in this respect, they will never falter in their efforts to accomplish it.

And now, perhaps, as this is the only occasion upon which I shall have an opportunity of expressing an opinion on the subject, you will allow me to point out to you the direction in which I venture to think your greatest efforts should be made in the Punjab.

The National Association set before itself three objects— medical tuition, medical relief, and the supply of trained nurses. It is to the first of these that I desire to draw your serious consideration. Medical tuition is the very foundation of a permanent supply of medical relief. Female hospitals and female dispensaries cannot succeed unless you have medical women to put into them; and as I believe that every part of India will have to provide and to educate its own supply of female doctors, it follows that each year that is lost in any particular place in sending pupils to the university must seriously retard the progress of female medical relief in that part of the country.

There doubtless is a vague idea abroad that Englishwomen, or native women from other provinces, can easily be got to officer new hospitals and dispensaries; but this is a false impression. The Englishwomen who are able and willing to come to India as doctors will always be exceedingly few in number; and as regards native women, each province will for many a long year have more than enough to do in providing for its own requirements, and will not be able to spare any of its educated medical women to other places. It is, therefore, from the Punjab itself that female doctors for the Punjab must as a rule be taken, and the question of finding them and of educating them admits of no delay.

So strongly have the central committee of the National Association felt the necessity of helping on the cause of medical tuition here that they have made a special donation towards building a home for medical students at Lahore. I trust you will complete that work; for, until a house for them, and a trustworthy matron to look after them, be provided, I do not think that it is possible for many pupils to come and reside in this place.

With regard to the other two objects of the association, I may congratulate you heartily upon the way in which they are being carried out in the Punjab. Female medical relief is receiving the attention of the branch committee, of private individuals, and of municipalities, at Delhi, at Kapurthala, at Gurdaspore, at Quetta, at Ludhiana, at Multan, and at many other places; while in the Lady Aitchison Hospital at Lahore you have a great central institution whose beneficent influence will be felt throughout the province. There too you have the means of giving practical instruction to your medical students, and of promoting the third object of the association by the training of native Dhais. You have also, in the institution presided over by Miss Hewlett at Umritsar, one of the most practical and one of the most successful training places for midwives that I know of in India. I think, therefore, that I may rejoice with you at the progress that has been made in promoting the objects of the association in this province; and when I learn, as I hope I shall ere long, that the Hindustani female medical class at the Lahore University numbers at least fifty pupils, I shall feel satisfied that female medical relief in the Punjab rests upon a sure foundation.

I again thank you heartily for the kind words of your address, and I wish you every possible success in your efforts to improve the condition and to increase the happiness of our Indian sisters.

SPEECH BY THE VICEROY AT DURBAR HELD AT PATIALA ON THE OCCASION OF THE MAHARAJA'S MARRIAGE.

On the 17th of November, 1888, the Viceroy arrived at Patiala to attend the marriage ceremonies of His Highness the Maharaja. The same afternoon a grand durbar was held in the Maharaja's palace, in the course of which His Excellency addressed the assembly as follows:—

YOUR HONOUR, CHIEFS OF THE PUNJAB, LADIES AND GENTLEMEN,—I need hardly say how much pleasure it gives me to be present on this auspicious and joyful occasion. I am sure that in offering my congratulations to the Maharaja of Patiala on his marriage, and in wishing him and his house all the happiness and prosperity that this world can give, I am expressing the unanimous sentiments of all present in this distinguished assembly.

When His Highness comes into possession of power, I feel convinced that he will worthily maintain the honour of his ancestral house, and take a high place among the princes of India as a loyal and brave feudatory of Her Majesty the Queen-Empress, as well as a conscientious and enlightened ruler.

And now, before I leave this assembly, I wish to say a few words regarding a subject of the utmost importance. You are all aware that three years ago, when war seemed imminent upon our north-western frontier, the native princes of India, both in the south and in the north, both Hindus and Mahomedans, came forward in a body to place at the disposal of Her Majesty's Government the whole resources of their States. Hostilities were then happily averted, but the feeling shown by the native chiefs could not be misunderstood, and I am convinced that their attitude in this crisis of our affairs not only created a very favourable impression in England, but produced a very striking effect in other countries. Again, last year, the year of the jubilee of Her Most Gracious Majesty the Queen-Empress, the rulers of many native states seized the opportunity of offering to contribute in a very liberal manner towards the defence of the empire, and their offers excited universal approval both at home and abroad.

Prominent among the princes who came forward on both occasions were the chiefs of the Punjab, the frontier province, who had already stood by the British Government more than once in the hour of trouble, and whose brave troops had fought and bled by the side of their English fellow-subjects. I remember with deep gratification, and they must remember with pride, that only ten years ago a contingent from the Punjab states marched to the Afghan frontier, and did its duty well under circumstances of great hardship and difficulty. Some among those around me wear on their breasts the medals earned by them for the service they then rendered to their Sovereign and country.

The Government of India has not failed to give earnest attention to the offers of the native princes, and, well knowing them to be as sincere as they were generous, has endeavoured to work out a scheme by which they might be turned to advantage in a manner both gratifying to the princes themselves and of material value to the empire. I believe we have succeeded in working out such a scheme, and this durbar seems to me to afford a fitting opportunity for its public inauguration. The Government of India does not think it necessary, or in all respects desirable, to accept from the native states of India the pecuniary assistance which they have so freely tendered. But in one very important particular we wish to enlist their co-operation. The armies of the native states are strong in numbers, but at present of various degrees of efficiency. Among many of them there exist warlike traditions and fine soldierly material, while some already contain regiments well worthy to share in any active operations which Her Majesty's troops may be called upon to undertake. What we propose is, in a few words, that we should ask those chiefs who have specially good fighting material in their armies, to raise a portion of those armies to such a pitch of general efficiency as will make them fit to go into action side by side with the imperial troops. For this purpose some extra exertions will be necessary, as troops in the present day, to be thoroughly fit for service, require very complete arrangements in the way of arms, transport equipment, and organization generally. But we shall in no case ask a native state to maintain a larger force of this description than it can well afford to support, and we do not doubt that under these conditions, the chiefs, knowing that the Government of India has no desire to take undue advantage of their loyalty in order to throw upon them an excessive burden, will be glad of the opportunity of making good their words by providing troops for the defence of the empire. I trust that the chiefs selected will in any case regard the acceptance of their offers as an honourable distinction, while those whose armies it is not found possible to utilize in the same manner will understand that if they cannot usefully contribute to the fighting strength of the empire, they can in other ways render services equally meritorious and equally sure to win the approval of Her Majesty the Queen-Empress.

To help these chiefs in setting on foot and maintaining the troops selected for service, a few English officers will be appointed as advisers and inspectors. These officers will have their headquarters at some central point in British territory, and will visit the several states in turn. Capable native drill instructors will also be lent to the native states from our own regiments. It is hoped that in this way, while each force will remain a purely state force recruited in the territories of its chief and serving within them, the troops composing it will gradually be made so efficient as to enable the imperial Government to use them as part of its available resources to meet any external danger.

The selected troops will be armed with breech-loading weapons presented to the several states by the British Government. These will be carbines for the cavalry, and Snider rifles for the infantry. In addition to this, each Punjab chief will receive from the British Government a battery of four guns.

The principal states of the Punjab and others elsewhere

have, I am happy to say, expressed their full concurrence in this scheme, and arrangements will be made to carry it into effect as far as they are concerned. I cannot but feel that I have been very fortunate in being able to announce before I leave India the inauguration of this important measure, which will, I hope, serve to show the world in what estimation Her Majesty the Queen-Empress holds the native states of India, and how she appreciates the conspicuous loyalty and attachment of their chiefs.

I have now, your Highness, to thank you for the eulogistic manner in which you have referred to Lady Dufferin's exertions to improve the system of medical aid for the women of this country. The splendid success of the fund inaugurated by her ladyship is due in a large measure to the munificent liberality of the chiefs of India; and the determination which Your Highness has arrived at of commemorating the occasion of our visit to you to-day by the establishment of a Zenana Hospital, intended to provide relief to both indoor and outdoor female patients, is one worthy of the high reputation which you already bear for concern for the welfare of your subjects and for noble public charity.

SPEECH IN PROPOSING THE HEALTH OF THE MAHARAJA OF PATIALA.

On the evening of the 17th of November the Maharaja entertained the Viceroy and Lady Dufferin and the other guests present in camp at dinner in a large Shamiana. His Highness was himself present on the occasion, and proposed the Viceroy's health. In reply, His Excellency said :—

LADIES AND GENTLEMEN,—In conveying to His Highness the Maharaja the grateful thanks of Lady Dufferin and myself for the honour he has done us, I am sure it will be agreeable to all present if I make myself their spokesman upon this auspicious occasion, and express to the Maharaja, in their name and on their behalf, our warmest wishes for his future happiness and prosperity. (Applause.) His Highness stands on the threshold of what we have every reason to hope will prove an honourable career and a happy life. He is surrounded by those who have known him from childhood, whose respect and love he has won; he is called upon to preside over the fortunes of a happy and contented people, and he enjoys the confidence of the Government of India. There now stretches before him, I trust, a long life of usefulness in discharging the duties for which his previous education will have well fitted him. He has been taught that, though called by Providence to one of the highest posts which this world can offer, he too is bound to be the servant of duty and the faithful guardian of the welfare of his people. (Applause.) These doctrines I have every reason to believe have sunk deeply into his mind, and as soon as the time shall have arrived for him to be intrusted with those ample powers which Her Majesty the Queen-Empress is always glad to confide into the hands of her feudatory chiefs, he will, I am sure, fulfil the promise of his early days, and, by a faithful adherence to the path of duty, take his proper place amongst those other princes who have already started upon so satisfactory a career, whose example, I trust, he will follow, and in combination with whom the stability of the British empire in India is so likely to be assured. (Applause.) It only remains for me, ladies and gentlemen, again to call upon you to drink long life, health, and prosperity to the Maharaja and to all his house. (Loud applause.)

ALIGARH COLLEGE.

On the 20th of November, 1888, Lord Dufferin, in the course of his autumn tour, visited the Anglo-Mahomedan College at Aligarh, and was presented with an address by Sir Syud Ahmed (the President) and the Committee of the college, in reply to which His Excellency spoke as follows:—

Mr. VICE-PRESIDENT AND GENTLEMEN,—It is a source of much pleasure to me that I have been able to visit your college before leaving India and to receive the address which has just been read on your behalf by the Principal of the institution. My only regret is that my stay in Aligarh this afternoon will be so short that I can only reply to you in the briefest possible way. I have listened with much interest to the splendid list of benefactions by which your college has been endowed, and my attention has naturally been much struck by the manner in which Englishmen, Mahomedans, and Hindus have vied with one another in assisting you to enlarge its buildings and increase its revenues. This noble institution with its rich endowments owes its foundation to the spirit of self-help and self-reliance which animated its founders, and the success which it has attained affords, I trust, a happy augury that we shall not have long to wait before there are in India numerous colleges and public schools maintained by those who use them, or supported by the liberality of private benefactors.

You have decided, and in my opinion, very rightly, to open your college to all, irrespective of their creed, and it is, I think, much to the credit of the managing body of this institution that it is conducted on non-sectarian principles, and that the Hindu scholar is as readily received as the Mahomedan, just as a native of Madras is as eligible for admission as one from these provinces. It is the opinion of the Government over which I have the honour to preside that our present State system of education is not sufficiently safeguarded by discipline and moral training, and it is a matter of satisfaction to me that you have recognised the need for giving religious, moral, and social instruction to your pupils and for following our Western methods in bringing to bear upon them during their leisure hours the influence of upright and high-minded tutors. The encouragement which you give to the boys at your college to become skilled in outdoor amusements is also, in my opinion, highly to be commended, and I have read with interest, of the success which they have from time to time achieved in the cricket-field.

SPEECH AT ST. ANDREW'S DINNER, CALCUTTA.

On the 30th of November, 1888, Lord Dufferin attended the annual dinner given by the Scotch inhabitants of Calcutta in celebration of St. Andrew's Day. In reply to the toast of his health, which was proposed by the Chairman, Sir Alec Wilson, His Excellency spoke as follows :—

GENTLEMEN,—Before attempting to return thanks for the kind and hearty manner in which you have drunk my health, I feel that, above all things, it is necessary that I should justify my presence amongst you upon this occasion. This is especially a Scotch dinner, and it is held in commemoration of an eminent personage, who was next door to having been born and bred in Scotland. (Laughter.) Well, gentlemen, I may claim as much right to your consanguinity as St. Andrew himself; for, in those distant days to which we both belong, I also, as represented by my remote forefathers, was a countryman of your own. (Applause.) Indeed, I may still call myself by that honourable appellation, the only difference being that I have been very much improved by having been an Irishman during the last three hundred years. (Cheers and laughter.) You, gentlemen, represent the raw material in its protoplastic condition; Mr. Barbour, my eminent financial colleague, whom I am happy to see keeping me in countenance, and myself, are specimens of the manufactured article and the developed organism. (Laughter and cheers.) But, for all that, the old Adam—I do not allude to the father of the human race, but to one Adam, an ancestor of my own, who, like his namesake, was turned out of your northern paradise, and that, too, for being too submissive to a lady, who was not even his wife, but Mary Queen of Scots—(laughter)—the old Adam, I say, will still betray itself and kindle a glow of brotherly enthusiasm in my breast whenever I find myself surrounded by a company of kindly Scotchmen. (Cheers.) And now, gentlemen, having made good my *locus standi* amongst you—my foot being, so to speak, on my native heath—I desire, from the bottom of my heart, and with all the earnestness that words are capable of displaying, to convey to you my deep sense of your goodness in having extended to me so friendly and so gracious a welcome. (Cheers.) Although I cannot take credit to myself for all the appreciative and indulgent encomiums which your chairman has been pleased to pass upon my administration, I am not the less sensible of the good-will and sympathy implied by the enthusiastic cheers which greeted his utterances. It is quite true, as Sir Alec Wilson has observed, that, in the four years of my Viceroyalty, I have had greater and more unexpected difficulties to contend with than have troubled the serenity of most of my immediate predecessors. The first and the greatest of these has undoubtedly been the fall in the value of silver, which, by depleting the revenues of India to the extent of more than three millions a year, has crippled the energies of my Government in every direction, and imposed upon me the ungracious duty of—well, I will not damp the gaiety of this joyous festival by alluding further to so disagreeable a subject. (Laughter and cheers.) Indeed, I do not intend to trouble you to-night with egotistical references to my own administration, or with any attempt to vindicate the general policy of the Government of India. The verdict upon both has passed out of my hands, and it will be the pen of the historian that will determine whether my colleagues and myself have succeeded in any adequate degree in contributing to the peace and security of the country, in dissipating some formidable dangers, and in inaugurating such reforms and improvements in its administration as the time and the circumstances of the case either permitted or required. (Applause.) Of one thing, at all events, I am certain—we have done a great deal more in these directions than is generally supposed. Still there is one misapprehension into which the public has fallen, which I am desirous of taking this opportunity of correcting once for all, lest it should crystallize into a popular belief, and that is that the difficulties which we have had to encounter in Burma arose from an attempt of the Indian Government to effect the conquest of that kingdom in too economical a manner, or, to use a vulgar expression, 'on the cheap.' Such an idea is entirely unfounded. There may have been mistakes, but they did not arise from that source. On the contrary, the Government of India has never, from first to last, refused the local authorities of Burma a single requisition, whether for money, for troops, for civil officers, or for police, which they have ever submitted to us. (Cheers.) Nay more, we encouraged them from time to time to make further demands on us in every one of these respects. With regard to the strength of the original force, it must be remembered that the expedition to Mandalay was essentially a riverine expedition, and that the number of troops that could be despatched upon it was limited by the riverine transport at our disposal. Though the means of transport afforded us by the existence of the Irrawaddy Flotilla Company were very considerable, they had to be strained to the utmost extent. Happily, they were amply sufficient for the immediate purpose in view, as was shown by the surrender of the Burmese army, the capture of the king, and the occupation of his capital in the course of a fortnight. (Applause.) The very day that Mandalay was taken we telegraphed to both our civil and military representatives to inquire whether or not the additional reinforcements which we had ready to start in support should be sent off; but both the civil and the military authorities considered that the forces at their disposal were sufficient for all immediate requirements. The difficulties which subsequently occurred were not difficulties which could be overcome by the application of mere brute force as represented by numbers. They were inherent in the very nature of the case, —the enormous extent of the country, its complete disorganization, the absence of all roads, and the vastness and impracticability of the jungles. Impediments like these could not be successfully dealt with at once, especially as the rainy season soon intervened to hamper our endeavours. Roads had to be cut, telegraphic communications established, military posts constructed, and a hundred other preliminary arrangements introduced. Above all, a military police had to be organized, for the Government of India does not keep on hand, as a grocer does pepper, a ready-made supply of military police for casual emergencies. Such a body, who are the real restorers of order, have to be painfully and laboriously enlisted and drilled. In spite of all these difficulties, as Sir Alec Wilson has stated, within a little more than two years and a half, we have succeeded not only in tranquillizing the country but in furnishing it forth with all the appliances of a civilized state. (Cheers.) All the big dacoit bands have been dispersed, and their leaders disposed of. Crime in Lower Burma is now less than it was before the war, and even the return of the dry season has not shown any perceptible recurrence of it in Upper Burma. It is true that, during the winter we shall have to punish some of the wild mountain tribes, both in the north and in the west, who have been raiding Burmese villages and head-hunting on Burmese territory. But these troubles are as common to the borders of India as they are to those of Burma. If we remember that, when Lord Dalhousie took possession of Pegu—though he undoubtedly displayed in everything he undertook the greatest vigour and energy, and though Pegu was only a sixth of the size of the country that we have recently dominated—it took him seven or eight years to reduce it to reasonable submission, I think we may be satisfied with the result. (Loud applause.) Indeed, it was only the other day that I was reading a life of Lord Minto, who mentions incidentally that in his time whole districts within twenty miles of Calcutta were at the mercy of dacoits, and this after the English had been more than fifty years in the occupation of Bengal; while, even in our own days, large bands of robbers in Central India are baffling all the efforts of the Indore Government to put an end to their depredations. The fact is dacoity is a peculiar sort of crime, and one far more difficult to deal with than even the organized opposition of regular armies. I have been led to dilate more fully upon this subject than I had intended; but I have felt it my duty to do so, not so much in the interests of the Indian administration as from a desire to vindicate the conduct of those eminent civil and military officers who, in the teeth of a great deal of mis-apprehension, have been carrying out with exceptional ability, and with acknowledged success, their responsible and thankless duties. (Cheers.) And now, gentlemen, what else am I to say to you? As a rule, I do not think it is a desirable thing for the Viceroy of India to make speeches. I have carefully avoided doing so as much as possible; but perhaps, as I am so near the day of my dissolution, I may be permitted to utter a few words of warning and advice to those to whose affairs I have been giving such unremitting attention for so long a period. You will understand, therefore, that it is not so much the Viceroy that is addressing you as a departing, pale, and attenuated shade, or rather, shall we say, some intelligent traveller who has come to India for three months, with the intention of writing an encyclopedic work on its Government and its people, and who is therefore able to speak in a spirit of infallibility denied to us lesser men. (Laughter.)

Well then, gentlemen, what is India? It is an empire equal in size, if Russia be excluded, to the entire continent of Europe, with a population of 250 million souls. This population is composed of a large number of distinct nationalities, professing various religions, practising diverse rites, speaking different languages—the Census Report says there are 106 different Indian tongues—not dialects, mind you—of which 18 are spoken by more than a million persons—and many of these nationalities are still further separated from each other by discordant prejudices, by conflicting social usages, and even antagonistic material interests. Perhaps the most patent peculiarity of our Indian "cosmos" is its division into two mighty political communities—the Hindus numbering 190 millions, and the Mahomedans, a nation of 50 millions—whose distinctive characteristics, whether religious, social, or ethnological, it is of course unnecessary for me to refer to before such an audience as the present. But to these two great divisions must be added a host of minor nationalities—though minor is a misleading term, since most of them may be numbered by millions —who, though some are included in the two broader categories I have mentioned, are as completely differentiated from each other as are the Hindus from the Mahomedans. Such are the Sikhs, with their warlike habits and traditions, and their theocratic enthusiasm; the Rohillas, the Pathans, the Assamese, the Biluchees, and the other wild and martial tribes on our frontiers; the hillmen dwelling in the folds of the Himalayas; our subjects in Burma, Mongol in race and Buddhist in religion; the Khonds, Mairs, and Bheels, and other non-Aryan peoples in the centre and south of India; and the enterprising Parsees, with their rapidly developing manufactures and commercial interests. Again, amongst these numerous communities may be found at one and the same moment all the various stages of civilization through which mankind has passed from the pre-historic ages to the present day. At one end of the scale we have the naked savage hillman, with his stone weapons, his head-hunting, his polyandrous habits, and his childish superstitions; and at the other, the Europeanized native gentleman, with his refinement and polish, his literary culture, his Western philosophy, and his advanced political ideas; while between the two lie, layer upon layer, or in close juxtaposition, wandering communities, with their flocks of goats and moving tents; collections of undisciplined warriors, with their blood feuds, their clan organization and loose tribal government; feudal chiefs and barons, with their picturesque retainers, their seignorial jurisdiction, and their mediæval modes of life; and modernized country gentlemen, and enterprising merchants and manufacturers, with their well-managed estates and prosperous enterprises. Besides all these, who are under our direct administration, the Government of India is required to exercise a certain amount of supervision over the one hundred and seventeen native states, with their princely rulers, their autocratic executives, their independent jurisdictions, and their fifty millions of inhabitants. The mere enumeration of these diversified elements must suggest to the most unimaginative mind a picture of as complicated a social and political organization as ever tasked human ingenuity to govern and administer. (Loud applause.) But, even within British India in the narrower sense of the term, we have not reached the limits of our accountability, for we are bound to provide for the safety and welfare not only of Her Majesty's Hindu, Mahomedan, and other native subjects, but also of the large East Indian community, of the indigenous Christian Churches, of the important planting and manufacturing interests which are scattered over the face of the country, as also to secure the property and lives of all the British residents in India, men, women, and children, whether employed in the service of the Government or pursuing independent avocations in the midst of the alien and semi-civilized multitudes whose peaceable and orderly behaviour cannot, under all circumstances, be implicitly relied on. (Cheers.) To these obligations must also be added the duty of watching over the enormous commercial interests of the mother country, represented by a guaranteed capital of over two hundred and twenty millions of pounds sterling, which, to the great benefit of India, has been either lent to the State or sunk in Indian railways and similar enterprises; for it would be criminal to ignore the responsibility of the Government towards those who have sunk large sums of money in the development of Indian resources on the faith of official guarantees, or who have invested their capital in the Indian funds at the invitation of the Imperial Indian authorities. The same considerations apply with almost equal force to that further vast amount of capital which is employed by private British enterprise in manufactures, in tea planting, and in the indigo, jute, and similar industries, on the assumption that English rule and English justice will remain dominant in India. (Loud applause.) If, again, we turn our eyes outwards, it will be found that our external obligations are hardly less onerous and imperative than those confronting us from within. India has a land frontier of nearly 6000 miles, and a seaboard of about 9000 miles. On the east she is conterminous with Siam and China, on the north with Thibet, Bhootan, and Nepaul, and on the west she marches, at all events diplomatically, with Russia. On her coast are many rich and prosperous seaports—Calcutta, Bombay, Madras, Kurachee, Rangoon—and every year we are made more painfully aware to how serious an extent our contiguity with foreign nations, whether civilized or uncivilized, and the complications arising both out of Eastern and Western politics, may expose us to attack. Every day we feel more keenly the necessity of walking both warily and wisely in respect of our international relations, and of taking those precautions, however onerous or expensive, which are incumbent on every nation that finds itself in contact with enterprising military monarchies or rival maritime powers. (Cheers.) It is then for the outward protection and for the internal control—it is for the welfare, good government, and progress of this congeries of nations, religions, tribes, and communities, with the tremendous latent forces and disruptive potentialities which they contain, that the Government of India is answerable; and it is in reference to the ever-shifting and multiplying requirements of this complicated political organization that it has been called upon from time to time to shape and modify its system of administration. In the earlier stages of England's connection with India, and even after the force of circumstances had transmuted the East India Company of merchants into an Imperial Executive, the ignorance and the disorganization of the peninsula consequent upon the anarchy which followed the collapse of the Mahomedan *régime* necessitated the maintenance of a strong uncompromising despotism, with the view of bringing order out of chaos, and a systematized administration out of the confusion and lawlessness which were then universally prevalent. But such principles of government, however necessary, have never been congenial to the instincts or habits of the English people. (Applause.) As soon as the circumstances of the case permitted, successive statesmen, both at home and in India itself, employed themselves from time to time in softening the severity of the system under which our dominion was originally established, and strenuous efforts were repeatedly made, not only to extend to Her Majesty's subjects in India the same civil rights and privileges which are enjoyed by Her Majesty's subjects at home, but to admit them, as far as was possible, to a share in the management of their own affairs. (Cheers.) The proof of this is plainly written in our recent history. It is seen in our legal codes, which secure to all Her Majesty's subjects, without distinction of race or creed or class, equality before the law. (Cheers.) It is found in the establishment of local legislative councils a quarter of a century ago, wherein a certain number of leading natives were associated with the Government in enacting measures suitable to local wants. It lies at the basis of the great principle of decentralized finance, which has prepared the way for the establishment of increased local responsibility. It received a most important development in the municipal legislation of Lord Northbrook's administration. It took a still fuller and more perfect expression during the administration of my distinguished predecessor, in the Municipal and Local Boards Acts; and it has acquired a further illustration in the recommendation of the Public Service Commission, recently sent home by the Government of India, in accordance with which more than a hundred offices hitherto reserved to the Covenanted Service would be thrown open to the Provincial Service, and thus placed within the reach of our native fellow-subjects in India. (Applause.) And now, gentlemen, some intelligent, loyal, patriotic, and well-meaning men are desirous of taking, I will not say a further step in advance, but a very big jump into the unknown—by the application to India of democratic methods of government, and the adoption of a parliamentary system, which England herself has only reached by slow degrees and through the discipline of many centuries of preparation. (Cheers.) The ideal authoritatively suggested, as I understand, is the creation of a representative body or bodies in which the official element shall be in a minority, who shall have what is called the power of the purse, and who, through this instrumentality, shall be able to bring the British executive into subjection to their will. The organization of battalions of native militia and volunteers for the internal and external defence of the country is the next arrangement suggested, and the first practical result to be obtained would be the reduction of the British army to one half its present numbers. Well, gentlemen, I am afraid that the people of England will not readily be brought to the acceptance of this programme, or to allow such an assembly, or a number of such assemblies, either to interfere with its armies, or to fetter and circumscribe the liberty of action either of the provincial governments or of the Supreme Executive. (Applause.) In the first place, the scheme is eminently unconstitutional; for the essence of constitutional government is that responsibility and power should be committed to the same hands. The idea of irresponsible councils, whose members could arrest the march of Indian legislation, or nullify the policy of the British executive in India, without being liable to be called to account for their acts in a way in which an opposition can be called to account in a constitutional country, must be regarded as an impracticable anomaly. (Applause.) Indeed, so obviously impossible would be the application of any such system in the circumstances of the case, that I do not believe it has been seriously advocated by any native statesman of the slightest weight or importance. I have come into contact, during the last four years, with, I imagine, almost all the most distinguished persons in India. I have talked with most of them upon these matters, and I have never heard a suggestion from one of them in the sense I have mentioned. (Cheers.) But if no native statesman of weight or importance, capable of appreciating the true interests of England and of India, is found to defend this programme, who are those who do? Who and what are the persons who seek to assume such great powers—to tempt the fate of Phaeton, and to sit in the chariot of the Sun? (Applause.) Well, they are gentlemen of whom I desire to speak with the greatest courtesy and kindness, for they are, most of them, the product of the system of education which we ourselves have carried on during the last thirty years. But thirty years is a very short time in which to educe a self-governing nation from its primordial elements. At all events, let us measure the extent of educated assistance upon which we could call at this moment; let us examine the degree of proficiency which the educated classes of India have attained and the relation of their numbers to the rest of the population. Out of the whole population of British India, which may be put at 200 millions in round numbers, not more than five or six per cent. can read and write, while less than one per cent. has any knowledge of English. Thus, the overwhelming mass of the people, perhaps one hundred and ninety out of the two hundred millions, are still steeped in ignorance, and of the ten or twelve millions who have acquired education, three-fourths have attained to merely the most elementary knowledge.

In our recent review of the progress of education, it was pointed out that ninety-four and a half per cent. of those attending our schools and colleges were in the primary stage, while the progress made in English education can be measured by the fact that the number of students who have graduated at the universities since their establishment in 1857—that is, during the course of the last thirty-one years—is under eight thousand. During the last twenty-five years probably not more than half a million students have passed out of our schools with a good knowledge of English, and perhaps a million more with a smattering of it. Consequently, it may be said that, out of a population of 200 millions, there are only a very few thousands who may be considered to possess adequate qualifications, so far as education and an acquaintance with Western ideas or even Eastern learning are concerned, for taking an intelligent view of those intricate and complicated economic and political questions affecting the destinies of so many millions of men which are almost daily being presented for the consideration of the Government of India. (Applause.) I would ask, then, how any reasonable man could imagine that the British Government would be content to allow this microscopic minority to control their administration of that majestic and multiform empire for whose safety and welfare they are responsible in the eyes of God and before the face of civilization? (Cheers.) It has been stated that this minority represents a large and growing class. I am glad to think that it represents a growing class, and I feel very sure that, as time goes on, it is not only the class that will grow, but also the information and experience of its members. At present, however, it appears to me a groundless contention that it represents the people of India. If they had been really representatives of the people of India—that is to say, of the voiceless millions—instead of seeking to circumscribe the incidence of the income tax, as they desired to do, they would probably have received a mandate to decuple it. (Laughter.) Indeed, is it not evident that large sections of the community are already becoming alarmed at the thought of such self-constituted bodies interposing between themselves and the august impartiality of English rule? These persons ought to know that in the present condition of India there can be no real or effective representation of the people, with their enormous numbers, their multifarious interests, and their tesselated nationalities. They ought to see that all the strength, power, and intelligence of the British Government are applied to the prevention of one race, of one interest, of one class, of one religion, dominating another; and they ought to feel that in their peculiar position there can be no greater blessing to the country than the existence of an external, dispassionate, and immutable authority, whose watchword is Justice, and who alone possesses both the power and the will to weld the rights and status of each separate element of the empire into a peaceful, co-ordinated, and harmonious unity. (Loud cheers.) When the Congress was first started, I watched its operations with interest and curiosity, and I hoped that in certain fields of useful activity it might render valuable assistance to the Government. I was aware that there were many social topics connected with the habits and customs of the people which were of unquestionable utility, but with which it was either undesirable for the Government to interfere, or which it was beyond their power to influence or control. For instance, where is there a population whose rise in the scale of social comfort and prosperity is more checked and impeded by excessive and useless expenditure on the occasion of marriages and other similar ceremonies than that of India? Or in what country is the peasant more hampered in the pursuit of his agricultural industry, than is the Hindu or Mahomedan ryot, by chronic indebtedness to the moneylenders? Where is there a more crying need for sanitary reform than amongst those who insist upon bathing in the tanks from which they obtain their drinking-water, and where millions of men, women, and children die yearly, or, what is even worse, become the victims of chronic debility, disease, and racial deterioration, from preventible causes? What system could be named more calculated to cause greater searchings of the heart than some of the domestic arrangements so ruthlessly insisted upon by Hindu society? Above all, what land is exposed to such imminent danger by the overflow of the population of large districts and territories whose inhabitants are yearly multiplying beyond the number which the soil is capable of sustaining? To this last topic I am especially anxious to call the attention of every lover of his country. The danger has long since been signalized by European writers, especially by that most acute of all observers, the late Sir Henry Maine; and it was almost the first subject that attracted my attention when I came to India. Perhaps the widespread misery which I had witnessed in Ireland, produced by similar conditions, had quickened my observation. (Applause.) I first of all commissioned Sir William Hunter to take the matter up, and after his departure the task of dealing with it was confided to Sir Edward Buck. A committee met at Delhi, and at the same time provisional reports were called for from various governments on the general condition of the people. The short resolution in which the general tendency of these reports and the lessons to be derived from them are contained, has, I understand, been denounced as an endeavour of the Government to impart a rose-coloured view to the situation. All I can say is that in ordering the inquiry my object was to obtain the means of awaking public opinion in India to the gravity and danger of our position, rather than to lull it into fancied security, and any one who can derive much satisfaction from the result must be either of a very sanguine or a very callous temperament; for although it has been clearly demonstrated that those who represent the poorer classes of India as universally living in a chronic state of semi-starvation and inanition, grossly exaggerate, and that the condition of these classes has been steadily improving, it is undoubtedly the case that in certain districts, whose inhabitants are to be numbered by millions, the means of sustenance provided by the soil are inadequate for the support of those who live upon it. When we reflect that, in the most thickly populated districts of Europe, there are only from 400 to 500 persons to the square mile, whereas in the localities I am referring to they exceed 700 and even 800 to the square mile, we shall be better able to appreciate the reality of the danger. Well, then, gentlemen, for such a state of things there are only two remedies—the expansion of manufacturing industries, and emigration. But it is not in the power of the Government of itself to apply either of these remedies. (Applause.) By removing restrictions on trade, and by the multiplication of roads, railways, and the facilities of conveyance, we can foster manufacturing and mercantile activity, which we are doing; but the actual creation of manufacturing centres must be the work of private enterprise. (Cheers.) To the same imperfect degree, and principally by the same means, the Government can promote emigration. (Cheers.) It can let or sell land under favourable conditions to would-be settlers. It can indicate the places where population is superabundant, and where comparatively unoccupied tracts are to be found; but it can neither prohibit by law imprudent marriages, nor compel the inhabitants of a village in any particular locality to transfer themselves to another. But what the Government cannot do, the gentlemen to whom I am referring might very usefully employ themselves in doing. They know the ways and habits of the people; they know the nature of their occupations; they know their needs; and as they themselves come from different parts of India, they know where labour is scarce, where land is plentiful, and where the new comers could be best accommodated either as cultivators or as coolies. By carefully examining the elements of the problem, they might put themselves into a position to place at the disposal of the Government both useful information and advice. (Loud applause.) Again, with regard to sanitation. And by sanitation I do not mean the inopportune and injudicious worrying and harrying of our villagers into the adoption of uncongenial ways and habits, or the forcing upon them of the latest principles of Western hygiene, but a gradual patient process similar to that which has banished cholera, jail fever, and many other ills from England during the course of the present century, and which consists in placing pure water within the reach of the people, and in indoctrinating them with those simple rules which add as much to the comfort as they do to the decency of domestic life. The Government has recently given its serious attention to this subject, and has laid down the lines upon which, in its opinion, sanitary reform should be applied to our towns and villages. It has given sanitation a local habitation and a name in every great division of the empire; and it has arranged for the establishment of responsible central agencies from one end of the country to the other, who will be in close communication with all the local authorities within their respective jurisdictions. But, after all, the most earnest endeavours both of the Supreme and of the Provincial Governments will be of little avail, unless seconded by the intelligent co-operation of the educated native classes. (Applause.) So again with regard to technical education. The Government of India may recommend to the local governments the policy and the arrangements which it considers to be suited for the establishment and spread of this useful and necessary branch of instruction, and the local governments may improve upon those suggestions, or may apply them with the utmost zeal and wisdom; but it is the educated classes—those who are most intimately acquainted with the internal economy of the homes of India and the natural aptitudes of their inhabitants—who alone can give energy and vitality to the movement. Well, gentlemen, as I have already observed, when the Congress was first started, it seemed to me that such a body, if they directed their attention with patriotic zeal to the consideration of these and cognate subjects, as similar Congresses do in England, might prove of assistance to the Government and of great use to their fellow-citizens; and I cannot help expressing my regret that they should seem to consider such momentous topics, concerning as they do the welfare of millions of their fellow-subjects, as beneath their notice, and that they should have concerned themselves instead with matters in regard to which their assistance is likely to be less profitable to us. (Applause.) It is a still greater matter of regret to me that the members of the Congress should have become answerable for the distribution—as their officials have boasted—amongst thousands and thousands of ignorant and credulous men of publications animated by a very questionable spirit, and whose manifest aim is to excite the hatred of the people against the public servants of the Crown in this country. (Cheers.) Such proceedings as these no Government could regard with indifference, nor can they fail to inspire it with misgivings, at all events with regard to the wisdom of those who have so offended. Nor is the silly threat of one of the chief officers—the principal secretary, I believe—of the Congress, that he and his Congress friends hold in their hands the keys not only of a popular insurrection but of a military revolt, calculated to restore our confidence in their discretion, even when accompanied by the assurance that they do not intend for the present to put these keys into the locks. (Loud applause.) But, gentlemen, though I have thought it my duty in these plain terms to point out what I consider the misapprehension of the Congress party as to the proper direction in which their energies should be employed, I do not at all wish to imply that I view with anything but favour and sympathy the desire of the educated classes of India to be more largely associated with us in the conduct of the affairs of their country. Such an ambition is not only very natural, but very worthy, provided due regard be had to the circumstances of the country and to the conditions under which the British administration in India discharges its duties. (Applause.) In the speech which I delivered at Calcutta on the occasion of Her Majesty's jubilee, I used the following expression:—" Wide and broad, indeed, are the new fields in which the Government of India is called upon to labour, but no longer, as of aforetime, need it labour alone. Within the period we are reviewing, education has done its work, and we are surrounded on all sides by native gentlemen of great attainments and intelligence, from whose hearty, loyal, and honest co-operation we may hope to derive the greatest benefit. In fact, to an administration so peculiarly situated as ours, their advice, assistance, and solidarity are essential to the successful exercise of its functions. Nor do I regard with any other feelings than those of approval and good-will their natural ambition to be more extensively associated with their English rulers in the administration of their own domestic affairs; and glad and happy should I be if, during my sojourn amongst them, circumstances permitted me to extend and to place upon a wider and more logical footing the political status which was so wisely given a generation ago by that great statesman, Lord Halifax, to such Indian gentlemen as by their influence, their acquirements, and the confidence they inspired in their fellow-countrymen, were marked out as useful adjuncts to our Legislative Councils." To every word which I then spoke I continue to adhere (cheers); but surely the sensible men of the country cannot imagine that even the most moderate constitutional changes can be effected in such a system as ours by a stroke of the pen, or without the most anxious deliberations, as well as careful discussions in Parliament. (Applause.) If ever a political organization has existed where caution is necessary in dealing with those problems which affect the adjustment of the administrative machine, and where haste and precipitancy are liable to produce deplorable results, it is that which holds together our complex Indian Empire; and the man who stretches forth his hand towards the ark, even with the best intentions, may well dread lest his arm should shrivel up to the shoulder. But growth and development are the rule of the world's history, and from the proofs I have already given of the way in which English statesmanship has perpetually striven gradually to adapt our methods of government in India to the expanding intelligence and capacities of the educated classes amongst our Indian subjects, it may be confidently expected that the legitimate and reasonable aspirations of the responsible heads of native society, whether Hindu or Mahomedan, will in due time receive legitimate satisfaction. (Cheers.) The more we enlarge the surface of our contact with the educated and intelligent public opinion of India, the better; and although I hold it absolutely necessary, not merely for the maintenance of our own power, but for the good government of the country, and for the general content of all classes, and especially of the people at large, that England should never abdicate her supreme control of public affairs, or delegate to a minority or to a class the duty of providing for the welfare of the diversified communities over which she rules, I am not the less convinced that we could, with advantage, draw more largely than we have hitherto done on native intelligence and native assistance in the discharge of our duties. (Loud applause.) I have had ample opportunities of gauging and appreciating to its full extent the measure of good sense, of practical wisdom, and of experience which is possessed by the leading men of India, both among the great nobles on the one hand, and amongst the leisured and professional classes on the other, and I have now submitted officially to the home authorities some personal suggestions in harmony with the foregoing views. (Cheers.) Gentlemen, I have sometimes seen in the newspapers formidable indictments drawn up against the British administration in India. I do not now refer to them for the purpose of controverting the charges which they formulated, but they have certainly indicated one blemish which the Government of India frankly recognises and had already begun to deal with; namely, the present constitution of the police. There are undoubtedly great defects in this branch of the public service. It is, however, by no means an easy matter to deal with. The difficulty lies in the low *morale* prevailing in the classes from which alone the police can be drawn, in the supineness and ignorance of the people themselves, and, still more, the additional expenditure which would be entailed by any really effective amelioration of the force. (Applause.) Again, with regard to the separation of judicial and executive offices in the early stage of the service and in the lower grades. This is a counsel of perfection to which we are ready to subscribe, though the reform suggested, where it has not been carried into effect—and it has been largely effected—is by no means so simple a proceeding as many people suppose. And here also we have a question of money. With regard to both these subjects, however, I have to make one observation. The evils complained of are not of recent date: they existed long before my time, and had they been as intolerable as is now stated, they would have been remedied while the existence of surplus funds rendered this practicable; but, as this was not done, it is fair to argue that, even admitting that there is room for improvement in both the above respects, we can afford to consult times and seasons in carrying these improvements into effect. (Applause.) Be that, however, as it may, I confess I always lay down these incriminating documents with a feeling of relief at finding that more serious shortcomings cannot be alleged

against us. (Cheers.) When I consider the difficulties of our task, the imperfection of the instruments through which we must necessarily work, the multiplicity of the interests with which we have to deal, the liability of our most careful calculations to be overset by material accidents over which we have no command, the complexity and centrifugal might of the forces we are called upon to harmonize and co-ordinate, the extraordinary tendency in the East for two and two to make five, and the imperfection which stamps the conduct of all human affairs, my wonder is that our miscarriages should not have been infinitely multiplied. In reading these criticisms I am reminded of a story of a young man who afterwards became a very powerful public speaker. On his first appearance on the hustings he was so embarrassed by the novel circumstances of his situation that he made but an indifferent attempt at a speech; but when some one in the crowd ill-naturedly jeered at him, he cried out, "You just come up here and do it yourself—you won't find it so easy," which pertinent observation at once won for him the sympathy of his audience. (Loud laughter.) At all events, we have the satisfaction of knowing that there is another side to the picture; for in these diatribes, to use Sir Auckland Colvin's eloquent words, "of the India of to-day as we know it; of India under education; of India compelled, in the interests of the weaker masses, to submit to impartial justice; of India brought together by road and rail; of India entering into the first-class commercial markets of the world; of India of religious toleration; of India assured, for terms of years unknown in less fortunate Europe, of profound and unbroken peace; of India of the free press; of India finally taught for the first time that the end and aim of rule is the welfare of the people and not the personal aggrandisement of the sovereign"
—he might have added of India that within the last twenty-eight years has accumulated 110 millions of gold and 218 millions of silver,—"we fail to find a syllable of recognition." (Cheers.) At all events, gentlemen, you may be sure that whatever our sins, whether of omission or of commission, the English Government in India will continue faithfully, courageously, and in the fear of God to endeavour to discharge its

duties, to amend whatever may be amiss, and still further to improve the good which already exists, indifferent to praise or blame, and as unresentful of the hard things occasionally said of us by those for whose sake we are labouring, as we shall always be grateful for the appreciation of those—and they are the great majority—of our Indian fellow-subjects who have the intelligence to understand and the generosity to acknowledge what we have done for them. (Loud applause.) And now, gentlemen, it only remains for me to thank you not only for your hospitality and for the friendly reception you have given to the mention of Lady Dufferin's name and my own, but for the patience with which you have listened to this somewhat lengthy speech. It is a great regret to me to think that I am looking round for the last time upon so many friendly and familiar faces. In another week I shall have discharged my trust, and transferred my great office to the hands of one of England's most capable statesmen, a nobleman in the prime of life, and already distinguished for his sound judgment, his moderation, his wisdom, and the industry with which he applies himself to public affairs. That he will by the intelligence, the impartiality, and the sympathetic character of his rule gain and maintain the good-will and the confidence both of Her Majesty's native and English subjects in India, I have not the slightest doubt, and this conviction to a great extent consoles me for my regret in quitting your service. Gentlemen, I again thank you from the very bottom of my heart for all your kindness and goodness. (Loud and long continued cheers.)

ADDRESS FROM THE NATIVE LADIES OF BENGAL.

On Tuesday afternoon, the 4th December, 1888, the *purda-nashin* ladies of Bengal presented a valedictory address to Her Excellency the Marchioness of Dufferin and Ava at Government House. The greatest privacy was observed in receiving the ladies, all male visitors being excluded. There were nearly seven hundred native ladies present, there being hardly standing room in the Throne-room, where the address was presented and the reception took place. Among those who formed the deputation were several Burmese ladies, some of the costumes worn being very picturesque. Lady Bayley and a large company of European ladies received the members of the deputation and conducted them to the Throne-room, where, after the usual formalities of introduction were over, Lady Bayley, on behalf of the deputation, read the following address:—

To Her Excellency the Marchioness of Dufferin and Ava, C.I.

MAY IT PLEASE YOUR EXCELLENCY,—We venture to address you on the occasion of your leaving India with our most heartfelt expression of gratitude for the inestimable boon which you have conferred on the women of India by your unwearying labour and watchful care on their behalf during the four years you have been among us. A memorable attempt has been made to alleviate the fearful amount of female suffering which prevails in India through the want of competent medical attendance, and it is under your auspices that a National Association has been formed for supplying female medical aid to women in all the provinces of the empire. The work of this Association, with which we are happy to feel that Your Excellency's name will always be associated, has now been successfully conducted through the difficulties which beset the early life of all similar institutions; and we are indulging in no hyperbole of speech when we say that it is through your sympathy with suffering, your devotion to the weak and helpless, your wisdom and enthusiasm, which has inspired others to charitable deeds, that the gratifying results already attained are to be attributed. You are now able to quit the scene of your labours with a serene conviction that the amelioration of the condition of the women of India, the cause which you have so much at heart, is a reality and not a dream; that it is a project which will not die with your departure, but is vigorous and instinct with life; and that your successors will take up the torch of further improvement and carry it on again to those who will follow after them with increasing lustre. We who now venture to address you on behalf of the women of India give utterance to the sentiments of all our sex when we assure you of our respect, affection, and admiration. To you and your illustrious consort we tender our thanks. We shall never be forgetful of your goodness, and we are sure of this also, that in whatever lot your life may henceforth be cast, your thoughts and interests and generous wishes will always be for the welfare of the women of India. We respectfully beg that on your return to England you will convey to her gracious Majesty the Queen-Empress our humble and grateful appreciation of the active interest she has been pleased to take in the work of the National Association, and of the encouragement she has afforded to the labourers in the movement by her august patronage. We bid you now a regretful farewell, and fervently hope that under God's providence you may evermore enjoy happiness and prosperity.

Her Excellency the Marchioness of Dufferin and Ava in reply said:—

MY FRIENDS,—It is indeed difficult for me to tell you how deeply I feel the kind words of your address. I am quite sure that no one in the fulfilment of a plain duty has ever received so great a reward as I have, in the sympathy and appreciation of those for whom I have tried to do something, and in the rapid progress and success of the work I undertook. That work is founded upon love and common sense, and built upon such sure foundations it cannot fail. If it has been my happy privilege to draw attention to the remediable sufferings and to the wants of the women of India, it is the quick response to that appeal emanating from the hearts and minds of their countrymen which has made the amelioration of their lot a reality and not a dream. I thank you also for your kind allusion to the Viceroy. You can readily understand that without his personal sympathy and encouragement and his hearty interest in the work of the National Association I myself could have done nothing; nor must I omit to acknowledge here the friendly aid and consideration my plans have always received from the Government of India. I shall have no greater pleasure in returning to England than that of conveying to Her Majesty the Queen-Empress your expressions of loyalty and gratitude, and in assuring Her Majesty of the stability and the vitality of the work in which she has taken so great and active an interest. Again I thank you with all my heart for your kindness to myself, and I pray that every year that passes may add to the happiness, may diminish the suffering, and may improve the condition of the women of India.

FAREWELL ADDRESS TO THE MARCHIONESS OF DUFFERIN AND AVA.

A deputation from the Public Health Society waited on Wednesday afternoon, the 7th December, on Her Excellency the Marchioness of Dufferin and Ava, to present her with a farewell address. The address, which was read by Mr. Simmons, honorary secretary, was as follows:—

MAY IT PLEASE YOUR EXCELLENCY,—We, the President, Vice-President, and Members of the Council of the Public Health Society, on behalf of the society, venture to approach Your Excellency on the eve of your departure from India, to tender to Your Excellency an expression of our appreciation of the great work it has under Providence fallen to your lot to perform for the women of this empire. And before dealing directly with the object of this address, we would ask permission to convey to Your Excellency and to your noble husband our sincere and heartfelt congratulations upon the honours conferred upon him by our most Gracious Sovereign in return for service to the State, the single-heartedness and devotion of which no one can know so well as you who have had the proud and wifely pleasure to share his cares and labours, and to grace his reward. Your Excellency, to a body devoted to the spread of sanitary knowledge, and to the extension of all measures tending to increase the comfort and secure the health of the people, such as the society we have the honour to represent, it is a source of peculiar satisfaction to bear testimony to the beneficent character of the institution you have provided in our midst, to the excellency of its methods of working, and to the promising and encouraging measure of success which has already attended its operations. The National Association for supplying female medical aid to the women of India has met a want long acknowledged and severely felt. It not only offers but affords help of the most valuable kind in quarters where help is most needed and has hitherto been most difficult to render. It is a boon to the women of India, for the gift of which future generations will hold your name in reverence, only to be measured by the affection which now surrounds you, and which, while lamenting the public loss caused by your departure from India, pours around your departing pathway the blessings and prayers of many nations for your future welfare, honour, and happiness. But valuable as the society which bears your name may be for the direct benefits it confers, it is equally valuable for the indirect impetus it gives to the improvement of the position of Indian women by the stimulus it affords for their education, and the outlet it furnishes for their energies, abilities, and talents. To Your Excellency it has been vouchsafed not only to accomplish a great work in a worthy and effective manner, but to see gathered in the first-fruits of your labours, rich in promise of future usefulness to those you have so willingly and so unstintingly served, and of a distinct and powerful influence for good on all that tends to promote the welfare of the people of India. In taking leave of Your Excellency, we are but repeating the sentiment which fills the hearts of millions of our fellow-subjects, when we say that we know we are parting from one of the truest, most disinterested, and most sincere friends this land and people have ever known, and we pray that the deep affection and respect you have evoked for yourself in every part of India may in the time to come be to you a precious solace, and a source of hope and happiness. We are, Your Excellency, with every expression of the most sincere and affectionate respect and admiration, Your Excellency's most obedient and most faithful servants.

Her Excellency in reply said :—

GENTLEMEN,—I thank you most sincerely for the kind address you have presented to me, and for the assurance you give me of your appreciation of the work of the National Association. That association has for its object the relief of suffering and the amelioration of the physical condition of the women of India; and having given considerable attention to this matter, I can heartily sympathise with the efforts of a society such as yours, which devotes itself to the improvement of the sanitary condition of the dwellings in this great city, and to the removal of the many preventible causes which produce disease and death. By the undoubted success of the movement in which I have been specially interested; by the eager way in which female hospitals and dispensaries are filled, and female doctors and trained nurses are employed wherever we have been able to establish them; by the good which even a few sanitary primers and useful rules have been able to effect; and, I may add, by the extraordinary kindness shown to me personally in return for the little I have been able to do towards promoting the objects of the association, it is abundantly proved that every effort made to increase the comfort and to secure the health of the people is warmly appreciated and gratefully acknowledged by them; and I feel sure that such considerations as these must be as great an encouragement to you in your work as they have been to us in ours. Again I thank you, gentlemen, for the very kind expressions of your address.

FAREWELL ADDRESS FROM THE CALCUTTA MUNICIPALITY.

On Friday afternoon, the 8th December, the Municipal Commissioners of Calcutta presented a farewell address to Lord Dufferin at Government House. The Commissioners were received by His Excellency in the Throne-room. The address was presented in a handsome silver casket, and was read by Sir Henry Harrison, the chairman.

His Excellency in reply said:—

GENTLEMEN,—I beg to thank you very heartily for the friendly terms in which you are pleased to congratulate me on the satisfactory auspices under which my term of office in India has concluded, and on the honour which has been conferred upon me by Her Majesty the Queen-Empress. I am also very sensible of the indulgent spirit in which you allude to my humble endeavours to contribute my small part to the general advancement of the people of India, and more especially to promote the welfare of the citizens of Calcutta. Our residence in Calcutta has always been most agreeable to myself and to Lady Dufferin, both as regards the climate, the life and colour which pervade your city, the important interests of which it is the centre, and, above all, on account of the many personal friends we have met among its inhabitants, whether English or native. We have never passed along your streets without receiving at the hands of the crowds that frequent them, not only that respect which you have always been ready to pay to the Representative of the Queen-Empress, but many marks of personal favour and consideration. Above all things, we shall never forget the liberal and enthusiastic manner in which all classes, high and low, rich and poor, converted your city into a realm of fairy splendour on the occasion of the Queen's jubilee. It is needless for me to say that I have watched the proceedings of your corporation, both in its deliberative and executive capacity, with the greatest interest and attention, and I esteem it a privilege to have been present at one of your discussions, which exhibited how successfully the art of orderly debate has been transferred from the West to the East. From the first moment that I landed in India, I have always shown myself a friend of local self-government, and anxious to give full play and every advantage to the working of those municipal institutions which my illustrious predecessor so liberally enlarged. It was not, of course, to be expected that a plant so foreign to an Oriental atmosphere should flourish with equal vigour and persistence in the great variety of soils over which it has been distributed; but, though even now, after four years' residence in India, I can only claim a very superficial knowledge of the country, I think I am justified in saying that local self-government is everywhere alive, and that in many districts it is green and flourishing; while the special Legislative Acts of the Government to which you refer prove, I hope to your satisfaction, that I have fulfilled my promise to foster its growth to the best of my ability. In bidding you good-bye, I trust you will not think it out of place that I should exhort you to continue with energy and perseverance those sanitary reforms upon which you have courageously embarked. The sanitation of a great city is not a very popular undertaking; its processes are impeded by long-established prejudices as well as by inveterate customs and habit; nor even are its benefits very readily recognised. It has great obstacles to contend with in Europe, though now it is fortunately triumphant along the line. Though it may be many a long year, or perhaps many decades, before any very considerable impression may be made upon the evils with which you are contending, you must not despair. There never was a truer saying than that cleanliness is akin to godliness, and a city that knows how to set its house in order, to adorn its thoroughfares, to garnish its chambers, and to clothe itself in robes of spotless purity, may well claim to be the imperial metropolis of the East. In conclusion, I beg to convey to you my deep sense of your generosity in recognising in such warm and cordial terms the efforts of Lady Dufferin in the service of the women of India. The very fact that the exertions of a single woman should have led to the inauguration of this great movement—to the introduction into India of a considerable number of female doctors; to the establishment at almost all the centres of population of female medical schools, in which already the native ladies are exhibiting remarkable proficiency in the studies they have undertaken; to the erection of hospitals for female patients; to the multiplication of female wards in those which already exist from one end of the country to the other;—and, above all, the tender, graceful, and grateful expression of thanks which Lady Dufferin has received not only from public bodies, municipal corporations, and political associations, but from hundreds and hundreds of princesses and the great ladies of India, as well as from their humbler sisters—is inexpressibly gratifying, for it shows how, even in the unchanging East, where improvement is too readily supposed to knock vainly at the gates of cast-iron tradition, if only sympathy, kindness, and practical good sense inspire the effort, the doors fly open and joyfully admit the train of blessings that follow the advance of all sound, well-considered, and rational progress.

REPLY TO AN ADDRESS FROM THE MUNICIPAL CORPORATION OF BOMBAY.

On the 12th of December, 1888, Lord Dufferin arrived in Bombay on his way to Rome at the close of the term of his Viceroyalty. In the railway station at Bombay, he was presented with an address from the Municipal Corporation of Bombay, to which he replied as follows:—

MR. PRESIDENT AND GENTLEMEN,—I am very sensible of your kindness in thus welcoming me again to your noble city —a city which, I am happy to think, has been continually increasing in splendour, in prosperity, and in wealth, under the joint auspices of your Governor's conscientious, wise, and painstaking administration, and the intelligent counsels of the municipal corporation. The solicitude of the Government of India, as you are aware, is in no sense confined to the limits of any particular province or city of the empire. It watches with impartial interest over the welfare of the whole peninsula, and we have always considered it a fortunate circumstance when it has been within our power, either directly or indirectly, to embark on any line of policy which was consonant to the wishes or conducive to the well-being of the loyal and enterprising population of Bombay. It is a great satisfaction to me to know that the intelligent classes of this part of India comprehend the obligation of providing for the security of the north-west frontier. India is so large a place that the nature and force of those considerations which impose upon the Government any special line of action at one extremity of the empire are scarcely appreciated or understood by those who live under different conditions at the other; but I think you may rest assured that the rulers of the country will never enter upon any expenditure of a warlike character, whether with the view of being prepared against possible contingencies of a serious character, or of repelling casual incursions of hostile tribes or of other enemies, except with extreme reluctance, and under the pressure of absolute necessity. In conclusion, allow me to thank you for the kind reference you have made to my wife's endeavours to improve the condition of the women of India. The encomium you have passed upon her cannot fail to be most gratifying to her feelings, and I at all events am at liberty to say that it is richly deserved; for, not only will she have done an immense amount of actual good in the present, but she will have shown what a powerful engine sympathy, common-sense, and judicious management can prove in overcoming or turning those special impediments to progress which are peculiar to the soil of India. In bidding you good-bye, I beg again to express to you my earnest wishes for the prosperity and welfare of your city and of its inhabitants, as well as of the magnificent and powerful province of which it is the capital. (Cheers.)

REPLY TO THE FAREWELL ADDRESS OF THE BOMBAY CHAMBER OF COMMERCE.

On the 13th of December Lord Dufferin was presented with a farewell address from the Chamber of Commerce of Bombay. In reply His Lordship, who spoke with considerable feeling, said:—

GENTLEMEN,—I am afraid I stand before you rather in the position of a defaulter. I have to confess to you that I have been quite unable to frame a written reply to your address. According to the conventional usage, it is necessary that the answer to such a document should in some way re-echo the paragraphs of the address itself, but when I came to take my pen in hand, I found that you had referred to the various phases of my administration in so generous and so kind a spirit that it became utterly impossible for me to write a word that could in any sense satisfy myself. I therefore thought that the best thing I could do would be to throw myself on your indulgence, and in a few brief words, coming directly from my heart, to tell you, with all the earnestness of which my nature is capable, how grateful I am for the terms in which you have spoken of me.

I assure you that I have never received an address during the long period of my service—in the course of which I have received many addresses—which has given me greater pleasure; and if ever hereafter I shall be called upon to defend my acts as a Viceroy of India, I do not know what better defence I can proffer than by simply submitting the paragraphs which have just been read. They will remain in my family as a proof of the reward which any one who endeavours faithfully and honestly to do his duty meets with at the hands of his countrymen. The only further reference which I will make to anything you have written is to assure you that my Government and myself have always considered it a matter of the greatest importance that, before embarking upon any considerable act affecting either commerce or the general commercial welfare of the community, we should take the utmost advantage of the experience and knowledge of business possessed by the leading commercial men of the various centres of the population in this country.

Among the members of the Supreme Legislative Council there is none more able than the gentleman who sits there by the right of his commercial and financial experience, and I am sure it will not have escaped your observation that during the last session I ran some little risk, and overstepped the usual practice, by taking the advantage of a technical excuse to allow the budget to be discussed in the Legislative Council, when under ordinary circumstances we should have been precluded by the regulations of business from so doing. In my own personal opinion there would ensue the very greatest advantage could such a practice be continued. However, gentlemen, I will not enter further upon the topics which I am sorry to say are no longer within my jurisdiction. I will simply conclude by again thanking you for your great kindness, and by asking you to accept, in lieu of the written reply to which you are properly entitled, a souvenir of one whose last day in India will have been gladdened by the kind words you have said to him.

SPEECH AT THE BYCULLA CLUB, BOMBAY.

On the evening of the 13th December, 1888, Lord Dufferin was entertained at dinner by the members of the Byculla Club, Bombay. In reply to the toast of his health, which was proposed by Mr. Justice Bayley, his Lordship spoke as follows:—

YOUR EXCELLENCY, YOUR ROYAL HIGHNESS, MR. PRESIDENT, AND GENTLEMEN,—I am very sensible of the honour you have conferred upon me by inviting me to this banquet, and I am still more grateful for the kind manner in which you have received the mention of my name, which has been brought to your notice in such eloquent and flattering terms by your chairman, Judge Bayley. (Cheers.) But, alas! when I shall have adequately thanked you for your hospitality, I feel that I have come to the end of my tether. I have made so many speeches lately that I stand before you in the position of a soldier called upon to fire a salute, but who has already expended all his gunpowder. (Laughter and cheers.) I have not even so much as a cartridge left in my pouch. (Laughter.) Nay, I am no longer even a commissioned officer, and am liable to be strung up as a *franc-tireur* if I begin discharging rhetorical fireworks in your midst. (Laughter.) Even were it otherwise, your younger sister—for it is in that light I understand that Calcutta is very properly considered on this side of India—has cheated you of your birthright. (Laughter.) Following a very ancient example, she came and beguiled me with a savoury dish in the form of a haggis * (laughter), and has stolen your blessing—that is to say, if you consider a political speech of an hour and a half a blessing after dinner, which it certainly is not to the person who has to deliver it. (Laughter.) For all that, I am glad of this opportunity of correcting a palpable mis-statement which crept inadvertently into my St. Andrew's deliverance, and which is now misleading the public of India. It was a gross error of figures; but, however humiliating, as an honest man I am bound to correct it. I then stated that in the East two and two

---

* Alluding to the Scotch dinner at Calcutta on St. Andrew's Day.

have a tendency to make five. I have now had time to square my private accounts, and I find that, as far as the rupee is concerned, so far from two and two making five, the very reverse is the case, and that they only make three. (Loud laughter.) But though, gentlemen, I am precluded, as I have said, owing to want of ammunition, and for other reasons, from inflicting on you a political discourse, I must at least try to make you understand how glad I am to find myself again beneath your hospitable roof. Probably, of all the variegated scenes that pass in succession before the eyes of an Indian Viceroy during the four or five years that he remains in this country—full of colour and picturesque splendour as they all are—the one which is the most ineffaceable, which makes the deepest impression upon both his physical and mental vision, is that which presents itself to his gaze when he first sights your historic shores. (Cheers.) Having traversed many thousand miles of barren ocean, he suddenly finds himself secure within the arms of one of the most magnificent harbours of the East. Standing on the threshold of his new life, about to assume a weight of cares and responsibilities such as is imposed on the shoulders of no other public man in the world, he looks abroad with a feeling of awe upon the new realms he is called on to govern. A display of military pomp, greater even than that which surrounds the monarchs of Europe, accentuates the solemnity of his landing, and when he passes through the thoroughfares of your city, ennobled by buildings which any Western capital might envy (cheers), he sees on every side, crowding every window and balcony, and thronging every street, lane, and alley, such innumerable multitudes of men and women gazing at him with earnest and expectant eyes, that he shrinks appalled at the thought that it is for the safety and welfare of these thousands, and for other thousands, nay, millions, similar to these—yes, almost for their daily food —that he, with his limited experience and finite capacities, has become answerable to his Sovereign and to the people of England. (Applause.) The thoughts which pass through his mind, gentlemen, on that occasion are never forgotten, and would be sufficient almost to overwhelm him were it not that the kindly greetings, the loyal addresses, the encouraging promises of support and of indulgent recognition which at once begin to pour in upon him from your rulers, your citizens, and your corporate and other associated bodies, reinvigorate his spirits, and give him the assurance that, after all, his lines are cast in pleasant places, and that his future work will lie in the midst of a kindly and sympathetic community, while it is shared and lightened by a public Civil Service that has neither its like nor its equal in the world. (Loud cheers.) But, perhaps, only second to these profound impressions are those which he experiences at the end of his term, when he finds himself again amongst you on the eve of bidding good-bye to those who so warmly welcomed him on his first arrival. (Applause.) Between the two events, though comprising after all but a short period of time, if merely counted by years, there stretches what in its retrospect almost seems a lifetime—so full has it been of varied experiences, of continuous anxiety, and of unremitting effort. The vague and only half-surmised troubles and difficulties which rose to his imagination then have since translated themselves into harassing realities. The labour, the worry, the need for constant vigilance, which he anticipated would be great, he has found infinitely more constant and imperative than anything known to his previous experience, while, in addition to the cares inseparable from the ordinary work of administration, many an unexpected crisis, thunderbolts out of a clear sky, occasioned by circumstances which could not have been foreseen or controlled, have been superadded to task his patience, his endurance, his courage, and his skill to the utmost. (Loud applause.) Well, then, gentlemen, happy is the man who, however conscious he may be that he has fallen short of his own ideal, that he has failed in some measure to accomplish all the good he might have desired, or completely to remedy the evils with which circumstances called upon him to contend—happy is the man, I say, who, coming back to you at the end of his term, receives at the hands of those who originally welcomed him such hearty greetings as you and my other friends in this part of the world, both English and native, have been pleased to accord to me. (Loud cheers.) And still happier is he if his conscience does not forbid him to hope that your favourable verdict will perhaps receive the *imprimatur* of history; for it is the future alone that can disclose the effect of a ruler's actions, or gauge the breadth and depth of the foundations he may have laid for further improvement. (Applause.) As regards the present, I think it may be fairly said that I have handed over India to my successor without a cloud on the horizon—for we may consider the Thibetan difficulty as settled, the Chinese Amban having arrived at Rinchingong to-day (applause)—with her princes and people contented; with her finances—in spite of Burma, Sikkim, and the Black Mountain—in a state of equilibrium—unless, indeed, the coming harvest should prove exceptionally short—and with no internal questions on hand which cannot readily be solved by that patience, firmness, and sympathetic sagacity which no one possesses in a greater measure than the present Viceroy. (Cheers.) I hope I have also done something towards enabling India to read her own thoughts, to discriminate between vain dreams and possible realities, and to comprehend that which she really wants as distinguished from that which she neither needs nor wants, and which cannot be given to her. (Applause.) Nor, gentlemen, have I been unmindful of your own immediate interests. The fortifications of your city have been set on foot—thanks to the energy of Lord Reay, who never ceases to trouble the tranquillity of our Simla Olympus whenever your interests are at stake (applause) —with as much expedition as the extraordinary faculty which able engineers possess of differing from one another will allow. (Laughter.) The works have already made considerable progress, and when the whole scheme has been developed and properly supplemented by torpedo fields, by suitably armed warships, and by a body of marine fencibles, you will be able to sleep in your beds in greater peace than the inhabitants of half a hundred towns in the mother country. (Loud applause.) Nor have I failed to recognise the importance of adequate railway communication between the Western Gate of India and its sister capital of Bengal, to the mutual advantage of both cities and of either province. (Applause.) Under these circumstances, gentlemen, I trust I am not called upon, like Cæsar, to put aside the parting wreath of approval which you have so generously offered to me. (Loud cheers.) Gentlemen, all governors and viceroys arrive on your shores with their heads jubilant and erect upon their shoulders; but, alas! it is always a question whether they may not return in the guise of St. Denis, decapitated by public opinion either here or at home. Well, gentlemen, you have been pleased to declare that my head remains as safely set in its place as when I first saw you. (Applause.) If it has been turned in the meantime, it has been turned by the universal kindness and good-will which I have received in all parts of India, and at the hands of every section of its inhabitants. Had it been turned by the ladies, that is an accident to which all Irishmen are subject. (Laughter.) Turned it certainly will be when I leave your shores—turned towards you with grateful thanks, with many a fond regret, and, as long as I live, with a still constant regard to your interests and welfare. (Renewed cheering.)

SPEECH AT BANQUET IN THE MANSION HOUSE.

On the 29th of May, Lord Dufferin was presented with the freedom of the City of London; and in the evening was entertained at dinner in the Mansion House by the Lord Mayor, the Right Hon. James Whitehead. In reply to the toast of his health, his Lordship spoke as follows:—

MY LORD MAYOR, MY LORDS, LADIES, AND GENTLEMEN,— In rising to return thanks to you, my Lord Mayor, for the flattering terms in which you have proposed my health, and to you, my lords and gentlemen, for the friendly manner in which you have received it, it is needless for me to express my deep sense of the honour which has been done me. After sixteen years of continuous service in distant parts of the empire and at foreign Courts, to return home and to find such a welcome awaiting one at the hands of the most powerful corporation in the world, and of those distinguished persons whom I see around me, is more than enough to gratify the fondest ambition and to make the recipient sensible that he is being rewarded far beyond his desert. This feeling is very much enhanced when I remember what famous and heroic men—the builders, the champions, and the benefactors of the British Empire—have stood where I am standing and received at your hands similar proofs of your favour. But, whatever misgivings I may entertain as to my personal right to have my name inscribed on your city's roll of fame, I draw a special encouragement from the fact that, having been called upon to act in three distinct capacities—as a colonial governor, as a diplomatic representative, and as an Indian ruler—in granting me these honours you are honouring the services with whom I have been connected, to whom I owe so much, and whose assistance has enabled me to gain your approbation. (Cheers.) During the period of my tenure of office in Canada—a country I shall never cease to regard with gratitude and affection—the affairs of the Dominion were conducted, as you are aware, through the instrumentality of responsible ministers; and, if my administration was successful, it is due to the patriotism, the wisdom, and the statesmanship of those eminent men— one of whom, Sir Charles Tupper, I am happy to see here to-night (cheers)—to whom the Parliament of Canada had confided the interests of the country. Again, in diplomacy, it is only those who are the ostensible heads of missions who can be fully conscious of the degree to which they are indebted for their success to the zeal, acumen, and tact of the members of the corps who are associated with them in the discharge of their delicate duties. But if this is the case in diplomacy and in colonial government, it is even more strikingly exhibited in the administration of Indian affairs. In common parlance, and in accordance with the language of ancient tradition, every act of the Indian Government, and every characteristic of its policy, is regarded as the outcome and the product of the Viceroy's personal initiative and will. And this undoubtedly is as it should be; for he, and he alone, is responsible for whatever is done in India. The minutest details of business come within his purview; every executive act requires his assent; it is he that finally pronounces on the frequently divergent views of the departments and between the competing suggestions of his colleagues, while he holds in reserve the absolute right of overruling his Council. Consequently, whatever may have been the genesis of this or that line of action, it is the Viceroy, and the Viceroy alone, who is properly held answerable by his countrymen, whether things go well or whether they go ill; nor, in the event of their going ill, have I ever heard of the principle being disputed. (Laughter.) But, for all that, it will be readily understood that no Viceroy, however arbitrary or self-reliant, however determined to impress his personal volition on the conduct of affairs, would be able to direct the movements of so vast and complicated a machine as that which regulates the destinies of 300,000,000 of our fellow-subjects in India, unless enlightened, aided, and advised by the most remarkable body of men that have ever laboured for the good of their country in any part of the world (cheers)—I mean the Civil Service of the Crown in India. Indeed, I may say, once for all, without disparagement to the accepted standard of public industry in England, that I did not know what hard work really meant until I witnessed the unremitting and almost inconceivable severity of the grind to which our Indian civil servants, and I will add our military *employés*, so zealously devote themselves. If, therefore, gentlemen, during the past four years things have on the whole gone well in India, the chief credit is due to a number of able and disinterested personages, who have been content to labour in what, from the force of circumstances, are spheres and positions which, for the most part, escape the attention of the British public, indifferent to their own fame, despising the snares of notoriety, provided only that the honour and the moral and material interests of the British Empire shall extend and flourish. (Loud cheers.) If, for instance, my Lord Mayor, the north-western frontier of India and our Indian seaports have been fortified and secured, it is thanks to the professional skill of Sir Donald Stewart (cheers), Sir Frederick Roberts (cheers), General Chesney, General Newmarch, Colonel Sandford, Colonel Nicholson, and the able engineers employed upon that business. If Quetta has become an unassailable bulwark, it is because Sir Frederick Roberts' practised eye discerned the strategical advantages of that position. (Cheers.) If the conquest and reorganization of Burma have been successfully accomplished in spite of difficulties the extent of which no one in this country can adequately appreciate, you are indebted for these results to such men as General Prendergast, General White, Sir Charles Bernard, and Sir Charles Crosthwaite, and those who have risked and lost, as alas! so many have done, their health and even their lives in the carrying out of this great task. (Cheers.) If our relations with the native princes of India have never been on a more friendly footing; if we have succeeded in maintaining amicable and confidential intercourse with the Amir of Afghanistan—a potentate of great force of character and of strong determination—whose advancement to his present position was accomplished through the skill and discrimination of Sir Lepel

Griffin (cheers); and if the general friendliness of our
neighbours, and especially of China, has been strengthened
and enhanced, it is because in regulating its foreign policy
the Government of India was enabled to rely for counsel and
advice upon its Foreign Secretary, Sir Mortimer Durand.
(Cheers.) If the army has undergone a marked improvement
in its organization and in every branch and department of its
several services, again we have to thank Sir Frederick Roberts,
General Newmarch, General Chesney, and Colonel Collen. If
a mobilization scheme has been initiated and a system of
reserves introduced and successfully established, the principal
credit is due in the one case to General Chesney, and in the
other to Colonel Collen, and the committee who assisted them.
(Cheers.) If, in spite of the considerable expenditure into
which we were forced by the war in Burma and the troubles
in the Black Mountain and on the border of Thibet, by the
increase to our army, by the Russian scare, by the fortification
of our frontier and of our seaports, and if, above all, in spite of
the depreciation of silver, we were able to arrive at equilibrium
at the end of the last financial year, with the prospect of a
surplus for the coming year, so remarkable an achievement
must be attributed to the financial skill of Sir Auckland
Colvin, Mr. Westland, Sir David Barbour, and Mr. Sinkinson.
(Cheers.) If large measures of land and other legislation of a
most important character have been most successfully passed,
and if the internal and domestic machinery of government has
worked smoothly and harmoniously, it is owing to the wisdom
and statesmanship of such men as Sir Alfred Lyall, Sir Stuart
Bayley, and Mr. Ilbert, who took such a leading part in the
passing of the Oude and Bengal Tenancy Bill; as Sir James
Peile, Mr. A. Mackenzie, and Mr. A. P. Macdonnell. (Cheers.)
If our legal codes have been improved and our legislative Acts
well drawn, it is because that task was discharged by Mr. Scoble
and Mr. Harvey James. If the revenue system is undergoing
a steady improvement—and it is constantly showing more
favourable figures—it is due to the judgment and fruitful
initiative of Sir Edward Buck. If our railway system in
India, whether designed for commercial purposes, for the

mitigation of famine, or in view of military ends, has been steadily extended, if the Indus has been successfully bridged at Sukkur, the Ganges at Benares, and the Hooghly near Barrackpore, and if the formidable Amran range was pierced, it is because the singular energy of Sir Theodore Hope has been ably seconded by the exertions of Colonel Trevor, Colonel Filgate, Colonel Conway Gordon, Colonel Pemberton, General Stanton, Sir Gilbert Molesworth, Mr. Robertson, Sir Alexander Rendel, Sir Bradford Leslie, Sir James Browne, Mr. Walton, and Mr. O'Callaghan. (Cheers.) If great economies are being introduced throughout the entire machinery of administration, the result is due to Sir Charles Elliott and his colleagues; and, in a like manner, we are indebted for the thorough investigation which has recently taken place into the whole status and condition of the Civil Service to Sir Charles Aitchison and the mixed commission over which he presided. If the late Viceroy of India has survived the labours of his office, and lives to dine with the present Lord Mayor of London, it is because he had in Sir Donald Wallace an incomparable private secretary, who relieved him of half his labours (cheers), who enjoyed everybody's confidence, who completely effaced himself and worked eighteen hours a day. (Laughter.) In fact, my lord, when I come to think of the hundreds and hundreds of persons through whose instrumentality, and thanks to whose unselfish and unrecognised exertions it is that I am occupying the proud position that I do to-night, I am afraid I should unfold so long a catalogue of names, both European and native, as would outrun your patience and the forbearance of this audience. In any event, my lord, it is a great satisfaction to me to have this opportunity of publicly repeating in England the grateful acknowledgments I had the pleasure of recording in their regard before I left Calcutta. (Cheers.) Nor is it altogether undesirable that the English public, so sedulously occupied as they naturally are with their own domestic concerns and the course of home and European politics, should be occasionally reminded by a competent witness like myself that away beyond the Indian Ocean, under alien suns, in a trying climate, amid homes in

which the laughter of children is never heard, a select body of
our fellow-countrymen are engaged in discharging duties of
whose onerous nature people at home can have but a very imperfect conception (cheers), and in dealing with administrative
and political problems, compared with which those for the
most part occupying the attention of the House of Commons
are the merest child's play. (Laughter and cheers.) Nor, in
referring to the labours of the European section of Her
Majesty's servants in India, ought we to leave out of account
the extent and degree to which those labours are supplemented
and rendered fruitful by the assistance and co-operation of
their native coadjutors. Indeed, it will probably be a surprise
to most of those I am addressing when they learn that the
whole covenanted Civil Service of the Queen in India comprises something less than 1000 individuals, while the
uncovenanted Civil Service includes nearly 120,000 native
members, many of them, especially among the higher ranks of
the judiciary, being persons of great capacity, learning, and
probity, while all of them, as a body, may be regarded as
eminently expert, industrious, and loyal. (Cheers.) And
now, my lords and gentlemen, in reference to this epithet
"loyal" which has instinctively escaped my lips, I hope it
will be understood as in no sense intended as a discriminating
appellation, for I do not hesitate to state my conviction that
the entire population of India is loyal to the throne and person
of Her Majesty, and to the modes of administration of their
English rulers. (Cheers.) I do not mean to say that we
English are beloved or are even popular in India, nor is there
any reason why we should expect to be so; not only are we
the representatives of a foreign domination, not only are
we aliens in race and religion, but the peculiar habits and
views of our Hindu fellow-subjects, the unwillingness of a
large majority to eat and drink with persons of a different
caste from themselves, their refusal to allow their ladies to
mingle in our society, naturally prevent the rise and growth
of that genial harmony and good fellowship whose happy
influences none know so well how to apply on similar occasions
as you, my Lord Mayor, and the hospitable companies of the

city of London. (Laughter and cheers.) But, though destitute of what may be called any strong sentimental element, the loyalty of India is based upon a far surer foundation; namely, that of self-interest. I believe that, leaving out of account the absolutely ignorant, some fanatical sects, the discontented sections of society which are to be found in all communities, and individuals with a personal grievance, but including those who vituperate us in the newspapers, there is not a subject of the Queen in India, whether prince, or landholder, or merchant, or artisan, or cultivator, who is not pretty well convinced that English administration gives him what he would get neither in an independent India nor in an India under the rule of any other power; namely, peace, security, justice, a free press, education, an enormous share in the Government appointments, a native magistracy, the conservation of the native dynasties as independent states, local self-government, the prospect of the gradual liberalization of our methods of administration, the supervision of the House of Commons, and a consciousness that English public opinion is always on the alert to notice any abuse of authority, and to temper the severity of that authoritative *régime* through which alone the vast congeries of nationalities, religions, and races inhabiting the peninsula can be effectually governed. (Cheers.) In fact, I have returned from India with a far deeper impression of the strength of our position, and of the solid character of our dominion, whether in relation to internal or external influences, than ever I had before. (Cheers.) Instead of diminishing, I believe that the moral ascendency exercised by Englishmen in the East is becoming more and more powerful, whilst the inventions of modern science, as exhibited in the extension of our railways, the acceleration of all means of communication, the shortening of the distances between London and Bombay and Australia and Calcutta, the improvement in artillery and arms of precision, the expansion of our trade and commerce with our Indian Empire, and the general infusion of English civilization, are extending and deepening the impression. (Cheers.) Nor have we less reason, I think, to congratulate ourselves on the general condition of affairs which prevails along the extensive frontiers of our Eastern empire. On quitting Bombay I was able with perfect accuracy to say that I left India without a cloud on the horizon, though I did not say that there might not be many a one below it. In establishing and extending our Indian possessions, as from generation after generation we have been compelled to do, we have given many hostages to fortune, but, even now, after six months have passed since I uttered the auspication, nothing has occurred in any degree to blot or obscure the prospect. The interior of the province of Burma having been pretty completely dominated and pacified, the next task was to teach the wild tribes inhabiting the hills to discontinue their head-hunting raids and predatory expeditions into the plains, and, thanks to the energy of my successor, this object seems to have been successfully accomplished both on the west, on the north, and on the east, and I am happy to observe that there is a prospect of a direct land route being opened up between the valley of the Ganges and the valley of the Irrawaddy. (Cheers.) On the North West our relations with the Amir of Afghanistan continue to be of a most satisfactory nature. The absurd rumours propagated by the press as to the hostile intentions of the Amir against Russia, which were never for a moment credited by the Russian Government, have been shown to be completely imaginary, the Amir himself acknowledging that he had nothing to complain of in the conduct of the Russian officials, and that his only desire is to remain at peace within his own borders. And in reference to this point I desire to seize this opportunity of publicly recognising the loyal and honourable manner in which the Government of Russia has observed and maintained its obligations arising out of the Afghan Demarcation Convention. (Cheers.) Before assuming the Viceroyalty I ventured to prophesy that this would be the case, for I had the utmost confidence in the wisdom and moderation of the Russian Foreign Minister, and, above all, in the high sense of honour and conscientiousness of His Majesty the Emperor. (Cheers.) As you are aware, on two separate occasions the Amir of Afghanistan found himself in great embarrassment and difficulty, owing at one time to the very serious insurrection of the Ghilzais and other tribes, and afterwards in consequence of the rebellion of his powerful relative Ishak Khan, the Governor of Balkh. There is no doubt that had the Russian Government condescended to falsify its engagements and to intrigue against Abdurrahman Khan, the affairs of Afghanistan might have been thrown into the utmost confusion—a circumstance which could not have failed to be productive of the most critical complications as between ourselves and Russia; for I hold it to be an essential principle that under no conceivable circumstance would it be compatible, either with the good faith of the contracting powers or the safety of the empire, that the agreement come to by us with Russia on behalf of the Amir, in regard to the northern boundary of Afghanistan, should ever be modified or ignored. (Cheers.) Any further approach of a great foreign military power towards the confines of India would entail upon the latter country such an intolerable amount of expense in the shape of additional fortifications and other measures of defence, as would become absolutely intolerable, and would be less preferable than any other alternative, however serious. Nor, in thus expressing my acknowledgments to the Government of St. Petersburg for their loyal and friendly attitude, must I fail to render a similar tribute to another great imperial administration—I mean that of His Majesty the Emperor of China. (Cheers.) Had the Chinese chosen to do so, they might, at the outset of our expedition to Burma, have greatly increased and complicated the difficulties of our task. (Hear, hear.) But I have great pleasure in bearing my testimony to the energetic and effectual manner in which the Chinese Government and the Viceroy of Yunnan have saved us from the endless worry and torment to which the French have been so unhappily exposed in Tonquin, by the operations of the Black Flags and Chinese freebooters. And now, my Lord Mayor, my lords, and gentlemen, I do not see that I have any right to intrude any further upon the kind attention of this company. In again thanking you for the honour you have done me, perhaps I may be permitted in Lady Dufferin's name to convey to you her heartfelt thanks for the kind and sympathetic manner in which you have alluded to her work in India, and which I, as an impartial witness, say cannot be overrated. (Cheers.) In saying that I am deeply grateful for these proofs of your favour, I am only expressing what I believe to be the dominant sentiment which inspires all those who, like myself, are called upon to serve our Queen and country outside of Great Britain. Removed as we are from the turmoil of party politics and the acerbities of party controversy, our thoughts and faculties are naturally more directed to the contemplation of the empire as a whole, and to devoting ourselves to its consolidated interests. To our fond imagination, in whatever distant lands we may be serving, amid all our troubles and anxieties, England rises to our view, as she did to the men of Cressy, like a living presence, a sceptred isle amid inviolate seas, a dear and honoured mistress, the mother of a race which it may truly be said has done as much as any other for the general moral and material happiness of mankind, and which has done more than any other to spread abroad the benefits of ordered liberty and constitutional government, which has learnt the secret of gradually interweaving the new material of progress into the outworn tissues of ancient civilizations, and of reconciling every diversity of barbarous tribe to the discipline of a properly regulated existence, whose beneficent and peaceful commercial flag illumines every sea, and pavilions every shore, whose language is already destined, ere the close of this century, to be spoken by a greater number of millions than any other tongue, and the chief necessity for whose prosperity and welfare is the continuance of universal peace, and the spread of amity and good-will among the nations. (Loud cheers.) Indeed, without such an ideal to stimulate and encourage them, their work would prove very unthankful to hundreds and hundreds of able and high-minded men who are wearing themselves out in the service of their country abroad, inasmuch as the one thought that sustains them in all their trials and temptations, when struggling with the depression occasioned by sickness, overwork, and debilitating climates, is the thought that they are making a good fight for the honour and welfare of England and her imperial renown, and that, in a greater or less degree, they are earning the approval of those of their countrymen who, like you, my Lord Mayor, and you, my lords and gentlemen, with so much superabundant kindness and generosity, have been pleased to testify to-night your approval of the humble endeavours to do his duty of one among the many thousands of your servants to whom the approbation of their fellow Englishmen is their greatest reward. (Loud cheers.)

SPEECH AT BANQUET IN THE ULSTER HALL, BELFAST.

On September the 19th, 1889, Lord Dufferin was entertained at dinner in the Ulster Hall, Belfast, by the inhabitants of that City and of the neighbouring Counties, on the occasion of his return from India. In reply to the toast of his health, which was proposed by Mr. Charles C. Connor, mayor of Belfast, his Lordship spoke as follows :—

MR. MAYOR, MY LORDS, AND GENTLEMEN,—Although I have had the good fortune, during a long and varied term of official employment, to be frequently called upon to return thanks for the kindly way in which my name has been mentioned at public entertainments, I can say with the utmost sincerity that I never felt it more difficult to reply in an adequate manner to the toast of my health than on the present occasion; for, as a rule, those who have hitherto been my hosts have sought rather to pay respect to the dignity of my office, or to the august Sovereign whom I was representing, or to the principles of government which my conduct of affairs embodied and enforced, than to give expression to their personal regard and sympathy. But in this magnificent demonstration, in the cheers which have greeted the flattering and eloquent utterances of the Mayor, what is principally brought home to me is the fact that I am surrounded by hundreds and hundreds of my life-long friends — (hear, hear) — by those who first encouraged my youthful and halting endeavours to be of some use to the country, and who have never missed an opportunity of manifesting the indulgent interest they have taken in my career, and of testifying to the world at large their general approval of my conduct. (Cheers.) And I assure you, gentlemen, I have found that the privilege of being able to display your *imprimatur* has been of no small practical benefit; for, whenever I have proceeded to discharge my official functions in the midst of strange communities who knew little of my character and antecedents, the fact of my bringing good credentials from Ulster was in itself sufficient to ensure me a favourable reception and an auspicious start. (Cheers.) But, although I am aware that private friendship and neighbourly good-will, and the natural indulgence you feel for one whom you have long known, have been the principal agents in bringing you here to-night, I may perhaps venture to hope that another sentiment of a more general character has added to the numbers of this assembly; namely, the desire of Irishmen to make a fellow-countryman feel that they are pleased at one of their own race and land having been able, without discredit, to take a considerable part in administering the affairs of the mighty British Empire, and to add another proof to the far more convincing ones so many of her sons have already given, that Ireland is as capable of producing men well fitted to undertake the great duties of the State as either of the sister countries. (Cheers.) At all events, gentlemen, I can assure you that at each successive stage of my career, at every fresh mark of my Sovereign's and of the country's approval, this thought has never been absent from my mind. (Hear, hear.) To do credit to Ireland, and to prove myself not unworthy of the native strain from which I am descended, has been the constant object of my ambition. (Hear, hear.) But in undertaking the government of India a more special anxiety forced itself upon my attention—the desire that if I could not emulate the merit—for I knew that would be impossible—I might at all events follow in the footsteps of those illustrious Ulstermen to whom India owes so much, and to whom England is chiefly indebted, during the most terrible season of trial that has ever overtaken her, for the preservation of her Indian Empire. (Hear, hear.) Though my labours and difficulties can in no sense be compared with theirs, yet to be allowed, through the indulgence of my fellow-countrymen, to occupy a humble niche in the temple of honour which enshrines the memory of the Lawrences—(cheers)—the Montgomerys—(cheers)—the Nicholsons—(cheers)—the Gillespies—(cheers)—and many another North of Ireland hero, would indeed be an ample reward. Nor, were this favour to be conceded to me, need those I am addressing fear that the cycle of distinguished Indo-Irishmen would be closed. Without disparagement to either of the sister kingdoms, I can say with perfect truth that both Ireland as a whole and Ulster as a province have imported a vast amount of ability, industry, and valour into the Indian civil and military services. (Hear, hear.) Why, gentlemen, to whom at this very moment has been entrusted as Viceroy the supreme conduct of Indian affairs? Is it not to a great Kerry nobleman, the Marquis of Lansdowne? (Cheers.) Who is governing thirty millions of Indian subjects in Madras with exceptional success and ability? Why, a Burke of Mayo, Lord Connemara. (Cheers.) Who is it that now commands the armies of the Queen in India with the universal acceptation both of the public and of the Government? Is it not a Waterford hero, the victor of Candahar, Sir Frederick Roberts? (Cheers.) And who is it that is in command of the army of Bombay? The Duke of Connaught. (Cheers.) Who, again, has succeeded in what, considering the difficulties of the task, was a marvellously short period, in reducing Burma to submission, or, what was even more troublesome, the hill tribes that surround Burma? Has it not been Sir George White— (cheers)—a most distinguished soldier, of whom his native Antrim may well be proud? (Hear, hear.) And, not to multiply further instances, who is the able financier that has contrived, in spite of the treacherous, debilitated, and ever-depreciating rupee, to evolve a surplus out of an impending deficit? Has it not been Sir David Barbour— (cheers)—whom we are entitled to claim as a Belfast man? (Renewed cheering.) No, my lords and gentlemen—and in saying this I feel that I am not trenching upon any burning political question—the British Empire could never get on without us Irishmen. (Cheers and laughter.) In the same way that too much decorum in individuals superinduces fatty degeneration of the heart, so the vitality of the British Empire would stagnate and become sluggish unless mercurialized by our livelier and more sunny temperament. (Cheers.) Not only our Indian but our colonial empire plainly shows that Irishmen have a positive genius for governing, if not themselves—(loud laughter)—at all events other people; and nowhere is this heroic talent more beneficently apparent than in the case of the Irish ladies—(loud cheers)—and the reason for this is not far to seek. Being extremely sensitive ourselves, and having a keen desire for sympathy, our lively imagination enables us more or less to put ourselves into the places of other people; to divine their thoughts, and to understand their wants and wishes, and this is the first quality requisite in those who are called upon to administer the affairs of an imperial dependency, or to rule over either kindred or alien populations. (Hear, hear.) But I freely confess that, of all the nationalities with which I have come into contact, the Indian races are those whose inner thoughts and modes of regarding the problems of life are the most difficult to discern. The inheritors of a civilization far older than our own, and the adherents of a religion whose subtle principles as held by their best thinkers it is almost impossible for a European understanding to analyze, our efforts to harmonize our intellectual methods with theirs, or to regard the economy of existence from the same point of view, end only too frequently in complete and sometimes comic failure. I will give you an instance of this. On one occasion the kind-hearted wife of some great official was attracted by the singular brightness and intelligence of the young lad who acted as her punkah boy. Thinking it a pity that so hopeful a youth should pass his whole existence in pulling day and night at a rope, she suggested to him one day that his prospects would be much improved if he would allow her to start him on some more promising career. For a long time the little fellow could not understand her meaning, or what was intended by a more promising career. When at last he grasped the import of her benevolent intentions, he rebuked her in the following terms:—" What for me change? I punkah puller, my father punkah puller, his father punkah puller; all my ancestors for thousand years punkah pullers; and the god from whom we are descended was punkah puller to Vishnu. Punkah puller to ladyship very good position." (Laughter.) Here, gentlemen, you have a specimen of the changeless East—bound in the fetters of caste—so unlike the seething, surging struggles of the entities in a modern European community, yet a system not without its compensations. But, though occasionally discomfited in this manner in our endeavours to ameliorate the condition of our Indian fellow-subjects, the English people may be fully content with the reflection that the history of the world does not exhibit a more splendid example of the way in which the material and moral condition of a vast congeries of nationalities may be elevated and improved than that which is manifested throughout the length and breadth of our Eastern Empire. Kingdoms and principalities which for hundreds of years had been continually devastated by successive wars and internecine conflicts now lie peaceful and secure in amicable juxtaposition. A justice which formerly was never known in India, and is not now known in any Oriental Government under the sun, protects alike the rights and property of the poorest peasant and the wealthiest zemindar. Extensive lines of railway—and the Indian population have an extraordinary aptitude for travelling —not only unite all the great centres of population and of industry, but have in a great measure penetrated all those districts which were once the theatres of the most disastrous famines, whose severity in future they will, at all events, mitigate. Universities, colleges, and schools offering free education to the entire population are to be found in every town—nay, almost in every village and hamlet. (Hear, hear.) British manufacturing energy and enterprise have not only supplied millions with cheap clothes and all the necessaries of life, but have taught them in their turn to establish in their own land rival looms and industries, while, above all, the standards of moral obligation which prevail in the West have vindicated their authority and planted their sanctions both in the courts of justice and in the counting-houses of Hindostan. (Cheers.) But, gentlemen, when once he is set going, an Indian official is apt to become only too garrulous in recounting his Indian reminiscences; nor is it desirable that an ex-Viceroy should become too discursive on Indian affairs. Rather let me turn and congratulate you, Mr. Mayor, and all those merchant princes I see around me, who themselves and their ancestors have created the North of Ireland as we now see it, on the splendid progress which has been made in Belfast and throughout the entire neighbourhood during these last few years. Although even to a resident the rate of progress which has taken place must have appeared very rapid, to one who, like myself, revisits this city after a considerable lapse of time, the change is simply marvellous; and well may we all be proud that a place which not so long ago was a place of comparatively small account, and was certainly not a county town, should now rank as the third commercial city in the United Kingdom. (Cheers.) All honour to those great organizers of enterprise and industry, the real paladins of the modern world, who have worked this wondrous change—a change both in its commercial, in its social, and in its political consequences of the greatest moment to the British Empire. (Cheers.) Gentlemen, to receive a wreath of laurel at the hands of so great a city is an honour of which any man might be proud; and the memory of this night, of the kindness you have shown me, and of the supreme favour with which you have rewarded my humble endeavours to do my duty, will never be forgotten either by me or by my remotest descendant. (Loud cheers.)

The mayor having proposed the health of the Marchioness of Dufferin and Ava, Lord Dufferin in response said :—

MR. MAYOR, MY LORDS, AND GENTLEMEN,—Although I have already trespassed at considerable length on your attention—(no, no)—I feel that you will be indulgent to a natural desire which animates me to be the interpreter to you of the deep gratitude which my wife experiences at the honour you have done her (Cheers.) It is indeed a very great honour for a lady to have been mentioned in such pleasing and kindly terms as those which have been adopted by Mr. Houston, but at the same time, as I am speaking on behalf of another and not of myself, I have no hesitation in saying that what has fallen from him and what has elicited your applause is richly deserved. (Cheers.) Words would fail me to describe the assistance I have derived in my public life from the happiness of having had, I will not say such a wife or such a companion, but such a colleague. (Cheers.) She ruled supreme indoors, and she has shared a considerable proportion of my authority outside. (Cheers.) And with regard to India, however humiliating the confession may be, I am bound to say that if there is one thing more certain than another, it is that the memory of Lady Dufferin, and of her goodness, and the beneficent results of her labours, will still live and flourish after the very fact of my ever having set foot in the peninsula will have been forgotten. (Cheers.) I only wish, gentlemen, that Lady Dufferin was beside me, in order that she might have replied in an adequate manner to your kindness. (Cheers.) You must, however, be pleased to accept my very imperfect expression of thanks on her behalf. (Loud cheers.)

Lord Dufferin, again rising, said:—

MY LORDS AND GENTLEMEN,—It is my pleasant duty to propose a toast, and that is "The health of the Mayor of the city of Belfast." (Cheers.) And I may say that the erection of Belfast into a city has been merely an act of common justice. (Cheers.) I trust that the time may not be far distant when perhaps I may have the good fortune to propose the health of the Lord Mayor of Belfast. (Hear, hear.) Certainly, on returning to England, I perceive a very remarkable change in one respect. It appears to me that the vitality of our municipal life in the United Kingdom has been very much enlarged and stimulated, that each great city of Ireland and England and Scotland is more and more assuming an individualized existence, and creating certain characteristics proper to itself. This principle, I think, will in time be so largely developed that the chief cities of England will come to assume the kind of existence which rendered the cities of Italy in the middle ages so remarkable, so prosperous—the patrons of art, the homes of architecture, and the centres of commerce. (Hear, hear.) At all events, I am certain of this, that the edict has already gone forth that the voice of Belfast is in future destined to exercise the very greatest influence upon the commercial, the social, and the political life of the British

Empire. (Cheers.) I am glad to think that a community—to use a vulgar American expression—so level-headed—(laughter)—so apt in business, possessing much determination and such calm good sense, should be in a position to make their influence extensively felt. (Cheers.) I have to express my personal obligations to the mayor for the kind and agreeable manner in which he has presided at this entertainment. (Cheers.) And perhaps, I may be permitted to add that, although it has been rather trying to me for the last two hours to sit opposite the date 1855, at the same time, amidst the many graceful marks of kindness I have received in various parts of the world, I do not remember one which has touched me so deeply, and which has been so grateful to my feelings, as the cornice * which runs round the foot of this balcony. (Cheers.) Gentlemen, I give you the health of the mayor.

* An embroidered inscription had been run round the whole hall, with the dates and places of Lord Dufferin's successive posts.

SPEECH AT A DINNER GIVEN BY THE LONDON CHAMBER OF COMMERCE.

On October 30th, 1889, the Marquis of Dufferin and Ava was entertained at dinner by the London Chamber of Commerce in the Hotel Métropole. In reply to the toast of his health, which was proposed by Sir John Lubbock, M.P., the president of the chamber, his Lordship spoke as follows:—

SIR JOHN LUBBOCK, MY LORDS, AND GENTLEMEN,—In rising to return thanks for the signal honour conferred upon me by this magnificent entertainment, I wish, in the first place, to express my extreme regret that a severe illness should have prevented me from placing myself at the disposal of the Chamber of Commerce on the date which had been originally settled, though the fact that you, Sir John, and your colleagues have been pleased to renew your invitation and to give me another chance of presenting myself before you greatly enhances the burden of my gratitude. (Hear, hear.) In the next, I desire to convey to you my warmest acknowledgments for the indulgent terms in which you have been pleased to propose my health, and to the august company which I see around me for the friendly spirit in which they have received the mention of my name. But however sensible I may be of so much kindness, I cannot help feeling that a higher and a wider interest than that of mere good-will to an indvidual has drawn together this distinguished concourse, and that in to-night's celebration is indicated the wise appreciation entertained, not merely by the London Chamber of Commerce, but by the representatives of the many great English interests I see around me, of the enormous benefit derived by the people of this country from their commercial relations with our Indian Empire—(hear, hear)—and consequently of the supreme necessity of maintaining to all time dominant and unimpaired England's ascendancy and dominion over her Eastern possessions. (Cheers.) I am aware that statistics, however important, are a somewhat ungracious element in an after-dinner speech; but inasmuch as during a period of four years a great portion of my thoughts and attention were directed to commercial questions, I may be forgiven if I at least call your attention to the fact that during the past year our trade with our Indian Empire was larger than our trade with any other country in the world, with the exception of the United States, amounting to no less a sum than 64 millions of pounds sterling. (Cheers.) If, again, we merely confine our attention to a comparison of our exports to India with our exports to other countries, we shall find that the same statement holds good; namely, that the exports of Great Britain to India are greater than those to any other country in the world except the United States, amounting as they do to 34 millions of pounds, whereas our exports to France do not exceed 24 millions, and to Germany 27 millions. (Hear, hear.) In fact, India's trade with the United Kingdom is nearly one-tenth of the value of the total British trade with the whole world. (Cheers.) Now, I think it is clearly evident that this remarkable and mutually beneficent commercial intercourse between the two countries may be regarded as the direct consequence and result of the stable condition of the political relationship in which they stand to one another; for, if we compare the figures I have quoted with the figures which give the measure of our business dealings with another great Oriental community, the population of which exceeds that of India by many millions—I mean China—an extraordinary disparity will disclose itself; for, whereas England's trade with India amounts, as I have said, to 64 millions of pounds, with China and Hong Kong it only reaches 17 millions. But not only do we derive the benefit from our Indian Empire indicated by the volume of our trade; it must also be remembered that India performs the function of a great storehouse and an opportune and fortunate reserve whenever any of our usual customers are unable to supply us with those exports upon which the prosperity of our trade and the welfare of our people intimately depend. (Cheers.) Thus, in years when Russia could spare comparatively little wheat, as in 1884 and 1885, India sent us 600,000 tons of that most necessary article, and by so doing undoubtedly mitigated the universal distress occasioned by a rise in the price of bread which would have inevitably supervened. (Hear, hear.) Again, in the time of the cotton famine, India, in response to Lancashire's demands, increased her raw cotton exports from 1¾ million cwt. in 1860 to a total of 5½ million cwt. in 1866. (Cheers.) That to Lancashire India is an invaluable customer is a well-known fact; but any one who has the interests of the two countries at heart cannot do amiss in bringing such facts within the purview of the English people. (Cheers.) In 1888 she took 21¼ millions sterling of our cotton goods and yarns out of a total value of 72 million pounds' worth exported to all countries, whereas China only took 6½ million pounds' worth, Germany 2½ million pounds' worth, and the United States two million pounds' worth. (Hear, hear.) Again, if we take another great section of British export, such as hardware, machinery, and metals, we find that out of a total export of 36 millions to all countries, India in 1888, took 5¾ million pounds' worth, whereas we only sent three million pounds' worth to France, 1¾ million pounds' worth to Russia, and three-quarters of a million pounds' worth to China. (Hear, hear.) These figures, I think, should be enough to convince the least receptive understanding what a fatal blow it would be to our commercial prosperity were circumstances ever to close, either completely or partially, the Indian ports to the trade of Great Britain, and how deeply the manufacturing population of Lancashire, and not only of Lancashire, but of every centre of industry in Great Britain and Ireland, is interested in the well-being and expanding prosperity of our Indian fellow-subjects. (Cheers.) Indeed, it would not be too much to say that if any serious disaster ever overtook our Indian Empire, or if our political relations with the peninsula of Hindostan were to be even partially disturbed, there is not a cottage in Great Britain—at all events, in the manufacturing districts—which would not be made to feel the disastrous consequences of such an intolerable calamity. (Cheers.) But, gentlemen, however satisfactory may be the present condition of our commercial relations with India, I am convinced that they will prove capable of indefinite expansion, especially if once the British investor could be induced to regard India as a favourable field for independent railway enterprise. (Cheers.) The Government of India undoubtedly has done and is doing every year a great deal in this direction, both by itself entering upon the construction of important lines, and by giving guarantees to private companies; but its action in both directions is necessarily limited, and it seems to me the time has come when unassisted private enterprise should step in to supplement and perfect the artificial exertions of the Government. (Cheers.) Were India only covered with a network of railways corresponding to its powers of production, and to the requirements of its population, the present volume both of our import and of our export trade, considerable as it is, would undoubtedly be greatly augmented. (Hear, hear.) And not only is this true of India proper, but I believe that a similar commercial expansion is upon the eve of being developed in Burma— (cheers)—and before no very distant date I prophesy that our chief means of communication with China will be either through the north or east of Burma. (Cheers.) And now, my lords and gentlemen, having trespassed upon your attention with these somewhat dry, though not unimportant, observations, I would willingly sit down; but I should be glad to take this opportunity of correcting a very wrong impression which, though by no means universal, yet has undoubtedly prevailed in some quarters in relation to the recent policy of the Indian executive with reference to the ruler of Cashmere. I do so the more readily as what has recently occurred is but the natural consequence of what happened during the course of my own Viceroyalty. As you are probably aware, the personal administrative functions exercised by the Maharaja of Cashmere were a little while ago considerably restricted, and the action of the Government of India in his regard has been criticised as an arbitrary and unjustifiable interference with the authority of a native prince, and as an indication of a desire to undermine and infringe the rights and jurisdiction enjoyed by Her Majesty's great Indian feudatories over their own immediate subjects. Now, my lords and gentlemen, let me assure you once for all that if there is one line of policy which would be utterly distasteful and abhorrent to the Government of India, and which would be completely foreign to all those principles by which its conduct is guided, it would be an attempt to minimize or belittle the personal prestige, or to interfere with the regulated independence of the princes of India. The tendency both of the wishes, instincts, and accepted traditions of the Government of India is entirely in the opposite direction—(cheers)—and I can assert, without fear of contradiction, that at no moment of their history have the princes of India had greater faith in the good-will, benevolence, and generosity of feeling of the supreme Government than at the present moment. (Cheers.) But, my lords and gentlemen, the case of the Maharaja of Cashmere was a very peculiar one. You all know how important is the situation occupied by Cashmere on our north-western frontier, and how absolutely necessary it is that the people of Cashmere should be prosperous and contented. During the later years of his father's government, who, when I arrived in the country, had already been attacked by a mortal disease, the affairs of the State had fallen into great confusion, and its prosperity into still greater decay; but in spite of these untoward circumstances, which certainly called for remedial measures, it did not appear to me opportune or desirable to trouble the fast-closing span of the dying prince's life by any harsh remonstrances. (Hear, hear.) When, however, the new heir ascended the throne, I took the earliest opportunity of meeting him, and did my best to make him comprehend both the nature of the great responsibilities to which he had been called, as well as the earnest desire both of myself and my colleagues to assist him in performing them. Though the young prince appeared both amiable and tractable, it was very evident that not only was he entirely devoid of experience, but that his limited, or shall we say his undeveloped abilities, scarcely fitted him for the position he occupied. This was undoubtedly a very grave source of anxiety, for a glance at the map will make it understood how important it is that the affairs of Cashmere should be administered by a strong, wise, and loyal ruler. Still, so loth were we to interfere with a native government that we allowed the new ruler without let or hindrance to enter upon the free and unimpeded discharge of his full powers. The results, however, of this forbearance had proved anything but satisfactory even before I left India, and the subsequent conduct, or rather want of conduct and of ordinary intelligence of the young Maharaja has left my successor no other alternative than that which he has adopted—(hear, hear)—for, however anxious and determined the Government may be to abstain from all unnecessary inteference with the heads of the several States in India, and indeed to remain passive even when their conduct of affairs falls very far short of the desired standard, still there is a point of misconduct and maladministration—implying as it does the permanent ruin of the finances of the State, and the consequent misery and oppression of its people—beyond which absolutely bad government cannot be permitted. (Cheers.) This point had not only been reached, but had been passed in the case of the Maharaja of Cashmere; but, at all events, we had the satisfaction of knowing that the incident in question was an exceptional one, for, although in every category of human beings certain unworthy members may be found, I have no hesitation in saying that, as a body, the present generation of the princes of India will compare favourably, both as regards their intelligence, their activity, and their desire to do their duty even with the general run of the sovereigns of Europe. (Cheers.) It would, of course, be invidious for me to cite instances of individual names; but were it not for that consideration, I could mention half-a-dozen young and promising rulers, each one of whom is actuated by the most earnest desire to do his duty, and is as equally distinguished by the purity and high moral character of his domestic life as by his industry, his intelligence, and his public spirit. (Hear, hear.) Indeed, not only are we anxious and thankful to be able to transfer a considerable portion of the enormous burden of our administrative responsibilities upon the ruling princes of India, but the whole tendency of the Indian Government is to decentralize as much as it can, and to interfere as little as possible either with the native states or with the provincial governments in the management of their own affairs. (Hear, hear.) And here, before concluding, I may perhaps be allowed to express my very great gratitude for the invariable assistance and loyal support I derived during the whole term of my office from the various Governors and Lieutenant-Governors who shared and lightened my responsibilities—to Sir M. E. Grant-Duff, to Sir James Fergusson, to Lord Connemara, to Lord Reay, to Sir C. U. Aitchison, to Sir Alfred Lyall, and Sir A. Rivers Thompson. (Cheers.) No one could have received more loyal support or kinder sympathy than I did from these gentlemen; and although, of course, I did not come so directly into contact with those distinguished civil servants who assisted them with their counsels, I am well aware that they as richly deserved my thanks, as those who immediately served under the Government of India, and to whom I endeavoured to pay a fitting tribute when I last addressed a London audience. (Cheers.) Each and all of them are engaged in very onerous and burdensome duties, of which their fellow-countrymen in England have a very inadequate idea. (Loud cheers.) And now, gentlemen, it only remains for me again to thank for your kind reception and for the attention with which you have listened to these very imperfect observations. I assure you it will be a great satisfaction to everybody in India, both natives and Europeans, that so influential a body as the London Chamber of Commerce should have been pleased to show their interest in Indian affairs by the honour they have conferred upon one of its Viceroys. (Loud cheers.)

www.ingramcontent.com/pod-product-compliance
Lightning Source LLC
Chambersburg PA
CBHW032047230426
43672CB00009B/1504